A
CHARGE
TO
KEEP

A
CHARGE
TO
KEEP

My Journey to the White House

GEORGE W. BUSH

Perennial

An Imprint of HarperCollins*Publishers*

Grateful acknowledgment is made to reprint the following excerpts: Page 106: Copyright 5/10/99 by The Texas Lawyer. Reprinted with permission. All rights reserved. Page 142-144 (excerpt from Karla Faye Tucker interview): Courtesy of Cable News Network. Page 158: Copyright 9/28/98 by Houston Chronicle Publishing Company. Reprinted with permission. All rights reserved. Page 215: Copyright 10/17/97 by Houston Chronicle Publishing Company. Reprinted with permission. All rights reserved.

A hardcover edition of this book was published in 1999 by William Morrow and Company, Inc.

HarperCollins books may be purchased for educational, business, or sales promotional use. For information please write: Special Markets Department, HarperCollins Publishers Inc., 10 East 53rd Street, New York, NY 10022.

First Perennial edition published 2001.

The Library of Congress Cataloging-in-Publication Data has been applied for.

ISBN 0-06-095792-1

01 02 03 04 05   10 9 8 7 6 5 4 3 2 1

for Laura and the girls

CONTENTS

CONTENTS

FOREWORD

When I was first approached and asked to write a book about my life, I was not inclined to do so. At age fifty-three, I feel that many chapters of my life story are yet to be written.

But I learned a political lesson during my first campaign for Congress more than twenty years ago, and that was to never allow others to define me. When I discovered that a number of other people were writing books about me, I decided to tell my story from my own perspective. Plus, in our family, even the dog has written a book.

A Charge to Keep is not intended to be a comprehensive look at every event of my life. It is not in chronological order and does not cover everything I have ever done. That would be far too boring. The book chronicles some of the events that have shaped my life and some of my major decisions and actions as governor of Texas. It is intended to give the reader a sense of my values, my philosophy, and how I approach and make decisions.

I thank my friend and communications director, Karen Hughes, for helping me put the words on paper. Karen has worked with me since my first campaign for governor. She persuaded me to write the book and did much of the work. I also need to thank her husband, Jerry, and son, Robert, for sharing her with us. I thank my attorney, Terri Lacy, for guiding the project from start to finish. I thank Stephen Garrison, a member of my policy staff who worked long hours to research and provide and check facts.

The book is not intended to replace the presidential campaign in which I will lay out a detailed agenda and a series of policy speeches outlining my plans for the future of America. I do hope it offers some insight into my life and leadership style.

The title of the book is based upon a hymn written by Charles Wesley, "A Charge to Keep I Have." A painting that was inspired by the hymn hangs on the wall in my office at the state capitol in Austin. A reproduction of it is on the back cover of this book. *A Charge to Keep* speaks of determination and direction; it calls us to a higher purpose.

I thank my publisher, William Morrow, for its support of this project. Because I believe that cultures change one heart, one soul, and one act of compassion at a time, I have donated my share of the proceeds from the book to four charities: the Boy Scouts of America, the Girl Scouts of America, the Boys & Girls Clubs of America, and Girls, Inc. (formerly Girls Clubs of America).

George W. Bush

REFLECTIONS

We were in the midst of an important campaign swing in Iowa, just a few weeks before the Ames Straw poll, when Governor Bush sent me home. My twelve-year-old son was playing that night in a baseball game that could decide the capital area's Little League championship. Early that morning, Governor Bush told me, "You need to get on the next flight home and go to see that game." I protested, worried about fulfilling my professional responsibilities to him; he insisted. I went home. My son's team (not that night, but in the next game that weekend) won the capital area championship, and advanced to the regional Little League tournament. My boss was running for president, but I made every game except one.

That is one story; everyone who works for Governor Bush could tell many of his or her own. I told the editor of this book that I was worried because there was no chapter that described what all of us love most about our boss—because he is too modest to describe his thoughtfulness and the genuine and unique way he relates to people. He and Mrs. Bush generously share the special moments of their lives as governor and first lady, inviting all of us to inaugurals, parties, dinners, and receptions. They invite every one of the several hundred members of the Governor's staff and their families to come to a Christmas reception at their home; we are all invited to bring our children to the Governor's mansion to trick-or-treat every Halloween. He invited Joe Allbaugh and his wife, Diane, to join him on the 50-yard line for the Texas vs. Oklahoma football game; Joe is from Oklahoma and Diane earned her law degree at Oklahoma University. Karl and Darby Rove and their son, Andrew, joined Governor Bush in his front-row seats at the Texas Rangers baseball game; Andrew sat in the Governor's lap. He invites the cooks, security officers, and personal staff of the Governor's mansion to a private holiday party where he gives out funny awards for unusual events that took place during the preceding year; he invites the senior staff and major appointees to a formal holiday dinner each year to thank us. He hosts a picnic for staff and friends who run in the Capitol 10,000 race. I can trace my son's growth, measured by pictures of him at events at the Governor's mansion.

I've seen Governor Bush stay for an hour after a graduation speech to shake the hand of every graduate. I have waited as he talked with every one of the hundreds of people who came to see him at huge community receptions. I've walked through countless hotel kitchens and back door entrances to buildings with him; he always stops to talk with the cooks, janitors, and elevator operators. He smiles, shakes hands, and establishes a warm and immediate connection. I never know how he does it; the people know it is genuine and heartfelt. He has hugged and comforted people after terrible floods, tornadoes, and fires. He attended church in Jarrell the Sunday after the devastating tornado there; he didn't speak or grandstand, he simply attended the service to lend his prayers and comfort. After the horrible shooting at a church in Fort Worth in early September, Governor Bush attended a community memorial service. Again, he didn't speak or sit on the stage; he sat with the crowd.

I've seen Governor Bush during the stress of campaigns and during the joy of election night celebrations. I've sat in on countless policy briefings and discussions with him; he always asks the best questions, the ones that get right to the heart of the matter. We used to joke in the 1994 campaign that no matter how much we all studied and tried to know every fact before a new policy announcement, Governor Bush could always find one question to stump us. He has assembled a great team of quality people, and it has been an honor for me to work with all of them. I have worked for Governor Bush for more than five years; I respect and admire him even more today than I did on the first day I joined his team.

Karen Hughes

Karen Hughes

ACKNOWLEDGMENTS

An impressive trio of women made this book happen. Terri Lacy, my attorney, Karen Hughes, my communications director, and Claire Wachtel, our editor at William Morrow, guided and directed the project from start to finish, and I am most grateful. They were helped day and night by the long hours worked by Stephen Garrison to research and provide policy information. I thank Mickey Herskowitz for his help and work in getting the project started.

I thank my family and friends for so willingly sharing their time and stories: Mother and Dad, my brothers, Jeb, Neil, and Marvin, and my sister, Dorothy, and their families, and Dad's chief of staff, Jean Becker; my lifelong friends from Midland, Don and Susie Evans, Joe and Jan O'Neill, Charles Younger, Robert McCleskey, and Don Jones, provided insight and recollections. Many friends shared memories and provided material. I am grateful to: Clay Johnson, Pastor Mark Craig, Hugh Aynesworth, Texas Railroad Commissioner Michael Williams, Texas Railroad Commissioner Tony Garza, Supreme Court Justice Al Gonzales, former Texas Education Commissioner Mike Moses, Monsignor Jude O'Doherty, Tom Schieffer, Roland Betts, Bill DeWitt, Mike Proctor, Peter Roussel, Rusty Rose, and Don Rhodes.

Many members of my staff gave valuable advice and direction. I thank Joe Allbaugh, Karl Rove, Mark McKinnon, Vance McMahan, Gail Randall, Elton Bomer, Mike Gerson, Margaret LaMontagne, Dan Bartlett, Johnny Sutton, Don Willett, Albert Hawkins, Harriet Miers, Sally Canfield, Josh Bolton, Darren Grubb, Danner Bethel, Polly Sowell, Jodey Arrington, Donna Davidson, Margaret Wilson, Terral Smith, Dan Shelley, David James, Charlene Fern, Shannon Smith, Cliff Angelo, Max Everett, Ashley Estes, Carrie Cavanaugh, Sarah Moss, Nancy Pilon, Bill Clark, Ted Cruz, Joel Shin, Marc Sumerlin, Carol Thompson, Logan Walters, Gordon Johndroe, and Israel Hernandez. I also thank members of my press staff—Mindy Tucker, Brian Jones, Andy Malcolm, and Scott McClellan—for taking on extra duties while Karen Hughes worked on the book. I thank my administrative assistant, Ofelia Vanden Bosch, for suggesting the title, and my wife's administrative assistant, Andi Ball, for her work with Kim Black to collect all the pictures.

I am grateful to Bill Wright and Michael Murphy for finding us a home at William Morrow; to Kim Lewis, Tom Nau, Lorie Young, Christine Tanigawa, Richard Aquan, Fritz Metsch, Liz Connor, and Jennifer Pooley for their tireless efforts to produce this book; and to Ken Lang for his patience with my attorney.

A
CHARGE
TO
KEEP

1

A CHARGE TO KEEP

Most lives have defining moments. Moments that forever change you. Moments that set you on a different
course. Moments of recognition so vivid and so clear
that everything later seems different. Renewing my faith, getting
married, and having children top my list of those memorable
moments. Mine also includes deciding to run for Governor of
Texas and listening to Mark Craig's sermon.

I've heard a lot of different sermons in a lot of different
churches. I grew up in the Presbyterian church in Midland,
served communion as an altar boy at an Episcopal church in
Houston, married into the Methodist church. I've attended re-
vivals with Billy Graham, chapel at Camp David, Easter sunrise
service in small-town Texas. I've been spellbound by the pas-
sionate preaching of Tony Evans and T. D. Jakes in Dallas. I even
spoke from a pulpit, when my friend Pastor Ed Young of the
Second Baptist Church in Houston invited me to visit his congregation. I've heard powerful sermons, inspiring sermons, and a
few too many boring sermons. But this sermon reached out and
grabbed me, and changed my life.

"I am going to give each of you a huge sum, $86,400," the minister told the several hundred people gathered in the downtown Austin church. "I'm going to give it to you right now. It's all yours—with just one small catch. You have to spend it all, every bit, today. Use it or lose it. No saving for a rainy day. No placing any of it in the stock market or a retirement account. No time for special orders or comparison shopping: $86,400. Right now. Buy a car or a boat or jewelry or all of the above, but you have to spend it all today."

Imagine the extravaganza of consumption. At what store would you start, how would you begin to spend all that cash? Just as we in the congregation got lost in the possibilities, the pastor called us back to reality. He wasn't talking money, he was talking time. Eighty-six thousand four hundred nonrefundable seconds every day. Use them or lose them.

The sermon was a rousing call to make the most of every moment, discard reservations, throw caution to the wind, rise to the challenge. And it came during the prayer service two hours before I would take the oath of office as Governor of Texas for a second time, pledging to uphold the Constitution and laws of the state of Texas and the United States of America, so help me God.

Most of my family and closest friends were in the church with me. Laura and our twin daughters, Barbara and Jenna, Mom, Dad, Laura's mom, and two of my three brothers, their spouses and children, various aunts, uncles, and cousins, all sat shoulder to shoulder, filling the first several rows of upright wooden pews in the First United Methodist Church in Austin. My sister Dorothy was ill, and my brother Jeb was home in Florida, putting together his new administration.

Just two weeks before, the family had gathered in Tallahassee to watch that Governor Bush take his oath of office. The day had been sunny but unusually bitter cold, the temperature in the low twenties, the windchill below ten.

That day had been a long time coming. A treasured picture from my first inauguration shows Mother and Dad and the rest of my family watching as I took the oath of office. Dad was wiping a tear from his face, Jeb was standing behind him in the second row, looking pensive, no doubt thinking of what might have been. He was the brother who was supposed to have won in November of 1994, the Bush brother given the better shot at defeating Florida Governor Lawton Chiles than I had to upset popular incumbent Texas Governor Ann Richards. But it had not worked out that way, and Dad spoke for the whole family on election night when he told the press, "Our heads are in Texas, but our hearts are in Florida."

I was so proud of my younger brother. Jeb hadn't let defeat deter him; in fact, he said it had made him a better man. He displayed no hint of bitterness, despite allegations that campaign shenanigans had unfairly cost him votes. He was that hardest thing to be, gracious in defeat. After the election, he had taken stock of his life, spent more time with his family, converted to Catholicism, started a charter school in inner-city Miami, and kept working, reaching out, preparing for next time.

I could identify on a smaller scale, having come in second in a two-man race for Congress in 1978. Defeat humbles you. You work, you dream, you hope the people see it your way, then suddenly it's over and they did not. It's hard not to take a political loss personally; after all, it's your own name spelled out there on the ballot. Yet if you believe in the wisdom of the voters, as I do, you get over the disappointment, accept the verdict, and move on. My father and mother, who taught us so many of life's most important lessons, modeled that for us, too, in 1992.

Nineteen ninety-two was a tough year for our family. I watched as my dad's approval ratings plummeted from a record-shattering high of 92 percent just after Operation Desert Storm to only 38 percent when the American people voted in November. I had watched during that long year from my North Dallas office window as cars pulled in and out of Ross Perot's headquarters across the street, picking up signs for yards that should have been home to Republican voters. I had watched as Bill Clinton's catchphrase—"It's the economy, stupid"—became the defining message of the campaign, even though the economists said and the economy showed (although too late to make any difference) that recovery was under way.

Our family had gathered for election day at The Houstonian Hotel, in Mom and Dad's hometown of Houston, Texas. The day before, I had traveled with Dad on what would be his last campaign journey. He campaigned hard, always optimistic about his chances. Just before our last stop, Dad, Mary Matalin (ever the loyal soldier), the Oak Ridge Boys and I gathered in Dad's cabin on *Air Force One*. At Dad's request, the Oaks sang "Amazing Grace." It was a touching moment; Mary and I wiped tears from our eyes as we both sensed the impending defeat.

My fears were confirmed at three P.M. on Election Day when a friend called to say that exit polls from key states indicated the race was over. Minutes after the call, Dad bounded into the room where the family was gathered. I broke the news. "Dad, unfortunately, the exit polls look bad." "Well, we'll just see how it goes," he said, and left the room to get dressed. A miserable election year ended five hours later. And the next morning, Mother, in her usual, unflappable way, said, "Well, now, that's behind us. It's time to move on."

And we all did. I went back to counting less agonizing, though fully engaging, wins and losses at the Texas Rangers baseball games, and trained for and ran in a marathon, the Houston Tenneco. Mother and Dad built a house in Houston, raised money for charities, wrote their memoirs, invited interesting people to summer dinners in Kennebunkport, planned and opened Dad's presidential library at Texas A&M, spent time fishing and golfing and reading and gardening, and traveled the world making speeches. Dad jumped out of an airplane; Mom (and most of the rest of us) thought he was crazy, but he savored the moment like a big, giddy kid. Life was good. And so was their example. We saw, firsthand, that you could enter the arena, give it your best, and leave with your integrity intact. We saw that there is life after losing. Jeb and I took it to heart.

And so all of us had traveled to Florida on a cold January day more than six years later, gathered for the peaceful transfer of power called an inauguration. Jeb's day started with prayer, as mine would two weeks later, but his was more tent revival than church service. The horns and cymbals and drums of a marching band filled the gymnasium on the Florida A&M University campus and U.S. Senator Connie Mack gave his faith testimony.

"I have never attended a prayer breakfast before in my life and to think that my first is in the presence of such dignitaries. I feel right at home with all these senators, governors, and a president," joked Monsignor Jude O'Doherty, the priest from Jeb's home parish, Epiphany Catholic Church. "I am from a little parish in Miami and there we specialize in one thing and one thing only and we do it very well: we send people to higher places." The crowd erupted in laughter, knowing he wasn't just referring to the Florida governor's office.

Later, outside in front of the old Capitol building, framed by a crystal-blue sky, Jeb placed his hand on two Bibles—one his own and one used by our dad during his 1989 inauguration as President—and took the oath of office. The Bibles were opened to Psalm 91. "Because he hath set his love upon me, therefore will I deliver him: I will set him on high, because he hath known my name. He shall call upon me, and I will answer him: I will be with him in trouble; I will deliver him, and honor him. With long life will I satisfy him and show him my salvation."

Jeb's oath finished, America now had two Governors Bush,

one from Texas, another from Florida. And as I listened to my brother's inaugural speech, I couldn't help but think that although we live in different states and face different issues, we come from the same place.

Jeb spoke eloquently of faith, and family, and friends. "It is here that most of life's principles are forged," he said. "Loyalty, empathy, generosity, and caring are cords of a rope that bind us together into something far stronger than we can ever be individually."

Faith, family, and friends. The three joined together on that cold January day, just as they have joined together on most major occasions in my life. They guided my father during twelve years as President and Vice President; they are the ways by which ultimately, I believe, all our lives will be measured. That day, the Reverend Billy Graham, who many years earlier had planted the seed of faith in my heart and has been a wonderful friend to our family, gave the benediction.

I could not be governor if I did not believe in a divine plan that supersedes all human plans. Politics is a fickle business. Polls change. Today's friend is tomorrow's adversary. People lavish praise and attention. Many times it is genuine; sometimes it is not.

Yet I build my life on a foundation that will not shift. My faith frees me. Frees me to put the problem of the moment in proper perspective. Frees me to make decisions that others might not like. Frees me to try to do the right thing, even though it may not poll well. Frees me to enjoy life and not worry about what comes next. I've never plotted the various steps of my life, certainly never campaigned for one office to try to position myself for the next. I am more spontaneous than that. I live in the moment, seize opportunities, and try to make the most of them.

The unconditional love my parents gave all of us also freed us. Growing up, my brothers and sister and I knew that while they might not approve of everything we did (and would certainly tell us when they didn't), our mother and dad would always love us.

Always. Forever. Unwaveringly. Without question. They said it and they showed it. During his twelve years as Vice President and President, my dad was never too busy to take one of our calls. He wrote us long letters or sent quick faxes; Mom called and sent us all copies of notes she wrote in her journal during travels. The whole family would gather for Christmases at Camp David and summer barbecues on the porch at Walker's Point. Dad E-mails now and is constantly in touch. He sees an article, wants to know how the campaign swing went or how the legislative session is going.

Reporters frequently ask Jeb and me whether Dad gives us political advice. I always laugh inside when I hear that question. I think they envision the Bush family growing up, gathered at my father's knee, discussing America's role in the world or the impact of monetary policy on our economy. As Dad would put it, "Didn't happen." We were more likely outside playing base-ball, basketball, or football. We discussed current events, just as any family does. But at the Bush family dinner table, the kids were usually most worried about whether Marvin would eat his vegetables so we could all have dessert.

My dad does have a wealth of knowledge and experience, and I'm sure Jeb sometimes calls on it, as I do. Right after I was elected Governor, Dad asked if I would like to join him at President Zedillo's inauguration in Mexico in December of 1994. Texas shares a long border and close ties of history, culture, and family with Mexico; a good relationship with that country and its leaders is important for my state. Dad, the "Father of NAFTA," is respected and revered in Mexico, and traveling with him was a great opportunity to meet the new President and begin a discussion that would be continued many times during my term as Governor.

But mostly, my parents are parents. They give parental, not political, advice. I joke that Dad gives advice when I ask, Mother even when I don't. They are, in private, the same people America knows in public. Mother tells it like it is. She is totally natural and down-to-earth. Dad is kind, gracious, always thoughtful. They love us, and Laura and I have tried to do the same with our twin daughters. "You can't make me stop loving you, so quit trying so hard," I joke when my girls are acting like the teenagers they are. Unconditional love is the greatest gift a parent can give a child. Once you know your family will always love you, you are free to try anything. You are free to fail. And you are free to succeed.

Today, two weeks after Jeb's inauguration, in the church in downtown Austin, the pastor was telling me that my reelection as the first Governor to win back-to-back four-year terms in the history of the state of Texas was a beginning, not an end.

The minister talked of visiting Yellowstone with his family. They joined a crowd gathered around Old Faithful, waiting and watching expectantly. He joined in as they counted down—five-four-three-two-one—and was surprised to feel tears welling in his eyes as he joined in the cheers for the erupting geyser. "And then I realized I had just clapped for a *geyser*," Mark Craig said, the crowd in the church joining in agreeable laughter at the absurdity of the scene. "What on earth moves people to applaud with tears in their eyes for cascading water?" he asked, then answered his own question: "Faithfulness. People are starved for faithfulness."

He talked of the need for honesty in government; he warned that leaders who cheat on their wives will cheat their country, will cheat their colleagues, will cheat themselves. The minister said that America is starved for honest leaders. He told the story of Moses, asked by God to lead his people to a land of milk and honey. Moses had a lot of reasons to shirk the task. As the pastor told it, Moses' basic reaction was, "Sorry, God, I'm busy. I've got a family. I've got sheep to tend. I've got a life."

"Who am I that I should go to Pharaoh, and bring the sons of Israel out of Egypt?" Moses asks in the third chapter of Exodus. The people won't believe me, he protested. I'm not a very good speaker. "Oh, my Lord, send, I pray, some other person," Moses pleaded. But God did not, and Moses ultimately did his bidding, leading his people through forty years of wilderness and wandering, relying on God for strength and direction and inspiration.

People are "starved for leadership," Pastor Craig said, "starved for leaders who have ethical and moral courage." It is not enough to have an ethical compass to know right from wrong, he argued. America needs leaders who have the moral courage to do what is right for the right reason. It's not always easy or convenient for leaders to step forward, he acknowledged; remember, even Moses had doubts.

"He was talking to you," my mother later said. The pastor was, of course, talking to all of us, challenging each one of us to make the most of our lives, to assume the mantle of leadership and responsibility wherever we find it. He was calling on us to use whatever power we have, in business, in politics, in our communities, and in our families, to do good for the right reasons.

And the sermon spoke directly to my heart and my life. Throughout my first four years as Governor, I had tried to approach every decision by the standard Mark Craig had just outlined, to "do the right thing for the right reason." And it seemed the pastor was challenging me to do more.

After the service, I went to a reception in my capitol office with previous Governors, then down the steps to the south porch for the inaugural ceremony. The sky was overcast. As I stood to take the oath of office and give my inaugural address, the sun broke through the clouds.

The future of Texas is bright, I told the huge crowd gathered on the south lawn of the Texas Capitol. The next century would be one of great opportunity for Texas, so long as we pursued policies of free markets, free trade, low taxes, and limited government. Yet I also saw a problem on the horizon.

"I am optimistic our children's lives will continue to improve in material terms. The risk is that their moral and spiritual lives will not improve. You see, the strength of a society should not be measured only in the wealth it accumulates or the technology it develops. The strength of a society should be measured in the values its people share."

Texas is a place where people hold fast to basic values: give an honest day's work for an honest day's wages; don't lie, cheat, or steal; respect others, respect their property, and respect their opinions. And Texas is a place where most people know they can improve their lives through hard work and education. I told the story of Al Gonzales, a brilliant, hard-working lawyer I had recently appointed to the Texas Supreme Court. His parents reared eight children in a two-bedroom house in Houston. They worked hard every day. They sacrificed so that their children would have a chance to succeed, and Al realized their dream.

But during my first four years as Governor, I had seen too many faces in too many places that questioned whether the hope of a better life was available to them. I had seen decaying inner cities whose young people saw no way out, wealthy suburbs whose children ruined their lives with drugs and alcohol, and children who were having children themselves, begetting a cycle of despair.

I had worked hard on my inaugural speech, spent a long time thinking about how to address those problems as Texas headed into the next century. "To achieve prosperity with a moral and spiritual center, the Texas of tomorrow must be open," I said, "educated, and, while diverse, united by common Texas values.

"All of us have worth. We're all made in the image of God. We're all equal in God's eyes. And all of our citizens must know they have an equal chance to succeed. It does not happen by telling them they are victims at the mercy of outside forces; it happens when they realize they have a worth, a dignity, and a free will given by God, not by government.

"Government can't solve all our problems," I said. "Economic growth can't solve all our problems. In fact, we're now putting too much hope in economics, just as we once put too much hope in government. Reducing problems to economics is simply materialism."

The real answer to improving people's lives is found in the hearts of decent, caring people who have heard the call to love their neighbors as they would like to be loved themselves. And so I pledged to continue to work to rally the armies of compassion that exist in every community in Texas, people of faith who extend a hand to help neighbors in need.

The second challenge, I told the inaugural crowd, is to become an educated society. "Now, by educated, I mean two things. I mean the obvious—our children must be knowledgeable. They must be literate in the language of the twenty-first century. They must be ready to compete. They must be challenged to be the very best students they can be. And we must never leave any child behind by pushing him forward. I refuse to give up on any child, and that is why I argue so passionately against social promotion.

"First things first. Every child must learn to read. We must start early; we must diagnose; we must get children the help they need. As my friend Phyllis Hunter of the Houston Independent School District says, 'Reading is the new civil right.' "

But our children must be educated in more than reading and writing, I argued; they must be educated in right from wrong. "Some people think it's inappropriate to make moral judgments anymore. Not me. Because for our children to have the kind of life we want for them, they must learn to say yes to responsibility, yes to family, yes to honesty and work . . . and no to drugs, no to violence, no to promiscuity or having babies out of wedlock."

The third challenge I outlined is how to unite a very diverse state through shared values. Texas is already diverse and is becoming more so. Children enrolled in schools speak nearly sixty-three different languages in Houston, fifty-seven different languages in Dallas. Diversity is something to celebrate, not shrink from, I told the audience.

"Nuestra diversidad le da a Texas nueva vitalidad, nueva energía, y nueva sangre . . . y no debemos temerla si no recibirla con los brazos abiertos," I said, which means, "Our diversity gives Texas new life, new energy, new blood . . . and we should not fear it but welcome it." I am not fluent in Spanish, but I make the effort to speak this beautiful language whenever I can. I think Texas Hispanics appreciate their Governor's acknowledgment of the richness of their heritage and culture.

We must not allow race to divide us, I warned. "There's a trend in this country to put people into boxes. Texans don't belong in little ethnic and racial boxes. There are such boxes all over the world, in places with names like Kosovo, Bosnia, Rwanda; and they are human tragedies. As we head into the twenty-first century, we should have one big box: American."

I finished with my favorite quote, written by a great Texas author and artist, Tom Lea of El Paso. It sums up my sense of optimism, my approach to leadership. "Sara and I live on the east side of the mountain. It is the sunrise side, not the sunset side. It is the side to see the day that is coming; not the side to see the day that is gone. My fellow Texans, as we head into a new century, Texas lives on the sunrise side of the mountain. And I see a very good day coming."

After the speech, my family and close friends joined me for lunch, and a daylong celebration of parades and inaugural balls.

Later that week, while filing away all the inaugural programs and speeches, we realized that no one had a copy of Mark Craig's sermon. The church service was a private one; there were no television cameras and no one had thought to run a tape recorder. We called the pastor to thank him, and asked for a copy of the text. It didn't exist, he said. He had spoken from the heart. In an era of instant replay, the sermon had existed only in real time.

Yet those fifteen or twenty minutes had made a difference. As I started my second term as Governor, I was struggling with the decision about whether to seek the Presidency, worried about what that decision would mean for my family and my own life. And Pastor Mark Craig had prodded me out of my comfortable life as Governor of Texas and toward a national campaign.

2

MIDLAND VALUES

To this day, I am certain I saw her, her small head rising barely above the backseat of my parents' green Oldsmobile as it drove up in front of Sam Houston Elementary School in Midland. I was walking down an outdoor hall with a friend, carrying a phonograph back to the principal's office. The instant I saw the car, I put it down and took off running, eager to welcome Mom and Dad and my little sister, Robin, back from New York, where Robin had been seeing a doctor because she was sick. I got to the car, still certain Robin was there, but of course, she was not. Mom and Dad had come to school to tell me Robin wasn't coming home, not then or ever.

I was sad, and stunned. I knew Robin had been sick, but death was hard for me to imagine. Minutes before, I had had a little sister, and now, suddenly, I did not. Forty-six years later, those minutes remain the starkest memory of my childhood, a sharp pain in the midst of an otherwise happy blur.

I was seven. Robin was almost four when she died of leukemia. Others have said I tried to cheer up my parents, told jokes and even stayed inside the house after school for weeks because

I was worried about my mother, but I don't remember much of that. I remember being sad. My friends Susie Evans and Joe O'Neill remember the same thing, a great sadness. Susie vividly recalls the day my parents' car arrived at school, although she, like me, did not know what had happened. "It was unusual. Back then, people didn't come to get children during the school day. They came and picked up George, and he didn't come back that day. I guess my mother told me what had happened, although I don't remember exactly. I just remember it was all so sad."

But no one talked about it much; the 1950s were a time when a death or any other personal tragedy in a family was viewed as just that: personal. I didn't know that, of course; I was only seven. My parents have told the story of attending a football game several weeks after Robin's death. I spoke up and said I wished that I were Robin. As Mom described it, Dad blanched, then asked why. "Because she can probably see better from up there than we can from down here," I replied.

I was young enough, and my parents loved me enough, that Robin's death did not traumatize me. I guess I learned in a harsh way, at a very early age, never to take life for granted. But rather than making me fearful, the close reach of death made me determined, determined to enjoy whatever life might bring, to live each day to its fullest.

I filled many of my days with baseball. Although I was born in New Haven, Connecticut, while my dad was an undergraduate at Yale, we moved to West Texas when I was two. My first memories are of Midland, and when I think of growing up there, baseball comes to mind first. We were always organizing a game, in the schoolyard, or in the buffalo wallow behind my house on Sentinel Street. We played for hours, until our mothers would pull us away. I remember Mother yelling over the fence, insisting I had to come home for dinner, right now. Sometimes, on weekends, my dad would join us, impressing my friends by catching the ball behind his back. Joe O'Neill and the neighborhood boys used to try for hours to imitate Dad, usually succeeding only in getting bruises and scrapes. I played catcher in Little League, and still remember the proud moment when my dad told me, "Son, you've arrived. I can throw it to you as hard as I want to."

Midland had a frontier feeling; it was hot and dry and dusty. We moved there in the midst of a long drought, famously described in a book by Texas writer Elmer Kelton, the title telling the story: *The Time It Never Rained*. I remember giant sandstorms blowing in. You could look out the back window but not see the fence because the sand was blowing so thick and hard. People had storm windows on their houses not because it rained, but to keep the sand out. At school, where they kept the windows open in the spring and fall, you had to brush a fine coating of sand off the desks every morning. Tumbleweeds blew into our yard. Once it rained and frogs came out everywhere, like the biblical plague, covering the fields and front porches.

When we lived on Ohio Street, my best friend was Mike Proctor. He lived across the street and we went everywhere together. To get to a friend's house, you would walk down a couple doors, climb someone's fence, cut through a yard, only crossing the street when you absolutely had to. You could ride your bike downtown and take in a movie.

We walked to school at Sam Houston Elementary School every school day for six years. I remember being embarrassed because my dog would follow me, and I would have to return all the way home, leading the dog, then run back to make it on time for classes. The playground at Sam Houston Elementary was next door to Midland Memorial Stadium, where the great Wahoo McDaniel played. He was our hero, the best player on the high-school team. Coach Thermon "Tugboat" Jones, the legendary football coach, was in his heyday at Midland High School, and we spent fall Friday nights cheering Wahoo and his teammates at the football stadium. Years later, I would bring our twin daughters to the same stadium to watch Friday-night high school football. The ritual never changed.

Most of our dads traveled quite a bit. Most of them were in the oil business, and they were often out at the drilling sites. Our mothers were the constant presence. I was on the seventh-grade football team, and Mother always came to see the games. "When I was cheerleader in the seventh grade, your mother didn't miss one game," Susie Evans reminded me. "My mother was in charge of driving the cheerleaders to Odessa for a game, once, and she got lost. We were really late when we finally arrived at the school, and you came over from the sideline, worried about where we had been. No one else on the football team seemed to notice the cheerleaders were missing, but you did."

Susie and I were on the safety patrol together; we helped the little kids safely cross the street in front of school. We all wanted to be assigned to the middle crosswalk, not the side ones, because more people came in that way and we could see all our friends. The boys wore blue jeans and T-shirts; the girls wore casual dresses.

Everyone played together. Everyone's parents watched out for everyone else's kids. Midland was a place where other people's mothers felt it was not only their right, but also their duty, to lecture you when you did something wrong, just as your own mother did. I'll never forget the time Mike Proctor's mom came running out of her house to yell at me for running out into the street without looking. She got my attention, and I never did it again.

My friend Charlie Younger remembers the time he and a friend took a cigarette out of someone's purse and went back to the alley to smoke it. All of a sudden, up drove the football coach, Tugboat, who hauled them to his office and delivered a stern lecture on the evils of smoking. Someone's mother had seen the boys in the alley and called Tugboat to the rescue. Charlie has not smoked a cigarette since.

Midland was a small town, with small-town values. We learned to respect our elders, to do what they said, and to be good neighbors. We went to church. Families spent time together, outside, the grown-ups talking with neighbors while the kids played ball or with marbles and yo-yos. Our homework and schoolwork were important. The town's leading citizens worked hard to attract the best teachers to our schools. No one locked their doors, because you could trust your friends and neighbors. It was a happy childhood. I was surrounded by love and friends and sports.

The seeds of my lifelong love for baseball were sown during these years; first on the Little League fields, then later as I began following players and teams. I remember visiting my grandparents, back east. My dad's youngest brother, Bucky Bush, loved baseball, especially the New York Giants. To this day, I can recite the starting lineup of the 1954 Giants team. Willie Mays was my hero. I didn't see him play much—the games weren't on television—but I followed his career and read everything I could find about him.

I remember the time I rode my bicycle to the house of a friend of my dad, Mr. John Ashman, to borrow his copy of the first-ever *Sports Illustrated,* August 16, 1954. The cover pictured Eddie Matthews of the Milwaukee Braves at bat with catcher Wes Westrum and umpire Augie Donatelli behind the plate. For Christmas one year, Dad gave me a subscription to *The Sporting News,* then known as the bible of baseball. I can remember eagerly awaiting the arrival of the newest edition to pore over the statistics and read the stories about the baseball stars of the 1950s.

My life changed after seventh grade, when our family made the long move from Midland to Houston to be closer to the Gulf of Mexico waters where Dad's oil rigs were operating. The biggest immediate change was the weather. Midland was dry and dusty; Houston was green and wet. Everything felt damp. For the first time in my life, I went to a private school, Kinkaid, for eighth and ninth grades. I quickly made friends and played football and other sports.

My family had attended the First Presbyterian Church in Midland; with the move to Houston we began attending the Episcopal church, the denomination my dad was raised in. I served communion at the eight A.M. service at St. Martin's. I loved the formality, the ritual, the candles, and there, I felt the first stirrings of a faith that would be years in the shaping. I had settled into a comfortable life when Mother and Dad began talking to me about attending a boarding school named Phillips Academy, Andover.

Dad had taken me to visit the school, and he and Mom felt it was important that I go. Dad had received a great education there, and Andover had earned a reputation as one of the best schools in the country. "Congratulations, George, you've been accepted at Andover," Mom told me one day. I wasn't sure what to expect when I flew up there, checked into my dorm, and began meeting people from all over the country. I was fifteen, and on my own for the first time in my life.

Andover was cold and distant and difficult. In every way, it was a long way from home. The campus was beautiful when I arrived in the fall of 1961, the New England foliage displaying a brilliant sunset of colors unlike anything I had ever seen in Texas. Yet forlorn is the best word to describe my sense of the place and my initial attitude. "Bush, what did you do wrong?" a friend in Houston had asked, only somewhat jokingly, upon hearing I was going far away to boarding school. In those days, Texas boys who got shipped off to school were usually in trouble with their parents. In my case, Andover was a family tradition; my parents wanted me to learn not only the academics but also how to thrive on my own.

It was a hard transition. My friend Clay Johnson, a fellow

Texan who arrived at the school the same time I did, still jokes that he spent his first six months at Andover trying to figure out how he could get kicked out without totally disgracing his family so he could leave and go home, but he could never find a way to do so.

My feelings of loneliness eased pretty quickly, though, as I made friends fast. The studies came slower. Andover was hard, and I was behind. I remember staying up late at night, long after lights-out at ten P.M., putting my book on the floor so I could read by the light from the hall, trying to keep up. I remember the first paper I wrote. I thought I was in over my head, so I consulted the *Roget's Thesaurus* Mother had given me, searching for some big, impressive words. I wanted to show off for my eastern professors. It was a story about emotions and I was trying to find a unique way to describe "tears" running down my face. My discussion of "lacerates" falling from my eyes did catch the teacher's attention, but not in the way I had hoped. The paper came back with a "zero" marked so emphatically that it left an impression visible all the way through to the back of the blue book. So much for trying to sound smart.

Andover was a formal place, much different from my schools in Texas. We wore coats and ties to class. We went to chapel every day, except Wednesday and Saturday. There were no girls. Life was regimented, very different from the happy chaos in the Bush household. I missed my parents and brothers and sister. It was a shock to my system. But I buckled down, worked hard, and learned a lot.

Andover taught me how to think. I learned to read and write in a way I never had before. And I discovered a new interest, one that has stayed with me throughout my adult life. It was sparked by a great teacher, Tom Lyons, who taught history. He had a passion for the subject, and an ability to communicate his love and interest to his students. He taught me that history brings the past and its lessons to life, and those lessons can often help predict the future. Tom Lyons's descriptions of events that shaped America's political history captured my imagination. Not only was he a great teacher, but also he was an inspiring man. Tom Lyons was a twenty-year-old football player at Brown University when he contracted polio. He would never walk again without crutches. The polio crippled his body but never hindered his enthusiasm for his subject or his profession. In college, I would major in history.

Andover was a serious place, and I took my studies seriously. But I would not allow the long hours and cold days to dampen my spirits.

My friends and I found ways to have fun. I have always looked for the lighter side of life, and I did so at Andover. For much of the year, dark came early there. The winters were long, bitterly cold, and confining. And so with spring came an incredible sense of freedom. The snow would finally melt, and warmth would return to the air.

It was during the spring of my senior year that my political talents first blossomed. I helped organize a stickball league and named myself the high commissioner. "Tweeds Bush" was my self-appointed nickname, a play on Boss Tweed, the infamous political boss of New York City's Tammany Hall. In the spirit of Tammany Hall, I named my cousin Kevin as assistant stickball commissioner; we had a league umpire, a league scribe, even a league psychiatrist. We organized a full stickball tournament. Each dorm had a team, with creative names. Spirits ran high. The final game drew a huge crowd of admiring fans from the school. For me, stickball was a way of spreading joy, sharing humor, and lightening up what was otherwise a serious and studious environment.

Andover taught me the power of high standards. I was surrounded by people who were very smart, and that encouraged me to rise to the occasion. I was a solid student, but not a top one. I did well in the courses I liked, such as history, math, and

Spanish, and not so well in others, such as English. When I met with the dean to discuss different college options, I told him I would like to go to Yale. Many in my family had gone there; they loved the school and their love was infectious. On several weekends, I had visited Yale to watch football games, and I was impressed by the campus. The dean tactfully suggested I might think of other universities as well. I told him that if I did not get into Yale, there was only one other option for me, the University of Texas. I was not sure what would happen. I looked forward to either alternative. It was chaos in the mailroom the day the college acceptance letters arrived. The fat envelopes brought good news, the skinny ones rejection letters. I received a fat envelope from Yale and so did thirty-eight of my Andover classmates. I decided on the spot to attend Yale, and that very day Clay Johnson and I began working out plans to be roommates.

Andover taught me independence. I recognized the value of the education it provided. Most of all, though, at Andover, I learned how, as the old saying goes, to bloom where I was planted. I would never again feel isolated. One of the most valuable lessons of Andover was what I learned about myself. I could make friends, and make my way, no matter where I found myself in life.

3

"WHAT TEXANS CAN DREAM, TEXANS CAN DO"

I VIVIDLY remember the night I first thought I might run for Governor. It was May 1, 1993, a special election day in Texas. Voters were casting ballots to choose a new United States Senator to replace longtime Democratic Senator Lloyd Bentsen, who had been named Secretary of the Treasury by President Clinton. And voters were also casting ballots on a school funding referendum strongly supported by Governor Ann Richards and known as "Robin Hood." As its name implied, the plan would have taken local taxes raised in property-wealthy school districts and redistributed them to poorer school districts in different parts of the state. To say the "Robin Hood" plan was not popular proved to be an understatement. Many Texans felt it was unfair to take local taxes raised in one community and redirect them to a different one. Plus, homeowners were feeling squeezed by rising property taxes, which had been soaring as real-estate values and school enrollment increased across Texas.

Laura and I drove to the Anatole Hotel in Dallas that night to watch election returns and root for the candidate we were supporting in the Senate race, Kay Bailey Hutchison. Kay and I are longtime friends, and when the time came for her to speak, she asked me to introduce her. I walked up onstage, and the crowd of activist Republicans started hollering, "Run for Governor," and "Governor Bush." I was surprised, but not completely so. Republicans were not happy with Ann Richards's policies and they were hungry for a candidate to run against her. There had been speculation that I might run in 1990, but I had been busy with our new baseball team and nothing ever came of it.

After the school funding proposition was overwhelmingly defeated, I saw Governor Richards interviewed on television, obviously upset by the defeat of the proposal she had so strongly endorsed. Despite her high personal popularity ratings and national celebrity as one of the stars of the Democratic party, only 37 percent of the voters in Texas had supported her plan; 63 percent rejected it. "In truth, I think those people should come forward and give us their plans. We are all, boy, eagerly awaiting any suggestions and ideas that are realistic," Governor Richards said. I remember turning to Laura and saying, "I have a suggestion. I might run for Governor."

I was worried about my state, not only about how we paid for our schools, but also about how we governed them. "We're doing it backward in Texas," I said thousands of times during the course of the campaign, "funding our schools locally but governing them centrally." A state's most important responsibility is educating children, I believed, so I felt the state, not local property taxes, should be the primary source of funds for the schools. Local property taxes are inherently unfair and unequal, because property values are different in different parts of the state. I wanted children in every part of Texas to get a quality education no matter whether their school district was property-rich or property-poor. I also believed strongly in local control of schools. I knew that local parents and teachers and locally elected school boards were far more accountable than a distant, centralized state education agency in Austin.

I was worried about crime, especially juvenile crime. Random, violent juvenile crime was exploding. Gangs had turned some neighborhoods into war zones; our juvenile justice laws were written for disobedient children of the 1950s, not the juvenile delinquents of the 1990s. We risked losing a generation of young people.

A number of states across the country had begun to realize the need to reform welfare, but Texas had not enacted any reforms and didn't have any plans to do so. "Dependency on government saps the soul and drains the spirit of our very future," I said again and again, arguing for placing time limits on welfare benefits and requiring recipients to work, train, or learn a skill in return for the taxpayers' assistance.

And I was worried about our state's business climate. Articles in major business publications had essentially described Texas as "tort heaven." Liberal court decisions had resulted in an unfair legal system, tilted in favor of personal injury trial lawyers, unfortunately making Texas a great place for people to sue one another. I wanted Texas to be a great place to do business, an entrepreneurial heaven, where dreamers and doers felt comfortable risking capital and creating jobs, not a haven for frivolous lawsuits.

Most of all, I worried about changing the culture, a culture I described as saying, "If it feels good, do it, and if you've got a problem, blame somebody else." The warning signs of the cultural crisis are everywhere. Boys father children and walk away to let others deal with the consequences. Young girls, children themselves, are having more and more babies. Criminologists warn of a new generation of "super predators"—kids who are fatherless, godless, fearless, and jobless. Too many of America's marriages end in divorce, and one-third of the babies in our country are born out of wedlock. I had seen our country's culture change dramatically during my lifetime, so I was convinced it could change again. I believed we needed to usher in an era of personal responsibility so that our state would be more prosperous and more peaceful.

Not many people gave me much of a chance to win. My mother told me I couldn't beat Ann Richards, then was a little put out with me when I gleefully shared her opinion with the world. When reporters would ask about my chances, I would turn it into a joke, saying, "Even my own mother doesn't think I can win." My friend Charlie Younger said I was crazy, and that I should wait four years because I could never beat Ann Richards. "To this day, I suspicion you had a secret poll, that you knew something the rest of us didn't, you were so certain," Younger now jokes. Don Jones thought my loss in a congressional race in 1978 spelled the end of my political career, and he was surprised that I would even consider running for office again. Don Evans, always the loyal soldier, was ready to give it a shot, but as he told me later, he secretly thought it was a long one. My wife was initially dubious; she wanted to make sure others weren't pushing me into the race and that campaigning for Governor was something I really wanted to do.

Laura knew how much I enjoyed our life in baseball. So she was surprised over the course of the next few months when all I could talk about was how I wanted to change Texas and become its Governor. After a lot of soul-searching, and with Laura's blessing, by late summer I decided to become a candidate.

The campaign began to gather momentum as I talked with more and more people. Premier Texas political consultant Karl Rove had been a friend of mine for years, since the early 1970s, when my dad was chairman of the Republican National Committee and Karl headed the College Republicans. Karl is the Lee Atwater of Texas politics, a brilliant strategist and student of political history whose successful campaigns and candidates have helped transform Texas into a Republican state. He started working on the political plan, and the Austin headquarters of his direct-mail company became temporary command central for the fledgling Bush campaign. We planned an announcement tour for November.

Israel Hernandez was the first person I hired for the campaign staff. Without knowing it, Israel made a brilliant move in our very first meeting. I was looking for a travel aide, someone whose personality would meld with mine, someone young and hard-working and willing to spend long hours on the road. Israel showed up in my office an hour early. "Are you here to see someone?" I asked the young man sitting on the couch in the outer office I shared with several other businessmen. "Yes, sir, I'm here to see you. I have an appointment with you later this morning," he replied. "Gosh, you're early," I said. "That's good. Let me return a phone call and I'll be right with you."

It was the beginning of a great friendship. I'm a stickler for being on time, especially in a political campaign. When someone takes time to come hear a candidate speak, that's a great compliment and I don't ever take it for granted. I ask my schedulers to allow plenty of time so I often arrive at events early, before the television cameras do, driving my staff into a frenzy of activity. "Drive around the block," they'll implore me, talking into their cell phones to alert the missing camera crews that they are about to miss the activity. "We told the media the event doesn't start until ten and you have to give them time to get here," my staff will remind me.

I don't wait well. I have been fairly accused of being impatient. When a member of my staff once asked why I feel so strongly about being on time, I succinctly explained, "Late is rude." If people take time out of their lives to attend one of my rallies or to come see their governor, I believe it is rude to make them wait. And so, by showing up early, Israel Hernandez aced an important test.

We spent the next hour and a half talking about family and business and religion and politics. Israel told me about growing up in Eagle Pass, a small Texas border town, and about being the first member of his family to graduate from college. I always want to know about people's backgrounds and families. I like people, and I am interested in learning more about them, plus I believe people's values and priorities are rooted in their upbringing. Within days, Israel was on board. For the next several years, he was always there with the Altoids, the speech box, the schedule, whatever I needed, and he was always loyal and good-humored and professional and on-time. Except once. He was running late, and I left without him. He never did it again. He is a wonderful and loyal friend who is still with me today in the press office of my presidential campaign.

As Israel walked out of that first interview, Vance McMahan walked in. Vance came to me by way of Stanford and a Houston law firm. A brilliant young lawyer with an interest in public policy, Vance had a friend who was working for California Governor Pete Wilson. He wanted to get involved in a governor's race and had met with my political strategist, Karl Rove. Karl highly recommended him, and sent him to meet me in Dallas. "I walked into your office and there was lots of activity, phones ringing, people coming in and out, baseballs and paper everywhere. My first impression was one of tremendous energy," Vance later told me.

"Sit down, and let me tell you what I'm thinking about," I said to Vance, proceeding to outline my ideas about decontrolling education but making it more innovative and entrepreneurial, taking power out of the central Texas Education Agency and returning it to local school boards and parents. The need to align authority and responsibility is a fundamental management principle that has been too often violated when it comes to running public schools. When you give local schools and teachers the responsibility for teaching, yet try to have a distant authority dictate how they do so, you have defied this management principle and created a convenient excuse for failure. There is a role for the state, but it is not to micromanage local districts. The state's role is to set clear standards, hold local districts accountable for results, and measure progress.

I told Vance I thought the juvenile justice system had been totally ignored; we needed to turn it around and send the right message to redirect kids' lives. I told him I was not interested in the status quo, that I was interested in different ideas and wanted my policy director to think outside the box, to find and develop innovative solutions to our state's problems.

"Well, do you want the job?" I asked at the end of the lengthy discussion. I could tell from our conversation that Vance and I shared a conservative philosophy and that he was excited about the ideas we had discussed. He later told me he was a little surprised that I had done most of the talking, instead of grilling him to test his thinking and knowledge. But I wasn't buying, I was selling. Vance had come highly recommended and I wanted him on my team. As director of my policy operation in state government as well as on the campaign, Vance has repeatedly proven the merits of that decision. I later learned that Vance had taken a year off between Stanford undergraduate and University of Texas law school to work in an Episcopalian literacy program, a tribute to his character.

The first few months were a scramble of planning. Vance took a leave of absence from his law firm, moving from the forty-first floor of the Texas Commerce Bank tower in Houston to a cramped back room in Karl Rove's Austin office, sharing a desk and one laptop with two student interns. Months earlier, Karl had started forming issue groups, bringing together a cross section of people with different expertise on various subjects. I met with them, in small groups or sometimes one-on-one, discussing ideas, asking questions, picking their brains. I set the philosophical framework; Vance's job was to flesh out the ideas, develop specific changes to the law and policy initiatives.

From the beginning, we knew it was important to be substantive. I had never held office before, and I knew people would be skeptical. Ann Richards was personally popular, but I was convinced her policies were not. I wanted to take Texas in a very different direction.

I outlined my values in the speech kicking off my campaign. "To stand for office, you must stand for something," I said. "I believe in the value of hard work. Without jobs there is no hope. And all public policy in Texas has to be based on the fact that entrepreneurs and small-business people are the backbone of our society . . . and the basis of hope. I believe the best way to allocate resources in our society is through the marketplace. Not through a governing elite, not through red tape and over-regulations, not through some central bureaucracy full of experts who think they know more than we do, but through the actions of free men and women in the marketplace. I believe all people should be held responsible for their individual behavior. All public policy should revolve around the principle that individuals are responsible for what they say and do. . . . I believe the family is the backbone of Texas society. . . . I believe results matter. Our leaders should be judged by results, not by entertaining personalities or clever sound bites," I said.

I talked about the need to reform education and make the public schools our state's top priority. "We must govern locally to encourage new kinds of schools, new kinds of teaching methods, new curriculum, new educational entrepreneurship, and new standards of excellence if our children are to compete in the next century. . . . This generation can make public education work for our kids and their parents. That's the number-one priority for George Bush for Governor." I talked about tougher laws to crack down on crime, especially juvenile crime. "Penalties for juveniles who use a gun in a crime will be tougher, much tougher. We will have zero tolerance for discipline problems in our classrooms. We must assure our teachers they are allowed to teach and guarantee students their right to learn without disruption or fear of violence. But we can't just throw discipline problems out on the streets, so that is why I want a new kind of school, tough-love academies, and boot camps, and, as the last stop, more beds in our juvenile justice system." I talked about the need to slow the dramatic growth of government. "What I offer the people of Texas is a modern-day revolution. It's a revolution of hope, change, and ideas. It can only be launched by a new generation of leadership taking responsibility and it can only succeed with your support." I was off and running.

We had a strategy to visit rural areas of the state throughout the early half of the year, before the fall, when I would have to make news in major media markets. I would travel all day, visit a school and a factory or a courthouse, then have a fund-raiser at night. I love campaigning, especially in small-town Texas. I enjoy meeting people and shaking their hands and listening to their stories about their lives. I don't particularly like raising money, although it's a necessary part of a campaign, especially against a well-funded incumbent. In the early days, it was tough going, person to person, one individual at a time. No one gave me much of a fighting chance, and not many people want to put money into what they suspect will be a losing cause. I'll never forget going to see Don Carter, a wonderful man who was the owner of the Dallas Mavericks basketball team. I gave him my pitch, talked about why I was running and how I wanted to change Texas. An hour later, he pulled out a checkbook and said, "I'd like to help you." He wrote the check, handed it to me, and said, "Good luck, son." There are no limits on campaign contributions from individuals for state elections in Texas, and Don is a wealthy man. From watching him write upside down, from across the desk, I thought the check said $10,000. But as I walked out the door, I looked down and saw it was actually $100,000. I had to restrain myself, because I felt like jumping over the desk to hug Don Carter. I told him, "I'm honored, I'm humbled, I'll work to always make you proud." To this day, Don Carter has never asked me for one thing; in fact, when I called to ask him to bring his family and grandkids down to Austin to visit and have lunch, I practically had to beg him to come.

That moment was a big boost. And after the first of the year, I began detailing a series of substantive policy proposals. The first was a comprehensive juvenile justice plan that called for increasing minimum sentences for violent offenders, building additional detention beds for violent juveniles, making juvenile records available to law enforcement officials, and prohibiting juveniles from possessing firearms except in supervised activities such as hunting. I proposed two sweeping welfare reform packages to place time limits on welfare benefits; require able-bodied welfare recipients to get a job, attend school, or train for work; require participating mothers to identify the fathers of their children so they could contribute to their support; and emphasize personal responsibility by requiring welfare recipients to sign an independence contract pledging to stay drug-free and keep their kids immunized and in school. I proposed education reforms and tort reforms to improve the business climate in Texas.

The policy operation was on target, but I felt we needed a stronger overall organization. I wanted a tough but fair campaign manager who would keep tight reins on the campaign budget, and I found him in our neighboring state, Oklahoma, where Joe Allbaugh was serving as Deputy Transportation Commissioner. Joe had worked as the chief of staff for Governor Henry Bellmon, who recommended him highly, and had spent several years in political work across the country. I was impressed by Joe's answer when I asked him whether he had any faults. He used to have a temper, he told me, but he had worked hard to control it. While I have occasionally seen him angry, to this day, I have never seen Joe lose his temper.

Margaret LaMontagne, another recommendation of Karl Rove's, left a high-paying job with the Texas Association of School Boards to come aboard as political director. I convinced the executive director of the Republican Party of Texas, Karen Hughes, to join our team. And we recruited Reggie Bashur, who had worked as Republican Governor Bill Clements's press secretary, to man the press operation in Austin while Karen traveled with me on the road. It was an impressive team.

But the critics continued to disparage my chances. They ignored the substantive proposals I was making. I was a lightweight trading on a famous name, they said. I was going to lose my temper, blow up, and lose the election. And everything I proposed would cost at least a billion dollars. That was the Richards campaign's standard response to any new policy proposal I made. I was derided as "shrub," a clever, but derogatory term meaning "son of a Bush."

Governor Richards had always been mildly disparaging about my candidacy. In March of 1994, she told reporters in Dallas, "This is not a job where the federal government gives you job training funds so you can learn as you go. You can't be shaving one morning and look at yourself in the mirror and think, 'I'm so pretty I'll run for Governor.' " But I was determined not to respond in kind. Texas politics has a reputation for being a contact sport. But I was not suiting up for that game. From the beginning, I treated my opponent with respect. I don't like negative campaigning, and I refused to engage in it. Campaigns should be about ideas, and I had substantive ideas to change our state. I talked about my proposals, which I presented on my timetable throughout the campaign. I criticized Governor Richards's policies, but I would not criticize her personally.

So it stood out in late August, when Governor Richards derided me as "some jerk," then said she really hadn't. "You just work like a dog, do well, the test scores are up, the kids are looking better, the dropout rate is down," Governor Richards said in a speech in Texarkana. "And all of sudden, you've got *some jerk* who's running for public office telling everybody it's all a sham and it isn't real and he doesn't give you credit for doing your job. So far as he is concerned, everything in Texas is terrible." Then she tried to say she didn't say it, that the reference was "generic," which Barbara White of KDFW–TV in Dallas wasn't buying. Barbara ran a tape that showed, quite emphatically, the Governor had said it, and it appeared to everyone that she was talking about her opponent, who just so happened to be me. It caused a flurry of interest at the end of a long, hot summer, and I was delighted, because it indicated my opponent was suddenly paying attention to me. Television cameras came to my Dallas office for interviews. How did it feel, being called a jerk? I laughed it off, saying I couldn't remember being called names like that since I went to grade school at Sam Houston Elementary.

The incident said a lot, it seemed to me. It said my opponent was frustrated at facing a surprisingly tough challenge from someone who had never held elected office. It indicated she felt her reelection should be easy, that perhaps she thought she had earned and deserved it before she had.

We had always worried that Governor Richards would launch an early television offensive and would hit the airwaves with a substantive, forward-looking agenda that would reinforce her popularity before my campaign was able to get a foothold. We worried we would not have the money to respond if she went on television in the spring or early summer. It never happened. She didn't begin television advertising until August and her first commercial was vague. When I started my series of issue advertisements in August, the incumbent found herself responding to me and my proposals for welfare reform and education and juvenile justice.

Heading toward fall, the campaign was building momentum. Then came the picture that went round the world. Me, in blue jeans, khaki shirt, and hunting vest, holding a shotgun in one hand and the wrong bird in the other.

No self-respecting bird would ever come near this gaggle of

people, and cameras, and noise, I thought to myself as we walked in the field on the southwest side of Harris County, outside of Houston. The sun was just beginning to come up on September 1, opening day of dove season, the day that some new criminal justice laws I had criticized would take effect. I had a predawn news conference about those laws, then, media in tow, marched out in the field to go hunting.

The trip had been the subject of some internal debate. Governor Richards had been pictured on the cover of a Texas magazine, shotgun in hand, looking every bit the Texas hunter. My communications director teasingly accused me of wanting to engage in some macho one-upmanship; I wanted to go hunting. And so we did, about thirty of us, in what was described by the *Houston Chronicle* as a dawn dove hunt to "counter the media-event dove hunt Gov. Richards held near Terrell in North Texas. Without a single bird of any species in sight Thursday, Richards sky blasted with her shotgun for the benefit of television and newspaper cameras. . . . Richards began the tradition of televised dove hunts in her 1990 race for governor to reassure rural Texans she was not an anti-gun advocate," the newspaper reported.

Guns are an issue in Texas, as they are in America. I believe law-abiding citizens should be allowed to own guns to hunt and to protect themselves and their families. I believe that our government should aggressively pursue and arrest people who illegally sell guns, illegally carry guns, or commit crimes with guns. I also believe that government should pass laws such as instant background checks to help keep guns out of the hands of felons and juveniles and others who should not have them. Governor Richards had been criticized for vetoing a referendum that would have allowed Texans to express their opinion on a conceal-and-carry law. I argued that Texas should have this law. I knew that many law-abiding citizens, including many women who worked late at night or alone, were carrying weapons to protect themselves. I felt strongly that people who were carrying weapons should be registered, should undergo background checks, and should be trained in gun safety. I campaigned on the issue and later signed it into law, and Texas is safer for it.

But the gun I was holding in the field was not concealed. I was looking for doves. The guide had said, "Dove. On your left." So I fired and hit a bird. I walked out to pick it up and handed it to the guide. We waited for another twenty or thirty minutes, but no more birds came by. Besides, the trip had already been successful, we thought, so we called it a day.

We stopped for breakfast, then went back to our motel rooms to shower and dress for the next event that afternoon in Dallas. Karen Hughes got the call from headquarters. "That bird he shot, are you sure it was a dove?" asked Reggie Bashur. "Of course it was a dove," replied Karen, who wouldn't know a dove from a parakeet. "Are you sure?" he asked. "Of course I'm sure. The guide said dove on left, and he shot and he hit one," said Karen. "Well, I mean, I guess I'm sure," she said as she thought about it. "No one said anything different. Why?" "Well, I just had a call from a television cameraman in Houston. He claims it was some endangered species. Well, not exactly an endangered species but some protected songbird," Reggie said. I'm sure Karen's life flashed before her eyes, as mine did, when she frantically knocked at my motel door minutes later. "That bird," she asked breathlessly, "was it a dove?" "Sure. Why?" I asked. She explained the call. "We had better find that hunting guide," I said. Someone on the staff tracked down the number, and I called. They said they would have to page him, so we waited. Minutes later, the phone rang, and Karen listened to my side of the conversation: "It was?" Long pause. "Why didn't you say anything?" The guide had known the bird was a killdee, but with all the cameras and reporters around, he had not known what to do. He stuffed the bird in his bib and didn't say anything about it.

Karen and I looked at each other. What now? "We confess," we both said, almost simultaneously. I sent Dan Bartlett, a young staff member who had helped organize the trip, to find a local justice of the peace, determine the proper fine for shooting the wrong bird, and pay in full, yesterday if possible. (The justice set the fine at $130.) I went out to the parking lot, where I found Ken Herman, at the time the leading political reporter for the now defunct *Houston Post*. I remember him shaking his head. He knew this was a big story, and maybe he felt just a bit sorry for me. I then called every reporter who had been on the trip. "I have a confession to make; I am a killdee killer," I told them. As we walked into the airport for our plane to Dallas, the television reporter on the noon news was reporting that she had just received a call from George Bush who told her the bird he killed was not a dove, after all, but a protected songbird known as a killdee.

I opened my Dallas news conference that afternoon with my confession, and a joke: "Thank goodness it was not deer season; I might have shot a cow." We were laughing, but we were also worried. One of the veteran political reporters in Texas had told Karen he thought this could really cost me. Texas is a big hunting state, and no one was sure how people would react to my misfire.

Karen said she felt as if she were holding her breath for the next twenty-four hours, and wasn't able to exhale until the next day, when she arrived at the airport for an early-morning flight. The newspaper deliveryman, a man with a gimme cap and without several teeth, was loading the rack of papers when Karen saw him stop and look at the huge picture of me on the front page. "A killdee," he said, in a classic Texas drawl. "I shot a bunch of 'em ma-self."

In the end, it did not hurt, and it may have helped. I think it showed a side of me that voters had not seen. I was able to laugh at myself, to make a mistake, admit it, and poke fun at it. People watch the way you handle things; they get a feeling they like and trust you, or they don't. The killdee incident helped fill in blanks the voters may have had about what type of person I was. Plus it gave me great joke material. Of course, I took a lot of good-natured ribbing from my friends and even my family. I was at the state fair in Dallas in early October. My girls were with me and I was walking down the midway, television cameras trailing, when Jenna stopped to play a game and won a weird-looking stuffed bird. She turned, and looking right into the cameras, handed me the toy: "Look, Dad, a killdee." You'll understand why some in my family joke that my feisty daughter Jenna is "Barbara's (my mother's) revenge on George."

With each new day, the campaign seemed to intensify. Pagers went off constantly as new commercials were launched and responded to, new statements made and disputed. The fall was an air war of competing television commercials, daily news conferences, shots and countershots, some delivered directly, others through the news media. I felt I was gaining momentum as we headed toward the October debate, the only one both candidates had agreed to.

Debates freeze a campaign. News coverage focuses on the buildup and preparation, nothing else gets through. The sponsors, *The Dallas Morning News* and KERA public television, had insisted on a dual format: a series of questions from a citizens' panel, followed by questions from a panel of state political reporters. When the citizens began their questions, it seemed to me as if every anti-welfare-reform liberal in Texas had been placed on that panel. It didn't seem exactly representative of the Texans I had been talking with on the campaign trail. The key moment, from my perspective, came when *Texas Monthly* political editor Paul Burka asked Governor Richards about her agenda for the next four years. She gave a response which prompted me to reply, "The campaign speech we just heard . . . could have been four years ago." I told the audience that either nothing was accomplished, or Governor Richards's vision for the future was the past. In the end, both sides claimed victory. There were no major mistakes, no knockout punches. I felt I had won by holding my own with an experienced elected official, someone who had debated many times before.

The morning after dawned crisp and cool, a fall morning that the rest of the country probably gets in September but only arrives in Texas in late October. Attending a parade in East Texas reinforced my feelings of confidence. We were in rural Democrat country, and a lot of people seemed to be supporting George W. Bush.

But a lot of people were not supporting George W. Bush as well. Two Sundays before the election, I visited Brentwood Baptist Church in Houston. A few members of the church had asked me to come by in the time-honored Texas tradition of candidates visiting African-American churches on fall Sundays close to Election Day. I knew I would be speaking in front of a skeptical audience of mostly Democrats, but I was prepared to talk about my dreams for equal opportunity and justice. Just before I was scheduled to speak, the doors of the church flew open and down the center aisle came Senator Rodney Ellis of Houston, pushing the wheelchair of the great Barbara Jordan, the former Congresswoman who had achieved national prominence as a staunch defender of our Constitution during the Watergate hearings. I was seated on the aisle of the second pew, and Senator Ellis wheeled her directly in front of me, facing the congregation. The entire congregation was holding its collective breath. No one moved. Someone handed Representative Jordan a microphone and she began to speak, her voice and presence filling every space in the church. She slowly began to dissect me in front of the entire congregation. "I am here because I support Ann Richards for Governor of Texas," she said, her melodious voice booming through the church. She cited Governor Richards's long-standing relationship with the African-American community and heralded her record of appointing African-Americans to state boards and commissions. Every ear was tuned to her every word. She finished to a chorus of amens and a standing ovation, which lasted as she was escorted out of the church. All eyes turned to me, knowing I was next. I walked up to the pulpit, looked out over the congregation, and said, "I must be doing something right. I must have my opponent worried. After all, she has just called on one of the greatest speakers in modern history to make her case. I am humbled and honored to follow the great Barbara Jordan. She is the epitome of a soldier for what is right. I just happen to disagree with her choice for Governor." I don't remember what else I said. I don't think I won over many votes. But I think I did earn a little respect.

With a little more than a week to go, we began hearing about a surprise announcement. Governor Richards was having a news conference, reporters told us, and her staff was saying it could change the dynamics of the race. I was in Houston for an event when we got the word: Ross Perot, who I believed had been instrumental in defeating my dad in 1992, was endorsing Ann Richards. I was visiting Mother and Dad at their house when we got the news. I remember Mother picking up a copy of her just-published memoirs and, trying to make me feel better, looking in the index for references on Ross Perot. "Well, let's see what I said about him," she said. After an hour or so of angst, I went to my campaign event. Sam Attlesey, a reporter from *The Dallas Morning News,* was waiting to get my reaction. "She can have Ross Perot, and I'll take Nolan Ryan and Barbara Bush," I said.

The endorsement didn't seem to affect any votes. I think the election had already been decided, based not on endorsements or personalities, but on issues. We were counting down the days in the "campaign of joy," as we described our travel team, feeling good about the possibility of pulling off an upset.

I voted at about nine in the morning on Election Day at a school in my hometown of Dallas. When I arrived at the polls I realized I had left my wallet with my driver's license and voter registration card at home. No matter, the election judge told me, they were pretty sure they could identify me. I spent the rest of the day waiting, calling people to thank them, checking in with campaign headquarters to see if they knew any more than I did. Of course they didn't, but it made me feel better to check in, to hear turnout was good in Houston and Dallas and people were showing up to vote.

Around four o'clock, a friend of mine from one of the television networks called and said, "Governor, I've got the mid-afternoon exit polls. You're going to win fifty-three to forty-seven." I got on the airplane to fly to Austin feeling great, but I was still nervous. You never know. The flight down was nostalgic. I thought about all the flights to all the far-flung cities in Texas, and all the faces of all the people I had been privileged to meet. I had spent the last year of my life preparing for this night.

As we drove to the Marriott Hotel, where our party was taking place, I saw the satellite trucks, one after another, lined up along the street. As we pulled into the parking lot, I saw Joe Allbaugh and Karen Hughes waiting to greet me. "Have you heard? The exit polls look great. Thank you," I told them, grateful for all their help and hard work. Laura and the girls and I went to our suite. Our close friends gathered, the Evanses, the Youngers, the O'Neills, the Johnsons, my next-door neighbors from Dallas, Mark and Patty Langdale, my cousins Craig and Debbie Stapleton, my campaign chairman, Jim Francis and his wife, Debbie, my longtime administrative assistant Shari Waldie, my friends Tony Garza and Senator and Mrs. David Sibley, Israel, and some of our campaign staff. The room was packed. The phones were ringing. My political guru, Karl Rove, was on several phones at once, constantly getting the latest numbers. As the polls closed, Texas news stations began announcing preliminary numbers from absentee voting. The atmosphere was one of celebration, camaraderie, and relief that it was almost over.

The room exploded when the first television network announced a new Governor in Texas: Governor George W. Bush.

I hugged my daughters and kissed my wife. I began preparing to go downstairs to declare victory and thank my fellow Texans.

Ultimately, the campaign proved the power of ideas. I was outspent by my opponent, but I won with the largest margin of any gubernatorial candidate in twenty years. The biggest swing was in East and Central Texas, conservative Democrat country, the areas where Ronald Reagan attracted the votes that became known as "Reagan Democrats." Thanks to the hard work of my good friend and chairman, Jim Francis, and my campaign manager, Joe Allbaugh, I ended the campaign with $500,000 still in the bank.

After a whirlwind transition, inaugural day arrived. I awakened with great anticipation. Mother handed me a letter from my dad. To this day, it brings a lump to my throat.

Dear George,

These cufflinks are my most treasured possession. They were given to me by Mum and Dad on June 9 that day in 1943 when I got my Navy wings at Corpus Christi.

I want you to have them now; for, in a sense, though you won your Air Force wings flying those jets, you are again "getting your wings" as you take the oath of office as our Governor.

I remember way back to that day in 1943. I remember the feeling of excitement and joy. I remember other feelings, too. Expectation was one. I even felt a little twinge of anxiety—maybe apprehension is a better word. I felt the same things years later when I was sworn in as President of the United States.

Maybe you'll have some of those same feelings. That would be very normal. But you are ready for this huge challenge. You'll do just fine. You'll be a strong, honest, caring Governor.

Maybe it will help a tiny bit to know that your mother and I will be at your side through good times and bad—right there, always, with total confidence in your ability; and with an overflowing sense of pride in you, our beloved oldest son, and in our wonderful Laura, too.

You have given us more than we ever could have deserved. You have sacrificed for us. You have given us your unwavering loyalty and devotion. Now it is our turn.

We love you.

It was signed, in his handwriting, "Devotedly, Dad." On the bottom Mom had added a note: "We are so proud of you. Mom."

Throughout that day, as throughout my life, I was touched and comforted by the power of their love. At noon, my hand on Texas legend Sam Houston's Bible, simple and worn, I took the oath of office and became the Governor of Texas.

I set the tone for my administration in my inaugural address. I began by welcoming the Governors of the Mexican states closest to Texas and highlighting our important friendship with Mexico. I thanked Governor Richards and said Texas owed her a debt. "The example she set gives heart to those who battle adversity, and hope to those who wonder if opportunity is limited.

"I share the sense of dedication that other new Governors must have felt," I told my fellow Texans. "Like them, I understand that I am responsible to all the people of Texas. I share the excitement of those who have come to this job before me, their sense of purpose, and their eagerness to get on with the task ahead. I share my predecessors' feelings of humility. The duties that I assume can best be met with the guidance of One greater than ourselves. I ask for God's help."

And I laid the groundwork for the legislative session. "I share my predecessors' knowledge that progress is only possible with cooperation with the Lieutenant Governor, the Speaker, and the legislative bodies they represent. I am eager to work with you, Governor Bullock and Speaker Laney. Our task is to serve the great people of Texas—to serve them well, and constantly, and unstintingly. Together, we will do that. I share the energy of one newly scrutinized by Texas. During the campaign, I sought to let people know what was in my heart by speaking plainly and simply about my vision for our state's future. It was that philosophy and vision which were endorsed in November. Texans can run Texas," I told my fellow Texans. "I will ask the federal government to return to us the power to set our own course. My guiding principle," I said, "will be government if necessary, not necessarily government."

I talked about the need to change our culture, and reform our schools and welfare and criminal justice laws. "I feel the wind at our backs," I concluded. "My enthusiasm for our mission is exceeded only by my confidence that we can succeed. And when we do, those who feel left behind will have new hope, those who have grown cynical will begin to care, and our children will grow up in a more prosperous and more peaceful state. The history of our special land tells us this: that what Texans can dream, Texans can do. To be your Governor is an unimaginable honor. Thank you for your confidence in me and God bless Texas."

I started the day with a church service. One of the hymns I selected is titled "A Charge to Keep I Have." Written by Charles Wesley, the words say:

A charge to keep I have,
A God to glorify,
A never dying soul to save,
And fit it for the sky.
To serve the present age,
My calling to fulfill;
O may it all my powers engage
To do my Master's will!

Several weeks later, Joe and Jan O'Neill called. They owned a beautiful oil painting by W. H. D. Koerner entitled *A Charge to Keep*. It had been a wedding present from Joe's dad. The painting was inspired by the hymn that had been sung at my inaugural service, and Joe and Jan wanted to loan it to me if it would fit in my state office.

It fit perfectly on the wall directly across from my desk, and it hangs there today. In April, I sent a memo about the painting to my "hardworking staff members." "I thought I would share with you a recent bit of Texas history which epitomizes our mission," I said. "When you come into my office, please take a look at the beautiful painting of a horseman determinedly charging up what appears to be a steep and rough trail. This is us. What adds complete life to the painting for me is the message of Charles Wesley that we serve One greater than ourselves. Thank you for your hard work. Thank you for your service to our State. God bless Texas!"

The hymn has been an inspiration for me and for members of my staff. "A Charge to Keep" calls us to our highest and best. It speaks of purpose and direction. In many hymnals, it is associated with a Bible verse, 1 Corinthians 4:2: "Now it is required that those who have been given a trust must prove faithful."

4

YALE AND THE NATIONAL GUARD

THE world as we had known it changed dramatically, but not until the spring of my senior year at Yale. The sit-ins and long hair and sometimes violent protests that came to symbolize the unrest on the college campuses of the late 1960s and early 1970s were just beginning, but they had not yet arrived on our campus as my friends and I prepared to graduate. We later joked that members of the class of 1968 were the last in a long time to have short hair.

The atmosphere at Yale for most of my first three and half years was traditional. College was a time of hard work during the week and parties on the weekend. The discipline and study habits I had developed in boarding school at Andover stood me in good stead, as I went from its rigid structure and rules to the free-form world of college. I took my classes seriously and worked hard. I was enthralled by history, which became my major, with emphasis on American and European history. And I made friends and played hard. The students at Yale came from all different backgrounds and all parts of the country. Within months, I knew many of them.

After our freshman year, Yale students were assigned to residential colleges, which were spread all over the campus. Fraternities provided a common gathering place and my four roommates, Clay and Terry Johnson, Rob Dieter, and Ted Livingston, and I all joined Delta Kappa Epsilon, DKE. I spent much of my spare time with my fraternity brothers; they became lifelong friends. One now works with me in the Governor's office, others have been business partners, and many are helping in my presidential campaign. Our DKE parties were known as some of the best on campus; we would hire bands and host big dances. My senior year I joined Skull and Bones, a secret society, so secret I can't say anything more. It was a chance to make fourteen new friends.

I loved sports. Baseball is my favorite, but my talent never matched my enthusiasm; I was a mediocre pitcher on the Yale freshman team. In my junior year, I was introduced to rugby, and I worked my way onto the first team for my senior year. Rugby is a great game, a game of speed and hard knocks with a tradition of postgame camaraderie.

When I wasn't playing, I was an enthusiastic and spirited supporter of Yale's teams. I vividly remember our elation when the fighting Yale Bulldogs, led by Calvin Hill and Brian Dowling, upset Princeton to win the Ivy League football championship in my senior year. We charged onto the field to take the goal post. Unfortunately, I was sitting on the crossbar when campus security arrived. The police were not nearly as impressed with our victory as we were. We were escorted off the field and told to leave town. I have not been back since. In another not-so-proud moment that I later described as the infamous "Christmas wreath caper," some friends and I decided to liberate a Christmas wreath from a local hotel to dress up the DKE house for an upcoming party. We were apprehended for disorderly conduct; we apologized and the charges were dropped.

I did not date a lot in college because I was dating a wonderful woman in Houston. I asked Cathy to marry me over Christmas of my junior year, but we later postponed the wedding and gradually drifted apart. I still think the world of her, and our parting was friendly. We were young, we lived in different places, and we gradually developed different lives.

The next year brought big changes. The events of 1968 rocked our previously placid world and shocked the country, Yale, and me. In many ways that spring was the end of an era of innocence. The gravity of history was beginning to descend in a horrifying and disruptive way.

By the time the ball dropped in Times Square to welcome 1968, the situation in Vietnam had escalated from a conflict to a raging war. Every night the newscast included a body count. On January 31, the North Vietnamese Tet offensive began. In March, President Johnson announced he would not run for reelection. In early April, Martin Luther King Jr. was assassinated on a hotel balcony in Memphis.

I was shocked by the Reverend King's assassination and stunned by the violence. I watched, appalled, as racial riots escalated across the country. Militant groups such as the Black Panthers argued that the Reverend King's assassination also put to death the notion that civil rights could be achieved in a nonviolent way. I disagreed and hoped America could remedy civil wrongs in a peaceful way.

Television brought vividly to life the discrimination that existed in many parts of America. I was horrified, as I watched the snarling dogs and billy clubs directed at America's own citizens. It was hard for me to imagine a society that would treat my friends as harshly and unjustly as what I saw on television. I was the president of our fraternity; the vice president, Paul Jones, was an African-American. So were my good friends Calvin Hill and Roy Austin. Ours was an easy, natural friendship. I was reared by parents who taught me to respect others. I had been taught, and I believed, that all people are equal, that we are children of a loving God who cares about the quality of our hearts, not the color of our skins. I was surprised by the depth of the racial hatred I saw on television. Although I came from the South, that was never the attitude at my house. As a very young boy, I had once repeated a racial slur I heard at school; my mother washed my mouth with soap, and delivered such a stern lecture that I knew immediately I had done something very wrong. I remember my dad teaching us that each individual mattered and that each individual had a shot at the American dream. The spring of my senior year, in 1968, Dad voted for the Fair Housing Act in Congress, a vote that outraged many of his Houston constituents. I was proud of him for standing his ground and bucking the temptation to succumb to popular opinion. His vote reflected his belief that housing and the opportunity for a better life should be open to all in America.

As the year went on, the violence escalated. Antiwar protests that started out as peaceful sit-ins became clashes with police. Classes were finished and we were counting the days to graduation, when Robert Kennedy was assassinated the morning after winning the California primary. We were young men trying to enjoy what should have been the last carefree days of youth. But we could no longer be the same cavalier college students. We all knew that something was fundamentally, frighteningly wrong.

It was a confusing and disturbing time. Suddenly, the President of the United States didn't want the job anymore. Two of our national leaders had been assassinated. Far too many Americans seemed to hate one another.

Dick Gregory, an African-American comedian and social activist, spoke at one of our graduation events. He said that he wanted to open our eyes and give us an insight into being a "Negro in America." "Think about going to buy a pack of cigarettes," he said. "You put your money in the machine, but nothing happens. You put more money in, and still nothing happens. You did what you were supposed to do, he said, but nothing happened. So you kick the machine, and you kick it again, but still nothing happens. It's frustrating as hell," he said. "That cigarette machine owes you a pack of cigarettes, but it doesn't deliver." It was a different perspective, and it made a lasting impression.

The other reality of the spring of 1968 was Vietnam. The war became increasingly personal as friends who had graduated the year before went into the military. The war was no longer something that was happening to other people in a distant land; it came home to us. We didn't have the luxury of looking for a job or taking time to consider what to do next. It was hard to get a job until your military status was resolved. Three months before I graduated, some Yale student body leaders signed an Ivy League manifesto, saying they were "seriously considering, or have already decided to leave the country or go to jail rather than serve in Vietnam." Some speakers came to campus to talk about the war, but my friends and I did not attend the speeches. We discussed Vietnam, but we were more concerned with the decision each of us had to make: military service or not. I knew I would serve. Leaving the country to avoid the draft was not an option for me; I was too conservative and too traditional. My inclination was to support the government and the war until proven wrong, and that only came later, as I realized we could not explain the mission, had no exit strategy, and did not seem to be fighting to win.

I was well aware of my dad's service as a Navy fighter pilot in World War II. I had heard the stories and seen the pictures of his dramatic rescue after he was shot down over the Pacific Ocean. I remember opening up a scrapbook that Mother kept, and seeing a small piece of a rubber raft glued into the book. It was part of the raft that had saved Dad's life, kept him afloat until he was rescued from the water.

I'm sure the fact that my dad had been a fighter pilot influenced my thinking. I remember him telling me how much he loved to fly, how exhilarating the experience of piloting a plane was. I was headed for the military, and I wanted to learn a new skill that would make doing my duty an interesting adventure. I had never flown an airplane but decided I wanted to become a pilot. Home in Houston for Christmas, I heard from contemporaries that there were openings for pilots in the Texas Air National Guard, and I called to ask about them. There were several openings, I was told, because many people who wanted to go into the guard were unwilling to spend the almost two years of full-time duty required for pilot training.

I took my pilot aptitude test at Westover Air Force Base in Massachusetts in January 1968. That May, I went to Texas to interview with Col. William "Buck" Staudt, a Korean War veteran and highly acclaimed Fighter-Group commander. I met the qualifications and was accepted into the Texas Air National Guard. After graduating in June, I started six weeks of basic training in July. Lackland Air Base in San Antonio in late July and August is hotter than hell and almost as unpleasant. "Welcome to the land of slick heads and slick sleeves," I remember an instructor saying. They shaved your heads, making them "slick," and you had no rank, no standing, no stripe on your sleeve until you made it through basic training.

My pilot training began in November at Moody Air Force Base in Valdosta, Georgia. I'll never forget one of the first flights with my new instructor, a tough, gruff, Georgian. I was intimidated by him and by the airplane. I was even more frightened when he suddenly pulled the nose up and deliberately stalled the plane. "Are you afraid of this thing?" he asked as we began losing altitude. "Because if you're afraid of this airplane, you'll never be a pilot." He was graphically demonstrating that he was the master of the machine. The lesson was that I did not need to fear the airplane, I needed to learn to fly it. It didn't take long for me to be comfortable in the cockpit. Some people never were. Our class was much smaller at graduation than it was on the first day of flight school.

I enjoyed flying. Every day was a challenge, and I had a lot to learn. I learned the basics in the T-41, the Air Force equivalent of a Cessna 172. I then moved up to the T-37, a subsonic jet, where I learned to fly instruments. Finally, I advanced to the T-38, a high-powered airplane that was a joy to fly.

I studied hard. When one of our instructors said he expected us to know the material, he meant backward and forward. I also learned the value of precision. I remember flying one day when the manual called for a 20-degree bank, a level glide path and a 90-degree turn. I banked at 18, my nose slightly climbing, not level, and the degree of my turn was closer to 100 than 90. I'll never forget the instructor's harsh admonition: "In the Air Force, when we say twenty, we don't mean eighteen. And level is level, and anything else is sloppy." The training was impressive. The need for precision and accuracy and exactness was drilled into us at every opportunity. We spent a lot of time responding to different situations, going through flight procedures time and time again.

I spent fifty-five weeks on active duty, learning to fly, and graduated in December 1969. My dad pinned on my second lieutenant wings, a proud moment for both of us.

I was then assigned to Ellington Air Force Base in Houston, my home unit and also home of the F-102 flight training school. There, I would learn to fly the F-102A Delta Dagger Interceptor. Almost fifty-seven feet long with a wingspan of about thirty-six feet, the F-102A is a single-seat, single-engine jet fighter, and putting it in the sky required single-minded focus and attention.

One of my instructors was Maury Udell, a 270-pound black belt in judo, who divided our training into academics and flight time. One week, we would study in the morning and fly in the afternoon, the next week it was reversed. We studied engineering, flight characteristics, navigation, formation, equipment, emergency procedures and ejections, radar, missiles, and instrument procedures. Colonel Udell quizzed us every day, went over the same information, time and time again. He required a "blindfold" position check of every switch and instrument in the cockpit. When I once questioned the need for the long, repetitive briefings, my instructor explained: "It might be uncomfortable to listen to the same things over and over, but when you are on final approach in bad weather, you'll be glad you remember what I'm teaching you."

Colonel Udell taught us how to fly in visual flight conditions, instrument conditions, night or day, and in bad weather. We learned the radar system acquisition of targets, how to best use it, how to be subtle or deceptive, the missile parameters, the flight envelope, the limits of the missiles, and the edge of the envelope for the airplane. The goal was to learn to use the plane as you used your hand, instinctively, without having to think about it.

We were taught to be precise. Colonel Udell used to say, "You don't miss. You don't use improper procedures. You plan your attack to be successful, and you execute it to be successful. Nothing else is acceptable."

After the study and training flights, I'll never forget my first solo flight in the F-102. I taxied out onto the runway, breathing through an oxygen mask, with a parachute jammed into my back. I was strapped tightly into the cockpit. I remember a tremendous rush of adrenaline and anticipation. The tower cleared me onto the runway for takeoff. The brakes were on full as I throttled the engine to full power. My brain was fully engaged, checking gauges and instruments. I released the brakes and the airplane began rumbling down the center of the runway. I shifted the plane into afterburner, and with a loud bang the acceleration intensified, with the sudden increase from 10,000 to more than 16,000 pounds of thrust. The movement was amazing. I guided the airplane with my feet, straight down the runway. At 110 knots, I pulled slightly back on the control and the aircraft lifted smoothly off the ground. I raised the landing gear, shut off the afterburner, and I was airborne.

It was exciting the first time I flew and it was exciting the last time. It didn't matter where you had been or where you were going. The only thing that mattered was the moment, getting that airplane off the ground. Cockpits of fighter jets are tiny and close, and they force you to learn economy of motion. They also force you to master yourself, mentally, physically, and emotionally. You have to stay calm and think logically. One mistake and you could end up in a very expensive metal coffin.

Several of my fellow pilots had participated in a program known as "Palace Alert," which rotated Guard pilots into Vietnam to relieve active-duty pilots. A friend and fellow pilot, Fred Bradley, and I were interested in participating and we talked with Col. Jerry Killian about it. He told us the program was being phased out, that a few more pilots would go, but that Fred and I had not logged enough flight hours to participate.

I continued flying with my unit for the next several years. We developed a great sense of camaraderie and teamwork. My fellow pilots were interesting people, a mix of airline pilots, businessmen, and entrepreneurs. We were different, but we worked well together. The military is good at fostering loyalty and cooperation and strong morale. The most challenging moments were flying in formation, within 3 to 5 feet of another jet fighter, at a speed of 350 knots, more than 400 miles an hour. You had to learn to trust your fellow pilots. Sometimes we flew at night, and sometimes in very difficult weather. The mission of the Air National Guard at the time was to protect the American coast. We were trained to shoot down other airplanes. Thankfully, I never had a close call in the air. I had a few tense moments, especially at night, when we were flying close formation in bad weather. Your head would tell you to go in one direction; the instruments another. It took all my training to fight my instincts and trust the instruments. We lost two men in our unit when I was flying. One pilot disappeared over the Gulf of Mexico; he was never found. Another crashed while flying a test flight for NASA. It brought a sobering reality to what we were doing. I served, and I am proud of my service. Yet I know it was nothing comparable to what our soldiers and pilots were doing in battle in Vietnam. I lost several friends there, pilots I trained with in flight school. They are heroes.

My time in the Guard taught me the importance of a well-trained and well-equipped military. It gave me respect for the chain of command. It showed me, firsthand, that given proper training and adequate personnel, the military can accomplish its mission. After all, the military took a novice like me and trained me to be a skilled pilot of high-performance jets. I also learned the lesson of Vietnam. Our nation should be slow to engage troops. But when we do so, we must do so with ferocity. We must not go into a conflict unless we go in committed to win. We can never again ask the military to fight a political war. If America's strategic interests are at stake, if diplomacy fails, if no other option will accomplish the objective, the Commander in Chief must define the mission and allow the military to achieve it.

5

HARVARD AND MOVING
HOME

WHEN you step outside in Midland, Texas, your horizons suddenly expand. The sky is huge. The land is flat, with not even the hint of a hill to limit the view. The air is clear and bright. The impression is one of the sky as a huge canopy that seems to stretch forever. Appropriately, "the sky is the limit" was the slogan in Midland when I arrived in the mid-1970s, and it captured the sense of unlimited possibilities that you could almost feel and taste in the air.

You can see as far as you want to see in Midland, and I could see a future. I visited Midland on my way to Arizona during spring break of my last year at Harvard Business School; my friend Jimmy Allison had written me a letter describing how exciting Midland was and inviting me to visit. I was immediately inspired by the energy and entrepreneurship of the oil patch. I had worked in Alaska the summer before, exploring job opportunities there; it was fascinating and beautiful, but West Texas was in my blood. After graduation in June of 1975, I visited Mom and Dad for six weeks in China, where Dad was the United States ambassador.

Then I packed my blue 1970 Cutlass with everything I owned in the world, and headed west to Midland.

Unbeknownst to me at the time, others who would become my closest friends had also moved to Midland that year. Don Evans and his wife, Susie, who had gone to elementary school with me, arrived in February after Don accepted a management training job with the oil company Tom Brown, Inc. He started out working as a roughneck, so he would learn the business from the ground up, then moved up the chain of command. Five years later, Don would become president and today he is the company's chief executive officer. Charlie Younger moved back to Midland in 1975 after completing his medical residency and working for two years as a doctor in East Texas. Joe O'Neill also moved home in 1975 after working for five years for an oil company in California. His dad had insisted he get training in the business elsewhere, before coming home to run the family company. "Go make mistakes and learn the oil business on someone else's nickel," Joe's dad had told him. That's what he did, and it's what Joe recommended I do when I arrived in Midland, ready to apply my Harvard business degree to the real world. "Go to work for a company, learn the business on their dime," Joey said.

I listened to that advice and rejected it. I hadn't gone to business school to work my way up a corporate ladder. If that had been my ambition, I would have stayed back east, gone to Wall Street or a Fortune 500 company. I wanted to be my own boss; Harvard had given me the tools and the confidence to do so.

I had applied to Harvard Business School because a friend of mine from Yale encouraged me. He had had a great experience there and felt I would benefit as well. I was almost finished with my commitment in the Air National Guard, and was no longer flying because the F-102 jet I had trained in was being replaced by a different fighter. When I saw the Harvard application I was intrigued. Completing it required taking stock of your life. It forced me to think about what I had accomplished and what I hoped to achieve. I had learned to fly jets and acquired a good education; I had not yet settled on a path in life.

At the time, I was working full-time for an inner-city poverty program known as Project PULL. My friend John White, whom I had met during my dad's 1970 Senate campaign, asked me to come help him run the program. John was a former tight end for the Houston Oilers who had convinced off-season professional athletes to help him mentor inner-city kids who needed attention and role models. I had just returned from the Red Blount for U.S. Senate campaign in Alabama, and I was intrigued by John's offer. I had worked in politics and in business. Now I had a chance to help people.

Project PULL was located in Houston's Third Ward. My job gave me a glimpse of a world I had never seen. It was tragic, heartbreaking, and uplifting, all at the same time. I saw a lot of poverty. I also saw bad choices: drugs, alcohol abuse, men who had fathered children and walked away, leaving single mothers struggling to raise children on their own. I saw children who could not read and were way behind in school. I also saw good and decent people working to try to help lift these kids out of their terrible circumstances.

I remember one day when former Oiler defensive back Zeke Moore and I were playing basketball with the children on a little indoor court. One of the kids, eleven or twelve years old, went up for a jump shot and a pistol fell out of his pocket. Zeke let out a loud yell; I was stunned. We took the boy to John White, who marched him down to juvenile court for carrying a weapon. The kids did not seem as surprised as we were; that was life on the streets of their neighborhood.

I befriended a young guy named Jimmy. He became like a little brother. He followed me around all day and waited for me to get there every morning. He showed up without shoes one

day, so I bought him some. I'll never forget taking him home
one night. The screen door was ripped, the front porch was rot-
ting, the room inside was smoky, and the music was blaring. I
walked Jimmy to his door and the woman who answered it was
clearly stoned. I don't know what she was taking, but she was
not in touch with reality. Jimmy was happy to be home, but I
was incredibly sad to leave him there.

When I received a letter of acceptance from Harvard, I asked
John White what he thought. John encouraged me to go. "If
you really care about these kids as much as I think you do, why
don't you go and learn more and then you can really help," he
said. John had become a mentor for me as much as for the kids.
He was a wise and wonderful man who endured terrible segre-
gation when he played pro football in the early 1960s. He could
have done many things with his life, but he chose to work with
kids because he wanted to leave a better world. Some of the kids
we worked with made it out of their circumstances; others did
not. Years later, when I came back to deliver John White's eulogy, I learned that Jimmy had been shot and killed.

I am sometimes asked why I went to work for Project PULL.
There are many reasons. John's concern for others was infectious.
I was raised by a mother and father who taught the virtue of
compassion. I had been concerned by the race riots that had
challenged America's soul. I wanted to make a difference. Those
who look for the source of my passion to "leave no child behind"
and make sure all children have the opportunity to pursue their
dreams can find it in the guidance of my parents, in my faith that
we are all equal in the eyes of a loving God, and in the time I
spent at Project PULL.

John's advice about Harvard was sound. Business school was
a turning point for me. By the time I arrived, I had had a taste
of many different jobs but none of them had ever seemed to fit.
I had worked as a management trainee for an agribusiness company in Houston, and worked in a couple of political campaigns.

One summer I delivered mail and messages at a law firm; I spent another on the customer service and quote desk for a stockbroker. One summer I worked on a ranch, and another I roughnecked on an offshore rig. It was hard, hot work. I unloaded enough of those heavy mud sacks to know that was *not* what I wanted to do with my life.

My favorite summer job was as a sporting-goods salesman at the Sears, Roebuck and Company on Main in downtown Houston during the summer between my junior and senior years of college. I was excited about the job and my second day at work I rang up the highest volume of sales in the store. I was really hustling. But then one of the two commissioned salesmen took me in the back storeroom. He didn't mind me working hard, he said, but this was only a summer job for me and it was his full-time living. "Commissions put food on my table," he said. "I would appreciate it if you would handle the little items and let me have the big-ticket sales." I understood, and became the leading salesman of Ping-Pong balls. I also became a friend of the salesman who was working on commission.

I had dabbled in many things, but I had no real idea what I wanted to do with the rest of my life when I arrived at Harvard Business School. "Here you are at the West Point of capitalism," the taxi driver said when he dropped me off, and he was right. Harvard gave me the tools and the vocabulary of the business world. It taught me the principles of capital, how it is accumulated, risked, spent, and managed. I was fascinated by the case-study method that Harvard used to teach. I was intrigued by the variety of cases and the course work involving international finance, marketing, and capital markets. This time in Massachusetts, my studies came a little easier than they had when I attended Andover years before.

I was a little older than some of the students who had come straight out of undergraduate school. I lived alone in a little apartment in Central Square in Cambridge. I studied, and ran and rode my bike a lot. I was there to learn, and that's exactly what I did.

The lessons were underscored when I visited my parents in China that summer. I'll never forget the contrast between what I learned about the free market at Harvard and what I saw in the closed isolation of China. Every bicycle looked the same. People's clothes were all the same—drab and indistinguishable. Central planners restrict choices; a free market frees individuals to make distinct choices and independent decisions. The market gives individuals the opportunity to demand and decide, and entrepreneurs the opportunity to provide. It was clear that China's restrictions of markets limited individuality and competition. Change was slow to come. My visit underscored my belief in the power and promise of the marketplace, and deepened my belief that by introducing capitalism and the marketplace, China will free her people to dream and risk. I was also reminded of how lucky I was to be an American, and I was looking forward to Midland and the promises it offered.

When I returned home, I drove to Midland, rented a little apartment in the alley behind Mr. and Mrs. Rutter's house, and put myself in business. I started my career in the oil business as a landman, the perfect entry point for a history major. A landman performs an elementary but necessary task. He reads the land records in a county courthouse to determine who owns the mineral interests that lie below a piece of property. He also determines whether the minerals are available for lease and, in many cases, negotiates a lease. I caught on fairly quickly thanks to the help of some veteran landmen who let me travel with them to the courthouses of West Texas. I pulled various deed records and watched as they recorded the mineral history.

Midland was booming in the mid-1970s. The price of oil had skyrocketed in 1973, and higher prices had prompted lots of action. The activity made it fairly easy to find day work as a landman, and I took on a variety of assignments from different companies that needed records checked.

I eventually learned to trade mineral and royalty interests. With some of the $15,000 left over from an education fund my parents had set up, I began to invest in small pieces of drilling prospects. The first well I participated in was a dry hole. It was disappointing, but I knew the risks and had not gambled very much. We learned from the first well, and drilled a second one close by that turned out to be the beginning of a solid gas field. The cash flow from the wells was enough to support me during my run for Congress in 1978 and was a good foundation for the company I would build after my race.

I was fascinated by the oil industry and the many characters who worked in it. An old-time Midland lawyer nicknamed "Loophole" introduced me to Buzz Mills, a respected independent oilman. My friend and accountant Robert McCleskey later joked that sharing an office with Buzz Mills taught me more than Harvard had. When it came to the oil business, that's true. McCleskey remembers visiting me in my office; it was so small that he had to sit on a case of soft drinks. All my friends were in the oil business in one way or another; conversations always turned to who was drilling which well and where. I realized I had made the right choice. I knew that if I worked hard and hustled I could make a living.

I formed my first company, Arbusto (Spanish for Bush) Energy, to hold the mineral and royalty interests I had begun trading. Eventually, Arbusto would become the general partner of the limited partnerships that I would form as an investment vehicle for people to participate in the energy business. After my race for Congress, I went right back to the oil business with the idea of building the company. My goal was a steady growth of assets. The energy business was hot. In 1979, oil prices surged again as a result of the Arab oil embargo. Investors were lured by the high prices and favorable tax laws. Over the next three years, I raised and invested a little more than $3 million in low-risk wells. My investors seemed pleased. They were treated honestly, and each of the partnerships was returning cash.

It was a heady time. The banks were willing to make big loans, betting on the expected rise in oil prices, and many people got in way over their heads. I was too conservative to make that mistake, but I made some others. In 1982, I tried to expand my company by taking a drilling fund public. My little company was not very well prepared for the public markets and the program was not successful. I approached growth in a different way later that year, by selling stock in my company to an investor. The capital helped me buy oil and gas leases and hire an engineer to oversee drilling operations, and several geologists and a geophysicist to develop prospects. I also employed a vice president of finance and a landman. The successor to Arbusto, Bush Exploration, had become a full-blown operating company.

Bush Exploration was growing, but I was constantly on the lookout for new opportunities. And opportunity knocked when Paul Rea, a geologist and friend who worked for Spectrum 7, introduced me to that company's owners, Bill DeWitt and Mercer Reynolds. At the time, Spectrum 7 had a one-man office in Midland and a great group of investors. Bill and Mercer were looking to expand with an operating company that could develop prospects and operate wells. I was looking for people who could help raise drilling capital. We both wanted to grow. So the merger that took place in 1983 was a perfect fit. I became the chief executive officer and man on the ground in Midland; Bill and Mercer raised money and ran their other businesses out of Cincinnati. It was the beginning of a great partnership and friendship that would continue years later when we bought the Texas Rangers together.

Our consolidated company picked up steam over the next several years, drilled millions a year, and built up a sound reserve base. But in the mid-1980s things began to change. OPEC could not maintain discipline among its members and the oversupply of foreign crude oil began to affect oil prices. The days of money pouring into the energy business came to a sudden halt. In late 1985, the softening of energy prices became a total collapse when the price of oil plummeted from nearly $18 a barrel to about $10 a barrel in six short months. Drilling stopped. People with debt went under overnight. Banks failed and so did many companies. Midland was suffering through its version of the stock market crash of 1929. At the time, we had seventeen employees and few choices.

I could have laid everybody off and hung on by liquidating the company's assets. But I decided a better route was to seek a buyer who might be interested in our reserve base. When the chief executive officer of Harken Energy, Mikel Faulkner, called on me, I was more than willing to talk. Harken was a bigger company, better able to wait out the crisis, and it wanted our oil and gas reserves. Harken was also a publicly traded company. We worked out a trade, our assets for Harken stock. That gave the investors in Spectrum 7 a tradeable asset. I would serve on Harken's board of directors and as a consultant to the company.

My days of day-to-day management in the energy business were behind me. Laura and I had decided to move to Washington to help in my dad's campaign for President. But before I left, I knew I had one other mission to complete. I wanted to help every one of my employees find another job, and I did so.

I learned a lot of lessons in the oil business. I learned the perils of entrepreneurship. I learned that sometimes you can do most things right, manage risk carefully, use resources responsibly, make good decisions, but still never hit the big gusher. I learned that slow and steady investment brings rewards. Some people in the oil business hit grand slams, but like baseball, success in the energy business is primarily a game of singles. I was able to support my family, meet a payroll, and build a business.

I learned how to manage, how to set clear goals and work with people to achieve them. I learned the human side of capitalism. I felt responsible for my employees and tried to treat them fairly and well.

I lived the energy industry. I understand its ups and its downs. I also know its strategic importance to the United States of America. Oil and gas are important pillars of our Texas economy. Access to energy is a mainstay of our national security.

I believe in the free market, in good times and in bad. Government should not try to control the price of a commodity. The Fuel Use Act and the Natural Gas Pricing Act in the late 1970s damaged the natural gas industry for many years. The Fuel Use Act kept utilities from using our domestic supplies of natural gas, a clean burning and environmentally sensitive fuel. And the Pricing Act put in place a Byzantine set of price controls on gas. Today, the gas industry has finally recovered from that folly.

I am optimistic about the natural gas business. The demand for gas is strong. Gas is a clean-burning fuel that is good for our environment, and more and more people are using it. Gas is also too expensive to import from overseas; the most efficient way to transport gas is through pipelines, and therefore the most competitive suppliers of gas exist in our own hemisphere. A strong gas business means a stronger America, less dependent on the foreign supply of energy.

Unlike gas, the crude-oil business is subject to international markets. The price of crude oil depends on distant nations. In 1999, when a glut of foreign oil drove prices below $12 a barrel, many of my friends in the oil business wanted the government to rescue them through price supports. I was criticized for not encouraging the federal government to enact an import fee. I understand the frustrations of people in the oil business, but I do not support import fees. I did advocate tax relief to help oil operators weather difficult times and to keep them from plugging marginal wells. I believe it makes sense to use the tax code to encourage activities that benefit America, such as encouraging the development of alternative sources of energy, and research and development to enhance energy recovery in known fields. But I do not want to put up fees or tariffs or roadblocks to trade. I believe the best way to help American oilmen and farmers and producers and entrepreneurs is to open new markets by tearing down barriers, everywhere, so the whole world trades in freedom.

6

READING: THE NEW CIVIL RIGHT

TEXAS Education Commissioner Mike Moses and I were sitting in the small state airplane, a King Air 200, flying over the flat, brown-and-green patchwork of fields that stretch for more than three hundred miles between the state capitol in Austin and the high plains of the Texas Panhandle. We were heading for Lubbock, to a homecoming celebration for Mike, and talking about the issue that would define much of my first term as Governor.

I had campaigned on a platform of fundamental reform in four major areas: welfare, juvenile justice, tort laws, and education. All four are important, but education is closest to my heart. As I said in speech after speech, education is for a state what national defense is for the federal government, the first priority and most urgent challenge. If a state doesn't educate children, if the federal government doesn't defend America from foreign threat, whatever important issue comes next seems a very distant second.

My education agenda was bold. I planned big changes, and they would have to be implemented by hundreds of thousands of people in more than 1,100 school districts across Texas. I needed someone educators would trust to lead them in a new direction. My Democratic predecessor had put a New Yorker in charge of Texas schools, a smart and knowledgeable man, but it never seemed to be a good fit. Texas educators had always viewed him with mild suspicion.

At the time, the education commissioner was recommended by the state board of education, but the Governor had to approve. My staff and I were involved in the selection process, which resulted in the naming of my first choice, Mike Moses. He shared my philosophy of local control of schools and high standards, and education was in his blood. His father was a longtime teacher who had retired as a professor and head of the Education Administration Department at Stephen F. Austin State University. Mike started his career as a classroom teacher, became a principal, then worked as a superintendent in three different Texas school districts, Tatum, LaMarque, and Lubbock.

He had earned a reputation as an innovator, someone who was not afraid to try new things. I liked what he had done in Lubbock, where he advocated early intervention for at-risk students, and established an alternative boot-camp school staffed by drill instructors to try to redirect the lives of students with discipline problems. He also gave parents and students greater choice and flexibility in selecting which schools to attend, created a new parent training program, and worked to increase parental involvement in the schools. His strong financial management had turned the school district's debt of $4 million to a surplus of more than $12 million in four years. I also liked the fact that he had experience in three very different school districts, experience that would offer a lot of insight into the problems and proper role of the state education agency.

Just the man, I thought, to shake things up from Austin. Mike described his appointment as a "vote of confidence" in Texas teachers and educators, exactly what I wanted, and his statement at his opening news conference was exactly in line with my goals. "We must sharpen our focus and emphasize excellence in a core curriculum of basic subjects," he said. "Texas has great teachers and great educators, but we aren't getting the results we want in Texas schools today. We need to be innovators and creative thinkers to achieve excellence." The tone was perfect. Change is coming. We want high standards and academic excellence. We want creativity and competition. We need better results, and we know the teachers and educators we have in place are up to the task. We were on our way.

Six months later, in the fall of 1995, on the airplane headed to Lubbock, Mike and I were discussing the most recent student test scores from the Texas Assessment of Academic Skills, known as TAAS, an annual measure of student achievement. The most recent scores cast a glaring light on a very troubling statistic. More than 350,000 children, including 90,000 third and fourth graders, could not read well enough to pass a minimum skills reading test. I was appalled. I decided then and there that we were going to war against illiteracy. "I know our public schools teach a lot of subjects, and a lot of them are important," I told him. "But let's strip it down to the basics. If you could do one thing, one thing only, to get every child in Texas the best possible start to a great education, what would it be?" "Teach them to read," the education commissioner agreed. "Then let's do it," I replied, and the Texas Reading Initiative was born.

A few weeks later, Nelson Brown, a Houston teacher, put a human face on the dilemma. "My students can't read." Brown's plaintive cry first sounded in his hometown newspaper, the *Houston Chronicle,* and was later picked up by a statewide magazine. His story gave power and momentum to the cause of reading, and began to change the future of Texas.

Nelson taught ninth-grade history at Sam Houston High School, one of Houston's inner-city schools. Ninth-grade students have to pass a state-administered end-of-year test to advance to the tenth grade, and many of Nelson's students were flunking. Nelson's ninth-grade classes, supposed to be full of fourteen-year-olds, had sixteen-, seventeen-, eighteen-, and even a few nineteen- and twenty-year-old students. Understandably discouraged, the older students often gave up and dropped out, which led to the school's unacceptable 13.3 percent dropout rate. Too many students were failing the math section of the state test, and the school was rated "low performing," which meant the school was in trouble and failing to meet minimum state standards.

I am a strong advocate of accountability. I believe in results. After all, I ran a baseball team. The box scores are delivered in the driveway every morning, for everyone to read. Wins or losses are right there in black and white. If you don't measure how students are doing in school, how do you know whether teachers are teaching and students are learning? But Nelson Brown didn't think the Texas school accountability system was giving him a fair shot. The system was shining a spotlight of shame on failure, Nelson agreed, but he felt the spotlight was misdirected. His students' failing test scores had little to do with how well or poorly he taught history, he argued. The problem was much more profound. His students could not read, and he felt the accountability system was creating a scapegoat: him.

Nelson's article painted a devastating picture. During the first two weeks of school, Nelson gave all 160 of his high-school students a twenty-five-question vocabulary test. They didn't have to come up with the answers themselves; the test was multiple choice. Asked to define the verb "wade," 32 percent of the students, the highest number, picked "admire." A close second, 22 percent, mistakenly thought "wade" meant "worship," instead of the correct choice, "walk in water." Almost half of the ninth-grade students picked the wrong choice for the verb "mask," believing it meant to "nominate," "go to church," "annoy," or "extend," instead of the true meaning, "to conceal."

On it went, question after question, a sad litany of failure. Thirty-five percent of Nelson's students, the largest number, thought "compulsory" meant "disgusting"; only 11 percent knew the verb "labor" meant "toil." Almost a third of the students correctly identified "inferior" as meaning "below," or "lower," but it may have been luck, because another third said "inferior" meant either "above and higher" or "equal," and almost as many mistakenly thought it meant "rude." When asked to define "futile," 80 percent of the students chose the wrong answer—almost a third thought it meant "shocking."

What is shocking is that there are Texas teenagers who are so illiterate they can't understand the word "rut"—which was the case with three-fourths of Nelson's students. Think about it—we've got high-schoolers well on their way to getting stuck in a three-letter noun they can't even comprehend.

Nelson knew he could not teach high-school history to students who didn't know "wade" from "worship," and who had no understanding of whether "inferior" was good or bad, up or down. "Their vocabularies are so woefully deficient that they can't read the textbook; too often, they can't understand oral explanations, and they can't take any kind of worthwhile notes," he concluded.

And it wasn't just a few students who were having trouble. The best score in the class came from a student who missed "only" four of the twenty-five questions; the second-best student missed five; two missed eight. The remaining 151 students missed between ten and twenty-four questions on this "simple" vocabulary test.

"Think about this: 87.5 percent of my students cannot identify the correct meaning of 52 percent or more of the words on the test," Nelson wrote. "A significant majority of them, 57 percent, do not know the meaning of 72 percent of the words. And these were simple words."

The picture was already grim enough. But then Nelson went

for the kill. Read the following excerpt, not a particularly difficult one, he said, just a random selection from his ninth-grade history text.

> The New Deal was intensely controversial in the 1930s, and it has remained so to some degree ever since. To its defenders, it was a long overdue response to social injustices— a transforming moment that created a more humane and responsible government. To its critics on the right, it was a dangerous radical experiment that defied the Constitution and trampled on individual freedoms and the sanctity of private enterprise. To its critics on the left, it was a timid defense of capitalism, making modest alterations in the existing structure to fight off demands for more basic changes.

When you juxtapose that paragraph with Nelson's vocabulary test, you understand that for Nelson's students, the history book might best be used as a doorstop.

But Nelson did not throw up his hands in despair. He believed, as I do, that the problem can be solved. He talked of promising results from a computer reading class where students spent time focused just on reading. A colleague of Nelson's had put students to work on a computer reading program that began at the student's individual reading level. Working just twenty minutes a day for six weeks, each student raised his reading level by at least one grade.

Nelson closed with a stirring challenge to our state, to put more computers in classrooms, to do what it takes to teach children to read. "Do you want to continue to put thousands and thousands of uneducated dropouts on the streets? Do you want more crime? More prisons? More poverty? More welfare? It's up to you, Texas. You can continue to create scapegoats and watch the growth of problems for society, or you can help us. What's it going to be?"

I knew my answer. One of my jobs as Governor is to set clear and measurable goals. And a measurable goal is that every child should be reading by third grade and should remain on grade level throughout his or her public-school career.

For the next few months, my office worked closely with Mike Moses and the Texas Education Agency to develop the Texas Reading Initiative, which I outlined in a speech to educators from across Texas in January 1996, one year after I had first been inaugurated as Governor.

"Our children are the faces of our future. So I know you share my deep concern when I say that nothing stands to disrupt that future quite like the crisis now at hand: too many Texas school-children cannot read.

"The crisis is obvious in the numbers," I said. "Last school year, one in four Texas schoolchildren who took the state's basic reading skills test failed. That's 350,000 of our children, including 90,000 third and fourth graders, who cannot read and therefore are not prepared to learn.

"The crisis is obvious in our classrooms," I told them, sharing Nelson Brown's story of trying to teach high-school history to kids who couldn't read the book.

"This crisis is also obvious in our society," I said. "The science is clear and unequivocal. Children who do not learn to read by the end of third grade will likely never learn to read. Many will drop out of school. As uneducated adults, they face a life of frustration and failure on the fringes of society. Large numbers turn to crime and wind up in prison. Many others eventually join the welfare rolls. In study after study, the empirical evidence is deafening: you cannot succeed if you cannot read."

I sounded the battle cry: "Reading is to the mind what food is to the body. Nothing is more basic or more essential. And, in this administration, nothing is going to take a higher priority. That is why, today, I am here to set the clearest and most profound goal I have for Texas: Every child—each and every child—must learn to read."

I could see the skepticism on some faces. "He doesn't know the problems we deal with," I am sure some were thinking. Children who come to school hungry. Children whose parents neglect or abuse them. Children who assault their teachers; children who won't sit still long enough to learn.

Society throws many of our problems on the doorstep of our public schools. We expect teachers to be surrogate parents, counselors, and child welfare workers. Teachers are often overwhelmed. I frequently say you can't pay a good teacher enough for the love and care they give to our children.

I know the problems teachers face are real and difficult. I also believe they are surmountable. And one of the problems to tackle head-on, I thought, was a lingering suspicion that some kids who speak a different language at home or have a different skin color or live in a certain part of town somehow can't learn. That attitude infuriates me. I believe every child can learn, I refuse to give up on any child, and I wanted these educators to know I meant what I said.

"I am talking about every Texas child," I told them unequivocally. "It does not matter where children live or how much money their families earn. It does not matter whether they grow up in foster care or a two-parent family. In Texas, all our children are going to learn the basic skill on which the rest of their lives depend. I want to raise the bar for every child."

I outlined how we intended to go about it. We would direct $29 million of Texas's allotment of federal education funds to specific programs to strengthen teaching of reading and basic academic skills from kindergarten through fourth grade. We would improve teacher training, and ask the legislature to appropriate $35 million to create special reading academies, schools within schools that would focus just on reading. You cannot solve a problem until you identify it, so we would develop a teacher- and child-friendly diagnostic tool to help districts monitor and measure and make sure students were developing building-block reading skills between kindergarten and second grade.

I would also rally resources outside of our schools, I told them, businesses, foundations, and other state agencies. The Telecommunications Infrastructure Fund, a state agency, had agreed to make elementary reading a top priority as it distributed funds every year for the next ten years to put computers and technology in our public schools.

I urged the educators to use the flexibility and freedom of the new education code, freedom I had campaigned for and fought for during my first legislative session, which gave local school districts more autonomy and authority. "Be creative, be innovative. Use that menu of opportunity—whether you set up skill centers or mini-schools or extended-day reading classes or one-on-one tutoring. I hope you use your newfound freedom to promote reading. You should consider new ways to structure your class days. I hope you recognize that some children may need more time to learn to read. Some may need to spend the entire morning or most of the day focused on reading."

I wanted them to know the Governor was interested in results, not excuses. No more claiming they would have done a better job if only Austin had allowed them to do things differently. "I know there is a vigorous debate going on right now about the best way to teach children. My interest is not the means, it is the results. If drills get the job done, then rote is right. If it is necessary to teach reading all day long—fine by me.

"The state of Texas and the Governor will not dictate how you should teach. But we will take our responsibility to measure your progress very seriously. We expect the TAAS reading scores to show continued improvement toward our goal—that every child must read on grade level."

I called on parents: "The parents are a child's first teacher; the home a child's first classroom. I urge Texans to give their children the tools to start learning early—introduce them to books as babies. Keep reading to them as they grow. I challenge all Texas parents to develop families of learners by reading with their children a half hour a day, at least three times a week. Read children's classics, read the Bible, read the newspaper."

I called on every Texan: "I refuse to believe that—in a state as great as Texas—we can master rocket science but not reading scores. I know we can teach our children to read. But it will take all of us working together. So join me—in our communities, in our schools, in our homes—and let's make this year one for the books."

I knew the press would say it sounded simple. Teach children to read. How obvious. The first speech did not attract a great deal of attention. The Associated Press covered it, and the major daily newspapers, but many of the television stations didn't even show up. But gradually, it became obvious that this was far more than just a speech. Editorial interest and attention grew. Momentum built as I stuck with it. This was a cause, and for the next year, I talked of little else.

I traveled the state, urging community leaders, educators, and business leaders to join the war against illiteracy. Every visit to a school was a chance to implore teachers. Every speech to a business group or chamber of commerce was an opportunity to urge them to provide computers or volunteers or resources. I challenged the Boy Scouts to get involved. We organized a series of reading summits across the state to bring parents, teachers, and administrators together with local businesses, libraries, and volunteer organizations. The Texas Education Agency hired a reading czar. And every time I see children, I still ask, "How many of you read more than you watch TV?"

Thousands of Texans began to write me or call our toll-free reading hot line. A fourth grader from Gladewater wrote that he had accepted my challenge to read more than he watched TV. Reading, he said, "is starting to be a blast." Newspapers editorialized about the importance of reading, and libraries offered after-school homework help and literacy tutoring. School districts responded with reading programs and hundreds of corporations and private foundations joined to help them. The Clyde Drexler Literacy Foundation in Houston, for example, funded reading programs in the Houston Independent School District. Football stars from the NFL Players Association went into classrooms to read to students and give motivational talks. In Katy, Texas, more than five thousand volunteers signed up to help tutor schoolchildren, and more than seventy businesses signed a pledge to help ensure a quality education for each and every child in the Katy community.

Hundreds of companies throughout Texas adopted schools, following the example of Texas Instruments. It used to be that adopting a school meant showing up occasionally and putting a plaque on the wall. But that was not TI's vision of adoption. They put dollars, volunteers, and computer equipment to work in classrooms with students at Julia Frazier Elementary School in Dallas, and the test scores soared.

The Barbara Bush Foundation for Family Literacy, working in conjunction with my wife Laura's First Lady's Family Literacy Initiative, began awarding grants to reading programs throughout Texas. The Boy Scouts responded with a special program: the Governor's Challenge: Turn the Page, Scouting's Good Turn for Texas. The Boy Scouts ultimately met their goal of providing more than one million volunteer hours of literacy tutoring, and they inspired Scouts in other states to replicate the program.

And other political leaders noticed as well. One month after I launched the reading initiative, on February 28, 1996, U.S. Secretary of Education Richard Riley used very similar language to talk about reading in his State of Education in America speech in St. Louis. That summer, during his 1996 reelection campaign,

President Clinton announced a new goal, that every child in America should learn to read by the third grade.

Our focus on reading has paid off for Texas. Thanks to education leaders, thousands of teachers, and parents all across the state of Texas, we have a success story to share.

- TAAS test scores have increased across the board, for every ethnic group, in every subject, at every grade level tested over the last five years—and this is even though we have expanded the universe of children who are taking the test, as we should.
- Math scores have shown double-digit increases.
- Minority achievement has improved dramatically.
- This year's TAAS scores broke records, particularly in third-grade reading.
- A recent NAEP report card on math achievement showed Texas's African-American fourth graders ranked first in the nation, as compared to other African-American students around our country.
- A recent national report card found Texas is a national leader when it comes to improving our schools.

This is proof that Texans can rise to the challenge when we raise the bar and expect the best for every single child in our state. The next step would be the boldest move of all, putting an end to the practice of promoting children who are not prepared for the next grade. I would make that challenge the centerpiece of my 1998 reelection campaign.

7

THE BEST DECISION
I EVER MADE

IF it wasn't love at first sight, it happened shortly thereafter. My wife is gorgeous, good-humored, quick to laugh, down-to-earth, and very smart. I recognized those attributes right away, in roughly that order, the night our friends Joey and Jan O'Neill conspired to introduce us at a dinner at their house.

They had tried to get us together several times before, when Laura would come home to visit her parents in Midland, but she discouraged them. She was just there to spend time with her parents and visit friends, she would tell them.

We had actually grown up together in Midland. She lived with her parents on Humble Street; I lived with my family a half mile away on Sentinel. I went to Sam Houston Elementary; she went to James Bowie Elementary. We both went to San Jacinto Junior High. When I moved to Houston after seventh grade, she stayed in Midland, graduating from Midland Lee, while I went to Kinkaid and later Andover. I went to Yale and then Harvard; she went to Southern Methodist and later the University of Texas. In an odd coincidence of fate, we lived in the same apartment complex in Houston in the early 1970s. She lived on the quiet side of the Chateau Dijon; I lived on the loud side, where we played volleyball in the pool until late at night. She was teaching school; I was flying jets for the Texas Air National Guard and working a variety of jobs. Our paths never crossed.

I had moved back to Midland in 1975, drawn by the entrepreneurial spirit of the energy business. Laura moved to Austin to go to graduate school, where she earned her master's degree in library science, and became the school librarian at Dawson Elementary School. Laura came home to Midland to visit her parents in the summer of 1977, before classes began again, and this time, when Joe and Jan O'Neill invited her to dinner, she agreed to come. Nothing had really changed, they had just asked several times, and she decided it would not hurt to meet me.

Jan and Laura have been close friends for years. They went to high school together and roomed together in Houston. She later told us that she was not really sure that Laura and I would be interested in each other because we are such different personalities. Laura is calm; I am energetic. She is restful; I am restless. She is patient; I am impatient. But our differing styles exaggerate our differences. We share the same basic values. We share a West Texas upbringing that taught us that each individual is equal and equally important, but also that each individual has a responsibility to be a good neighbor and a good citizen. We both love to read, we both love spending time with our friends, and we both, very quickly, fell in love with each other.

The O'Neills later told me they knew something was different when I stayed until midnight. I go to bed early, and usually when I visited their house, I was almost always out the door no later than nine. The next night we all went to play miniature golf, and the next weekend I visited Laura in Austin. I was scheduled to go to Maine to visit Mom and Dad; I went and stayed one day, then flew back to Austin to see Laura. That's when my mother said she knew I was smitten.

Our friends were surprised, then not so surprised, then delighted. "Don came home and told me the O'Neills fixed you up with Laura Welch. I never would have thought of it," Susie said. "Then, when I thought about it, it made sense. Opposites attract."

We are not really opposite, although we are different. Laura is naturally reserved; I am outgoing. Laura stays in her own space; I've always invaded other people's spaces, leaning into them, touching, hugging, getting close. Some might mistake her calm for shyness, but they are wrong. She is totally at ease, comfortable and natural, just calm. I, on the other hand, am perpetual motion. I provoke people, confront them in a teasing way. I pick at a problem, drawing it to the surface. She is kinder, much more measured, arriving at a conclusion carefully, yet certainly.

I have always confronted uncomfortable subjects head-on. I think it's the mother in me. As Governor, when I visit important people and they make my staff feel unimportant, putting them in a back room, I will tease about it. "Is this the place for the little people?" I will ask. "I would rather be back here with the little people." Everyone else is thinking it; no one else usually says it. I have found that by directly confronting a slight or a hurt, you can minimize it. Placing it out on the table, in full view, also breaks the ice and usually makes people feel better. My friends in Midland remember when I would call to ask what they were doing and find out they were headed to a party to which I had not been invited. They would be uncomfortable; I would tease: "I guess I didn't make the cut." Or if everyone I knew was invited somewhere, I would call it a "phone-book party. They must have invited everyone in the phone book." My wife is nice enough to laugh out loud when I say things like that, but she would never say them.

A few months after we met, I asked Laura to marry me, the best decision I have ever made. I joke that I am not sure it was the best decision she has ever made to say yes, but she did. We told my family the first time they met Laura, during a trip to

Houston for the christening of my niece Noelle, Jeb's daughter. After the church service, we went to Mother and Dad's house. Laura and Mother went for a walk, and later, we told my parents we planned to get married and we wanted them to help us pick a date so they could be there. They were delighted; they were happy for me and they immediately loved Laura, just as I had. Dad looked at his schedule and we picked the first weekend he was available, November 5, 1977.

When I returned to Midland, I had dinner with my future in-laws, Jenna and Harold Welch, to formally ask for their daughter's hand. Fortunately, they said yes, and they became my family, too.

Our wedding was small, only seventy-five people, just our friends and immediate family. It was more spontaneous than elaborate; at the rehearsal dinner, my dad and our great friend Jimmy Allison heard a barbershop quartet playing at a party next door. They walked over and recruited them to come play for us. We didn't have bridesmaids or groomsmen. We were both thirty-one that year, the last of our friends to get married; we had each been in a lot of weddings and we didn't want anything complicated. No fuss, we just wanted to get married and we wanted our closest friends and family there to celebrate with us.

Laura and I went to Mexico for our honeymoon, then moved into a house that I had bought earlier that year. Laura said the weeds were as tall as she was. I had traded some oil leases for furniture. My favorite piece was a big, soft brown leather sofa that we never had the heart to get rid of; it sits in the girls' study at the Governor's mansion today.

For our extended honeymoon, we campaigned for Congress. It turned out to be a wonderful way to spend our first year of marriage. We were united on a common mission; we spent lots of time together. We had a young driver and the three of us drove around West Texas in our white Cutlass, meeting people and making friends. It was Laura's first real exposure to the political process, and she remembers it as a great deal of fun.

She tells a story about asking my mother for advice on being the wife of a candidate. Mother said, "Don't ever criticize his speeches." And Laura took that advice to heart, until one night, late in the campaign, when we were driving home from Lubbock. I knew my speech that night had not been good, and I pestered Laura for her reaction all the long way home. I guess I was expecting her to cheer me up, to tell me I had done better than I thought I had. As we drove into the garage, I gave it one last try. "I didn't do very well, did I?" And Laura replied, "No, it wasn't very good." I was so shocked, I drove the car into the wall of our house. Laura jokes that she doesn't criticize my speeches anymore, but that's not exactly accurate. The truth is, she is very smart. She doesn't criticize very often, so I really pay attention when she does.

After we had worked our hearts out for almost exactly a year, friends came to our house on election night to await the returns. As soon as the votes from Lubbock came in, I knew that I had lost. We were disappointed, but Laura does not remember it as a great setback. She was proud of the way I had conducted my campaign, and heartened that I had done so well in our home area of Midland.

The end of the campaign did, abruptly, change our life. For the first year, all our plans and activities had been directed toward one date, Election Day, then suddenly everything stopped. Laura and I took some time off, visited friends, and spent Christmas in Houston with my family. Then life settled into a normal routine we had not known thus far. I went to work at my energy company during the day, and we relaxed at home at night. Friday nights we joined the Evanses for Mexican food at Doña Anita's, Sunday brought church and lunch afterward with friends. Everything we did was casual; my friends still laugh that I was so casual,

I always looked as if I had just rolled out of bed in the clothes that I slept in. I was notoriously frugal. For a while, my only expensive dress shoes were a pair of alligator loafers my uncle had sent me. They were too big, but I didn't need to wear them very often. Once, when Vice President Bush came to town to give a speech, Don Evans literally took the shirt and tie off his back and insisted I wear them because he thought my shirt was too wrinkled for the occasion.

Laura and I were eager to have children. We were approaching our mid-thirties and began to feel the pressure of our ages. After Laura did not get pregnant for several years, we began to explore adoption. We had friends who had adopted children; Laura's parents had visited the Gladney adoption home in Fort Worth when she was little, after her mother had had a series of miscarriages. Laura and I visited the Gladney home. We filled out applications and had friends write letters of recommendation. By the time the Gladney home called to give preliminary approval for a home visit, Laura was pregnant. We were thrilled by the news we had awaited so eagerly; shortly thereafter, we went for a sonogram. I'll never forget the doctor saying: "Here's the baby. Oh, wait a minute, there are two babies, two beautiful babies." I remember hugging Laura, both of us weeping with joy.

The next day I sent Laura two dozen roses "from the father of twins." We were elated, but our excitement was tempered somewhat by the doctor's warning that twins were a high-risk pregnancy and Laura had to be very careful. We had waited so long that Laura was afraid to get our hopes up. She was cautious and superstitious; she wouldn't set up a nursery or buy baby furniture because she didn't want to count chickens before they hatched. Laura didn't go to Maine that summer because she was worried about traveling that far; I went for one day, then returned home, not wanting to be away from Laura and our growing little babies. In September, Laura went to bed. She and her doctor were worried that movement could cause premature labor, and the girls were not yet big enough to survive.

Laura developed toxemia in October. The doctor told her she had to check into the hospital right away, the next day. We had picked a hospital in Dallas where Laura's uncle was a surgeon and where we felt more sophisticated intensive care would be available for the babies. We had great doctors, one of whom was Dr. Delores Caruth, a neonatologist who was herself the mother of twins. When Laura arrived in Dallas, her condition stabilized and they were able to keep her in bed in the hospital for two more weeks, vital weeks for our babies to grow.

"You are having your children tomorrow," the doctor called to tell me. "Are you sure? It's five weeks early," I replied. "Well, unless you want your wife's kidneys to fail," the doctor replied. I rushed to Dallas and was in the room when the girls were born, the most thrilling moment of my life. Barbara came first, then Jenna, and they were large for twins, five pounds four ounces, and four pounds twelve ounces, both healthy. Because my dad was the Vice President, there was a lot of interest in the new granddaughters; they held their first press conference two hours after they were born.

Laura and I didn't know anything about babies, and suddenly we had two. In the early days, they cried, and cried, and cried some more. I still shudder today when I remember the helpless feeling that comes to all new parents when your precious little charges wail and cry and you can't seem to do anything to console them. "What's the matter with them?" I would ask Laura, help-lessly, but of course, she had no idea either.

I would pace through the house, holding both of them in my arms, juggling them, making faces, singing the only song I knew that seemed appropriate for children, the Yale fight song: "Bull-dog, bulldog. Bow wow wow." Laura has a picture of me en-gaged in this frantic exercise in the girls' baby book. The caption she put under it is, "Marching and singing Yale songs." My daughters howl with glee when they look at it.

There was never any question that I would help take care of them; I was a modern dad, plus we had our hands more than full. For a while we had a nurse, but I learned to change diapers, give baths, and feed them. We took them for long walks in the stroller. Weeknights, I came home from work and played with the babies. We would put them to bed early, sneak away, then run to the other side of the house so they wouldn't hear us and cry. Laura and I would sit outside in the backyard; she would putter in the garden and we would talk. My father-in-law, Harold, came by almost every day to check on the girls; we had dinner with Laura's parents often. They are kind and wonderful people. Harold passed away several years ago, and I miss him greatly; Jenna visits us a lot and I wish we saw her even more often.

The girls were baptized when they were eight or nine months old, and that's when I joined the Methodist church. Before then, Laura and I had attended both the Methodist church where she belonged and the Presbyterian church where I taught Sunday school when I first returned to Midland. I became an active member of the First United Methodist Church and served on the finance committee. On the Sundays when it was my job to count the money, my friends would give me a hard time by emptying their pockets, dumping all their change into the collection plate so it would take longer to count. I spent Sunday afternoons at meetings of the church administrative committee; I also became involved in the United Way and ultimately chaired one of its campaigns. Laura volunteered with the Junior League; we both believe in serving our community.

I loved being a dad and playing with the girls. A friend once told me he never realized how to enjoy his children until he watched me play with mine. I made faces at them, tickled them, wrestled with them on the floor. As they grew older, I helped with their homework. I was the only one in the family who could type, so when the girls tired of hunting and pecking on the keyboard, they would bring their school projects to me and I would finish typing them. They've learned to type now, but I'm still occasionally pressed into duty on big projects.

Although they are twins, the girls have always had very different personalities. We didn't have to encourage their differences so much as make sure that one did not abandon a pursuit because the other was involved in it. They would stake out territory. Jenna was the early bike rider, so for months, Barbara would not ride a bike. Barbara liked to cut and paste, so Jenna decided she was not interested. Our job was to discourage competition and encourage each of them to try things even if her sister did them earlier or better.

We all remember wonderful family times at the ballpark. Baseball was our life, starting in April, when the nights were still cold and we would stretch a blanket across us to keep the girls warm. It would end the same way, in October, in cold, with a long summer stretched out in between, its heat and humidity blanketing us during many long and leisurely nights. Barbara and Jenna also went to camp during the summers and they usually visited their grandparents in Maine for several weeks. We jokingly called it "basic training," hoping my mother was instilling some discipline into our feisty daughters.

They are normal girls, and as they grew older, the normal embarrassment of preteens and teenagers about the mere existence of parents was probably exacerbated by my increasingly high profile. I may have been a candidate for Governor, but I didn't have much status at my house. I will never forget one night in 1994. After a long day on the campaign trail, I went to pick the girls up at a party at eleven P.M., well past my bedtime. They had ordered me, "Do not come in," so I sat outside, waiting and watching other parents walk in and out to retrieve their children, until mine finally came to the car thirty minutes later.

When I won the Governor's election, we had an early lesson

in the importance of protecting the girls from the media spotlight. A television station did a feature showing our family decorating our Christmas tree. It was a happy holiday story and the girls seemed fine about participating, until the phone rang in the midst of the taping. Without thinking, I teased Jenna that it must be her latest boyfriend, naming the young man and embarrassing my daughter. "Dad," she exclaimed, stomping her foot, mortified, a wonderful little family vignette that the television station shared with the world. Jenna was furious. It was a good lesson. We've tried to shelter the girls. They don't give interviews, and they don't come to any events unless they want to. They are now seniors at Austin High School and their life in Austin has been normal; Laura and I are grateful that the media has respected their privacy.

Laura and I knew that having children would change our lives, but we didn't know how much. While the girls have had different needs at different times and different stages, our relationship, Dad to daughters, is forever, and its most enduring aspect is love. They try my patience as much as I try theirs. My job as a dad is to share my wisdom and teach them the lessons I have learned, and that sometimes requires tough love. It always requires complete love. I frequently talk about the unconditional love I received from my parents, and I hope someday my girls will say the same about me.

One of the most difficult things for a dad and mom is to recognize that there is a time when you must give your children additional responsibility and trust them to make decisions on their own. The most visible sign of that independence is a driver's license. It took me longer than I would like to admit to get accustomed to the idea of our girls driving alone, at night, through the streets of Austin. I worried. I worried they would fail to yield. I worried the radios would be blaring. I worried they would be distracted, talking with friends. But I came to realize the best thing parents can do is to teach their children right from wrong, clearly explain the consequences of bad decisions, surround your children with love, and hope and pray they remember the lessons and know when to put on the brakes.

No discussion of our family would be complete without mentioning our pets. The cats came first, when we returned from Washington, after my dad's presidential campaign. We had promised the girls they could have cats at our new home in Dallas, so the first weekend after we unpacked, we drove to an animal shelter and picked out two kitties. One of them died and we replaced it; Willie and Cowboy have lived at our house ever since. Our dog, Spot, was born in the White House to my mom's famous dog, Millie, on March 17, 1989. Six weeks later, Mother flew to Dallas to deliver her to Barbara and Jenna. Spot belongs to all of us, but she thinks she is my dog. Spot and I spend a lot of quality time together. She loves to play ball, and she has trained me well. Almost every day we play fetch.

Another kitty acquired us last year. I was out in the backyard and noticed Spotty making a great commotion in front of a tree. I thought it must be a squirrel and went to investigate. It was a scrawny, tiny kitty, which had somehow survived the streets of downtown Austin and ended up in a tree in the only backyard for miles, the backyard of the Governor's mansion. The kitty was skittish and afraid of us at first, but we began putting out food and it gradually warmed up. The kitty has six toes. Its little paws look like baseball gloves, and we named it Ernie because Ernest Hemingway had six-toed cats. Ernie is now a member of our family, claiming any comfortable spot as his own. I tell kids that the lesson of Ernie is no matter what tough circumstances you find yourselves in, never give up. Ernie went from the streets to the Governor's mansion, all because a dog chased him into a tree.

When I won the Governor's election, Laura felt her first priority was to get our family moved to Austin and our girls comfortable in their new home and school. But there was a hint of things to come when she hosted a reading for Texas writers as part of our inaugural-week festivities. I wanted Laura to do only what she wanted to do, no more and no less. I didn't push her to make speeches or public appearances; I didn't want my decision to lead a public life to dictate her choices. During the campaign, she had made some speeches to Republican women's clubs, but she wasn't really comfortable doing a lot of campaigning, which was fine with me.

I used to joke that Laura's idea of a speech was to put her finger to her lips in a school library and tell the children, "Shhhhhhh!" But I've quit telling that joke because Laura doesn't like it. She thinks it reinforces a negative image of librarians as mean people who tell children to be quiet. Her view of a librarian's role is much different, as she explained when she participated with Mother and me in an antidrug rally in Houston. Laura introduced Mother, who introduced me to a crowd of schoolchildren in a football stadium, not an easy place to give a speech. A member of my staff who had never heard Laura speak before was impressed. "Mrs. Bush, you are a wonderful speaker," she told her. My wife calmly replied, "I'm a librarian. Librarians are storytellers."

Laura had seen how effective Mother had been promoting literacy as America's First Lady. She knew that she wanted to make a difference in Texas. And as we settled into life in Austin, she gradually began working on a variety of projects, most involving her love of reading, art, and history, and her interest in children.

Laura has a Texas-size passion for books, a passion that is a part of our grand Texas history. When Texas hero Stephen F. Austin was jailed in Mexico in 1834, he bribed a guard to sneak a book into his jail cell. Austin wrote about the incident in his diary. "I prefer bread and water with books," he pronounced, "to the best of eating without them."

Laura views reading as food for the soul; I frequently come home to find her engrossed in a book. She has strengthened and revitalized Texans' love for books with a wonderful three-day celebration that has become an annual event, the Texas Book Festival. In 1996, Laura worked with the Texas Library Association, the Texas State Library and Archives Commission, and the Austin Writers League to start the festival, which features authors reading from their works, panel discussions, and book sales and signings. Authors who have given their time and prestige to the festival are as diverse as the literary landscape of Texas, from John Graves to Sandra Cisneros, Larry McMurtry, Frank McCourt, former President George Bush and General Brent Scowcroft, Mary Karr, Larry L. King, Kinky Friedman, Elmer Kelton, Mary Willis Walker, Joe R. Landsdale, and Robert James Waller. The festival is a family affair with children's activities, storytellers, music, and food. A gala dinner that kicks it off raises funds for Texas libraries. Approximately 230 libraries have received grants totaling almost $600,000 since the book festival started three years ago.

Laura also worked with the Texas Capitol Historical Art Committee and with Jan Bullock and Nelda Laney, the wives of our Speaker and Lieutenant Governor, to locate and collect historic Texas paintings for display at the state capitol. Her office at the capitol features a rotating display of the works of modern Texas artists; members of the public are invited to drop in to see the diverse works.

Laura launched the First Lady's Family Literacy Initiative for Texas, a statewide family literacy initiative designed to complement the education and reading reforms I have championed in our schools. Working in partnership with the Barbara Bush Foundation for Family Literacy, the program has awarded almost a million dollars in grants to programs, including a literacy program for the deaf, a pediatric medical clinic program, and programs working with Head Start, Even Start, and local libraries. She has traveled the state to promote Rainbow Rooms, a program to provide a safe haven for abused and neglected children.

She has championed breast cancer awareness and women's health issues. Last year she launched an early childhood development initiative, designed to arm parents with vital information to help their children get a healthy start in life.

Each Christmas, Laura displays unique holiday treasures at the Governor's mansion for the public and our guests to enjoy. One year, she displayed Texas folk art; another time, she collected treasured holiday decorations from former Governors to portray echoes of Christmases past.

A reporter once asked whether Laura had lost her voice, felt drowned out or overshadowed by the limelight. To the contrary, she has found a powerful voice. Hers is a voice for reading and literacy. A voice for authors and artists. A voice for abused children. A voice raising awareness about breast cancer.

Many people who don't like my politics love my wife. Writers, who tend to be more liberal than most Texans, appreciate Laura. She has helped celebrate their work, and she has done so in a knowledgeable and comfortable way. *Texas Monthly* magazine hosted a twenty-fifth anniversary celebration and asked Laura to be the speaker. She talked about the magazine and the way it has chronicled much of the modern history of Texas. "Since I can't possibly be as witty, as irreverent, or as insightful as a magazine that is known for its excellent writing, I plan to quote liberally," she said. "It's about the only thing a Republican knows how to do liberally." The audience howled.

I joke that the same thing that happened to my old man has happened to me. Both our wives are far more popular than we are. Laura has pursued her interests in a unique way, with grace and style.

The first time it hit home how at ease my wife has become in her new role was at the Republican National Convention in 1996. Laura was asked to speak, during prime time, about the importance of reading. "Reading is to the mind what food is to the body," she said. "In Texas, nothing will take higher priority."

I watched her deliver flawless remarks before a national television audience with awe and respect and love. During my reelection campaign, I used to say, "There are many reasons I want people to reelect me as Governor of Texas. The most important one may be to keep Laura Bush as our First Lady." It was always the biggest applause line.

Laura and the girls and I talked extensively before I decided to seek the Presidency. They were understandably reluctant. The girls don't want attention, and when your father is a presidential candidate, attention is almost impossible to avoid. Laura and I have been heartened that the media has respected Chelsea Clinton's privacy, and we hope they will do the same for our daughters. Laura remembers vividly how much it hurt both of us when my dad was criticized during his years as President. She dreads the thought of seeing similar attacks directed at me. But Laura also believes I have an opportunity to change the direction of our country. She believes, as I do, that America is at a critical moment in her history and that we must renew its promise and opportunity for all her citizens. She has seen firsthand the opportunity to make a difference as the First Lady of Texas, and I know she would be a fabulous First Lady of America. When I made my first campaign trip to Iowa and New Hampshire, Laura was by my side. She has already traveled to several states to campaign on my behalf. As America gets to know her, they will love her as I do.

Earlier this year, Laura and I went back to the Southern Methodist University campus in Dallas, from which she had graduated thirty-one years ago. For Laura's Christmas present, I gave a gift to the school in her name, the "Laura Bush Promenade," a beautiful and restful tree-lined brick passageway leading to the campus library. SMU students also contributed as their senior class gift. In honor of Laura, many of her friends, as well as my parents, put benches along the path.

"Laura and I both believe we have a responsibility to give

back—to share our many blessings with others," I told the audience. "And so as we were thinking about charitable contributions last year, Laura mentioned to me that she would like to give something to her alma mater, Southern Methodist University.

"Laura has fond memories of her years in school here. She credits SMU with nurturing her love for reading and learning and teaching. This is a gift that reflects its namesake: this is a serene and peaceful place, just like Laura.

"This promenade reflects a lot. It reflects a visionary, a decent soul, one who loves books and loves literacy. And it reflects my love for Laura." Tears in my eyes, I couldn't finish. My wife had to come to the podium to hug me, and walk with me back to my seat.

8

NAMING THE TEAM

THE "Icebox" some members of the Texas Senate called him, although only behind his back. "Big. White. Cold."

My staff and I thought the mildly disparaging label was hilarious. Not that we agreed. Clay Johnson is one of my lifelong friends (you first met him way back in the chapters on Andover and Yale, where he was my roommate). He is an intelligent and successful businessman who has a great sense of humor. But at the state capitol in Austin, Texas, where most people breathe politics like they breathe oxygen, Clay was the ultimate fish out of water.

I sent an important signal when I named him as my Appointments Director, a signal that the new Governor would not be doing business as usual. Clay was not a part of my political team and he knew little about politics; he was from the business world of bottom lines and results. The title Appointments Director is somewhat misleading; Clay was not in charge of haircuts or doctor visits. One of the Texas Governor's most important responsibilities is to appoint citizens, almost three thousand of them over

the course of a four-year term, to the various boards and commissions and agencies that oversee much of Texas state government. This widespread citizen participation is good and healthy,
but I knew the system was also ripe for abuse. Governors are
frequently criticized for appointing only major contributors to
key positions; I could only imagine that legislators and lobbyists
and trade groups and special interests would all try to pressure a
Governor to appoint their friends, contributors, supporters, and
advocates. Previous Governors had had some trouble with the
massive appointments job; one had famously appointed a dead
man.

I wanted to recruit and appoint people of quality, who would
serve the state, not selfish or personal interest. And Clay was the
perfect person to lead the charge. I could trust him, absolutely.
He was financially independent, and thus would not be looking
to curry favor or line up a job for the future. He had no agenda,
other than serving the state and helping me. And he loved Texas
as much as I did.

Clay would never be accused of being a good old boy. The
"you scratch my back, and I'll scratch yours" world of political
wheeling and dealing was totally foreign to him, and thus the
nickname "Icebox." The translation: Clay would not play the
political game. He was "cold"; no one could cozy up to him or
convince him to abandon his high standards to help a friend or
two or three. A legislator once called to ask Clay to appoint a
few people from his district to some "insignificant" boards, just
to "throw my area some bones." Clay politely informed him, "I
am not in the bone-throwing business."

Clay and his wife, Anne, were among the close friends who
celebrated with us in Austin on my first election night. The next
morning, I asked him to join with senior members of my campaign staff at an eight A.M. meeting in my suite at the Marriott.
Some of the staff grumbled at the early start after a late celebration, but I was eager to begin. My staff later said I looked different

that morning. I was about to become the Governor. I felt the weight of the responsibility and I wanted to make sure they did, too. We had a little more than two months until I would be sworn in as Governor and I would need every minute to set up my new administration.

"We are going to do two things," I told the assembled group. "We are going to enact a profound agenda that will change the future of Texas, and we are going to have the most ethical administration in our state's history." I wanted to start on the right foot, so I had asked my personal lawyer, Harriet Miers, to brief us on the state ethics laws that would govern our conduct. As she spoke, a hotel employee knocked on the door, bearing a huge basket of congratulatory flowers, underscoring the need to know the new rules about gifts and lobbying to avoid any potential conflicts. We didn't even have an office, but we were on our way.

The seventy-day transition was a blur of decisions. The first challenge of leadership, I believe, is to outline a clear vision and agenda. I had done so during the course of my campaign, and because I had outlined specific policy proposals, the people of Texas had endorsed my plans by electing me. The next challenge was to build a strong team of effective people to implement my agenda. I worked hard to recruit the very best.

I had decided I wanted a flat organizational chart rather than the traditional chief-of-staff approach; I wanted the senior managers of different divisions in my office to report directly to me, instead of working through a chief of staff. I like to get information from a lot of different people, plus I knew that high-powered people would be frustrated unless they had direct access to the boss. I had seen that problem in my dad's administration. Key members of his staff had felt stifled because they had to go through a filter to get information to the President. I did not want to replicate that environment.

I asked Joe Allbaugh, who had been my campaign manager,

to serve as my executive assistant, the first among equals. Joe doesn't try to block or restrict access to me. He's fair and even-handed. I knew he would be an honest broker of any differences on the staff. I was impressed that at a luncheon to thank our campaign workers, they had given Joe a standing ovation for his work. Joe had previously filled a similar role for the Governor of Oklahoma, so he knew how a Governor's office operates and how it interfaces with the legislature. Joe's role was to make sure my decisions were implemented and to oversee the administration of the Governor's office and our executive branch agencies; he also became a key part of our dealings with the Lieutenant Governor, Speaker, and legislators.

I recruited Al Gonzales, a smart and talented young lawyer from Houston, to serve as my general counsel. Al impressed me with his thoughtful approach to the law. He is straightforward and has good judgment and common sense. I felt he was a strong, independent person, who would give me an objective evaluation of the law and an honest opinion about how to apply it.

I asked Mike Weiss, a longtime friend and accountant from Lubbock, who had valuable experience with state government as a member of the governing board of the massive Employees Retirement System, to come to Austin to help me get a handle on the state budget. Mike quickly identified the brightest budget mind in the state of Texas, Albert Hawkins, and told me I needed to persuade Albert to join my office as our budget director. Albert had been with the Legislative Budget Board for more than twenty years, and he was reluctant to leave the relative security of that role. When Albert came to the transition office to meet with me, he told Joe Allbaugh that he had come as a courtesy, indicating he probably wouldn't accept the job, but I put on a full-court press. I outlined my vision for Texas and told Albert it was time for him to put his years of experience to work in a leadership role that would help set the tone for all state government. I assured him that not only would he have the freedom to run the Governor's budget division, he would also be part of the decision-making process on every major issue in the Governor's office. Albert joined our team; the other directors quickly learned to rely on his knowledge and judgment. After years of performing budget analysis on state agencies, Albert knew almost everything worth knowing about state government.

I knew my dealings with the legislature would be critical to the success of my administration, and I also knew the legislature would be most comfortable with one of its own. I asked Dan Shelley, a Republican state senator who had decided not to seek reelection and had previously served in the Texas House of Representatives, to serve as legislative director. Joe suggested I should add a few additional senior advisors. "It will take us some time to build credibility with legislators," he told me. "We need to start off by hiring some, and that will buy us time while we develop our own." It was great advice. We added Cliff Johnson, a former conservative Democrat state representative who had many close friends in the legislature, and Reggie Bashur, who had worked in my campaign press office and as Governor Clements's Press Secretary. Both were highly regarded in Austin; they had great antennae, and were plugged in to the back rooms of the legislative process.

We also gained credibility with the legislature when I asked State Representative Elton Bomer, a conservative Democrat from East Texas, to resign his seat and come to work as insurance commissioner. Insurance is a volatile and important consumer issue. I wanted someone who would be tough and fair. Bomer was highly regarded, close to Speaker Laney, and had been named to *Texas Monthly* magazine's respected list of the "ten best" legislators. He blended a business background with the political savvy that the insurance job needed. Some Republicans criticized the decision, even though it opened up a legislative seat that was ultimately won by a Republican. Elton was the right man for the job, and by the end of his tenure, Republicans were among his biggest fans.

Vance McMahan, the bright Stanford lawyer who had overseen our policy development in the campaign, would direct the Governor's policy operation, Karen Hughes would continue her campaign role as Communications Director, and Margaret LaMontagne, the campaign's political director, would be my chief education policy advisor and would help provide some balance for Clay's lack of political knowledge in appointments. My chief strategist, Karl Rove, would run the Bush committee, an ongoing political operation to make sure we did not blend taxpayer and political business, and manage my political efforts to help elect candidates and build the Republican party.

I was proud of my senior team, and at one of our first meetings, I gave them a piece of advice: "Always return each other's phone calls first." I felt that would foster good communication and make sure my senior people would seek one another's advice and guidance. Many of them later told me it set the tone and was key to the team approach they developed.

My first major appointment other than members of my own senior staff was to name Tony Garza Secretary of State. Tony is an articulate, bright young leader who had been the first Republican ever elected to the chief leadership job in county government— county judge in Cameron County, a heavily Hispanic Democratic stronghold in the Rio Grande Valley. The Secretary of State has a great deal of stature; he is the state's chief elections officer, responsible for administering all election laws. I also wanted Tony to be an active member of my senior staff. I saw the Secretary of State's role as an opportunity to build a diplomatic bridge to Mexico. Tony, who had worked closely with Mexican officials during his tenure as Cameron County judge, was a good friend and the perfect choice. The appointment also allowed me to reach out to the Hispanic community and to an area of the state,

South Texas, where I had received very few votes, to clearly demonstrate I intended to be the Governor of all Texans.

Clay approached the appointments process as a start-up business. He set up systems and criteria to help him find people whose experience and expertise matched the various job descriptions. I had suggested he meet with people who had advised former Governor Bill Clements on appointments, which he did. Separately, I asked a friend, Chase Untermeyer, the former Director of Personnel in the Bush White House, to review the appointments process and prepare a summary of the boards and commissions, which he gave to Clay.

They included groups as diverse as the Air Conditioner and Refrigeration Contractors Commission, the Fire Ant Research Management Account Advisory Committee, the State Commission of Examiners in Fitting and Dispensing of Hearing Instruments, the Acupuncture Board, and the Barber Examiners Board. There was a three-member Egg Marketing Board that was finally abolished in 1997. Our appointments staff joked that only about three people in the entire state were eligible to serve on it. The boards and commissions also included the governing bodies of virtually every major public university and agency in Texas: the University of Texas, Texas A&M and Texas Tech, and agencies that govern everything from the environment to law enforcement to work force training to public utilities to teacher and employee retirements systems to health and human services.

Clay initially worried that he might make some big political mistake, that because of his business background and lack of political knowledge or sensibilities, he might unknowingly cause me harm or embarrassment. I reassured him, "You worry about finding good people. I'll take care of the politics."

The appointments office is a good case study in how I make decisions. For each appointment I make, generally three or five or ten or sometimes twenty people want the job but are not selected. The appointments staff jokes that I make appointments, they are in charge of the disappointments. All kinds of people seek appointments. One applicant, on the education section of our form, wrote that she "has attended the school of hard knocks, but hasn't yet graduated." The appointments team looks carefully at why someone wants an appointment, mindful of the admonition of a state senator who cautioned, "In the public arena, you should never attribute to chance what could possibly be explained by a conspiracy." The staff generally categorizes applicants in one of two groups:

Some people:

Want to pad their résumé.
Want to gain power and control over some aspect of their profession.
Want to get involved in politics.
Have been recruited by their local community to try to bring more influence to their part of the state.
Don't have much experience to prove they can work effectively with board members from different perspectives and backgrounds.
Are seeking an appointment as a reward for past political service or involvement.

Other people:

Have demonstrated their ability to serve effectively on local or professional boards.
Have broad state, not narrow parochial, interests.
Have shown they have the strength of character to do the right thing even when it may not be popular.

As Clay says, wryly, we prefer the "other" people to "some" people. The selection process usually begins with an evaluation of the needs of the board or agency. A college or university may need someone with a fund-raising or marketing background to help expand an endowment or recruiting program; the environmental agency may need someone with a scientific background or expertise. Geographic balance is often important to make sure state agencies treat all parts of the state fairly. Diversity is another consideration. I don't believe in quotas or racial preferences, but I instructed Clay to seek and recruit qualified appointees who reflect the diversity of Texas.

What I want from my staff is thorough research and unvarnished opinion. I don't want them to tell me what they think I want to hear; I try to create an atmosphere where they feel comfortable expressing their ideas and opinions. Whether in a policy or appointments or legal briefing, I'll frequently stop, go around the room, and ask different individuals what they think and why.

I make decisions by understanding the background of an issue first. I will read about it and ask for additional information. The history major in me comes out when I seek to understand the background behind the issue of the day. I don't like long pre-programmed meetings. When state agency directors come in to brief me on a subject, they sometimes bring prepared notebooks and try to flip through them, reading out loud, page by page. I've usually already read the briefing books. I've been known to ask the directors to close the book and tell me in their own words what is really important, what they recommend and why.

I want members of my staff to know I think about what they say. It's important to listen, and I often call to follow up or ask about something someone said in a conversation. I do like people to make their points and express their opinions directly and concisely. If I know and trust someone, I would rather have him or her make the case in person. I read a lot of memos, but I enjoy the give-and-take that comes with a substantive discussion. I want to probe logic, ask questions and test ideas by talking about them.

I put a lot of faith and trust in my staff. I look for people who are smart and loyal and who share my conservative philosophy. My job is to set the agenda and tone and framework, to lay out the principles by which we operate and make decisions, and then delegate much of the process to them. The final decision often rests with me, but their judgment has a big influence. Clay screens and interviews applicants for appointments, then brings his recommendations to me.

The choice for a district judge came down to two well-qualified and highly regarded lawyers, one older and more established in the community, the other younger, higher energy, and a loyal and active Republican who had worked hard for my campaign. Clay outlined the qualifications of each, then recommended the older man. I asked why. "I just think the main reason the younger lawyer wants this appointment is because he wants to be part of the George Bush team," Clay told me. "What's wrong with that?" I asked. "Surely having the good sense to support me doesn't disqualify someone," I teased my Appointments Director. The reply came back, serious and stubborn. "I just think he wants to be a part of your team more than he wants to be a judge. What happens if he is still on the bench and you are no longer Governor? Will he still come to work trying to do the right thing every day?" Sometimes, Clay is a fifty-three-year-old Boy Scout. But he had a good point, and I wanted to think about it. Later that week, at a reception, I spotted a community leader I respected from the city in question. I told him the names of the two candidates we were considering and asked his advice. Unbeknownst to him, he confirmed Clay's judgment. "They are both well thought of," he told me. "The younger guy is a mover and shaker and wants this for his résumé," he said. "The other wants to be a good judge." I went with Clay's recommendation.

Sometimes legislators or contributors or supporters try to pressure my office to appoint a candidate of their choosing. We've sent a clear message that we don't play that game. Clay and I don't react very well to attempts at pressure; Clay is obstinate enough that he might not recommend someone if he feels pressure is being applied; I am obstinate enough to stand up to the critics when they complain about Clay.

My appointments decisions have made some people mad. We try to explain the reason for the decision and move on. When legislators are unhappy with me, I tell them they would do the same thing if they were Governor, explaining a larger worldview than the confines of their individual districts.

I am loyal to my friends, so it is sometimes hard to say no. One of my close friends very much wanted to be appointed to a state board, and he would have been a great member. He was smart and hardworking and well qualified. But Clay and the appointments staff had interviewed the agency's executive director, who felt the agency needed specific expertise in construction management and environmental law, and some geographic representation from a different part of the state. Although he would have been outstanding, my friend didn't meet those needs. So I did what I thought was best for the agency and the state and appointed three other people. One of the adages in the appointments office is that the real measure of a person is how he responds to bad news. My friend was disappointed, but he understood and respected the process. He confirmed the good things we all thought about him.

I have appointed four members of the Texas Supreme Court, almost half of our nine-member highest court. Texas elects our judges; the Governor appoints them only in case of a vacancy such as retirement or resignation. It happens more often than you would imagine.

Judicial appointments are long lasting and extremely important. In each case, I wanted a judge who would strictly interpret the constitution and laws of Texas and would not attempt to legislate from the bench. In each case, I wanted a person of impeccable character and integrity. In each case, I wanted someone smart and hardworking. And I found them in each case in the justices I appointed to the Texas Supreme Court: Justices James Baker, Greg Abbott, Deborah Hankinson, and Al Gonzales.

The *Texas Lawyer,* which, as the name implies, covers legal and judicial matters, paid Clay's appointments team a great compliment recently when it wrote an article on May 10, 1999, headlined: IT TURNS OUT THAT GEORGE W. & CO. DO HAVE A LITMUS TEST FOR JUDICIAL APPOINTMENTS. IT'S CALLED CHARACTER. The article reported:

> *Texas Lawyer* spoke with a wide range of lawyers and politicos about Bush's judicial selection method and the results it has yielded. The consensus among 25 diverse lawyers— from hard-scrabble criminal-defense types to high-rise-dwelling big-firm partners to champing-at-the-lawsuit-bit plaintiffs' lawyers—is that if President Bush goes about appointing federal judges as Governor Bush has gone about appointing some 88 state judges, the federal judiciary will be all the better for it. . . . Bush appointees are seen as extremely intelligent men and women who are well-qualified for the job.

The article noted that we choose people as if we are running a business. Clay's team carefully checks out backgrounds and references. He seeks the opinions of local lawyers who have seen a candidate practice law, and he especially likes to talk with those who have been in trial against a potential judge. But as I told Clay from the very beginning, the most important standard is to find judges who will be strict constructionists and will not try to be lawmakers in black robes.

One of my judicial appointees, Judge Manny Alvarez, told the newspaper the story of his appointment:

> Alvarez says he was up against a white male, a white female and an African-American male for the same bench. . . . "I

told them that I didn't want to be appointed because I was Hispanic; I wanted to be appointed because I was the best qualified," Alvarez says. A year after he was appointed, Alvarez was the highest rated criminal judge in Dallas County, according to the 1997 Dallas bar poll.

One of my favorite parts of the job is administering the oath of office to my new appointees. They invite family and friends. Their parents and children are bursting with pride. I always feel honored to look through this window into someone's life. I think of the day I traveled to Edinburg, in south Texas, to administer the oath of office to Micaela Alvarez (no relation to Manny), the first Hispanic woman ever to serve as district judge in Hidalgo County. I listened as one of her lifelong friends spoke of Micaela's integrity, her love for her family, her fairness, and her conservative philosophy. I watched as her parents, husband, children, sisters, cousins, and nieces and nephews crowded around to have their pictures taken with her. They all wanted to participate in this glorious moment in the life of their family.

Micaela's parents were migrant farm workers who traveled from job to job on farms throughout Texas and the southern United States. For them, Micaela was not just a success story. She was living proof of what they had lived for and promised their children: that in Texas and in America, if you work hard, get an education, make good choices in life, you can be whatever you want to be. And I can assure you, when her mother held that Bible for Micaela to take the oath of office to serve the state of Texas as a district judge, there wasn't a dry eye in the packed house.

Another memorable moment came the day I administered the oath of office to an old friend, Michael Williams. I told the crowd I got to know Michael when I was living in Midland. He ran for County Attorney in 1984; I was his campaign manager. "If you ever think of running for office, I strongly suggest you get another campaign manager," I told Michael and the crowd. "We didn't do so well. But we became friends. He is a good, honest man. He was raised in the oil patch." Michael's wife, Donna, was there, and his parents, to watch their son become the first African American ever to serve on the Texas Railroad Commission, which regulates the state's oil and gas industry.

"We stand on the shoulders of a wide number of folks who came before us," Michael said, talking of previous railroad commissioners and elected officials. "The state of Texas has had great leaders . . . and a whole bunch of unnamed and unknown folks that quite frankly, on a day like this, I'm proud to say look a whole lot like me. So today, let me just simply say that as we move to serve this state, we will move with the spirit that they brought us."

And none of us will ever forget the emotional moment when I administered the oath of office making Al Gonzales, who started out as my General Counsel, then served as Secretary of State, a justice of the Texas Supreme Court.

I told a story about when Al was twelve years old and sold soft drinks during football games at Rice Stadium. He remembers staying long after the crowds had gone home, watching the students wander back across campus, and daydreaming about how wonderful it would be to be a college student with unlimited possibilities.

My speechwriter, Gail Randall, was sitting in the upstairs gallery, and she watched as some Hispanic teenagers wandered in during their sightseeing trip to the capitol. They took seats and, after a few minutes, seemed spellbound by what they were seeing and hearing: A guy who looked just like them, who started out like them, was putting on the robes of a Texas Supreme Court justice. And he and the Governor who appointed him were hugging each other.

Gail told me the young tourists never budged; they stayed until the very end of the ceremony. And it occurs to me that—just like Al Gonzales perched in Rice Stadium—those kids, perched in the House gallery, got a glimpse that day of what can happen when you dare to set high goals and dream big.

A Governor's appointments are a lasting legacy. Long after I leave office, many of the judges and officials I appoint will still serve. The terms of many members of boards and commissions are longer than my own term of office. I hope my appointees will be known as quality people who brought new ideas and different approaches to state government. I believe I have helped put in place a new generation of leaders for my state.

9

WORKING TOGETHER

I NEVER used the nickname to his face. But I'm sure he heard about it, and was probably secretly pleased. It was an affectionate way to recognize his power and influence, and the way he could bulldoze those who got in the way of doing what he thought was right for Texas. Call "Bully," I would say to my staff, check in and let's see what "Bully" thinks about it.

"Hi, I'm Bullock," the slight man had said, beckoning me into the living room of his west Austin home. "Yes, sir, and I'm George W. Bush," I replied, an inauspicious beginning to the most unusual friendship of my life.

Bullock—"Bully" in my Rolodex of nicknames—was Bob Bullock, the Democratic Lieutenant Governor, most often described as the most powerful politician in Texas. Lieutenant Governors are independently elected in our state; Bullock was the last remaining giant of a past era, when Texas politicians and their personalities seemed larger than life. Adjectives cannot begin to describe him. He was a man of outsized passions and famous faults. He was frequently outrageous, sometimes crass, often funny, always cunning. He was unpredictable, volcanic in his language, rough-hewn, yet surprisingly tender-hearted.

His temper was legendary. At one point or another, he fired almost all of his staffers, many of them several times. They wore it as a badge of honor. You hadn't arrived as a true "Bullockian," as they proudly called themselves, until you had made Bullock mad enough to fire you at least once. He was difficult—no, impossible—to work for. He demanded that his employees wear beepers, which he would use to find them in the middle of the night. If they arrived at the office anytime after 6:00 or 6:30 A.M., he was already there, and that meant they were already behind. He would tear up work that he felt wasn't adequate. "This is for Texas," he would tell them. "You can do better."

Bullock had been an institution in state government since 1956. He served two terms in the Texas House, was an assistant attorney general, a Governor's appointments secretary, the secretary of state, and then was elected and served sixteen years as the Texas comptroller. He controlled the money, and thus much of state government. As comptroller, he set the revenue estimate that determined how much money legislators could spend. He controlled the timing of the estimates, could choose when to make revenue updates that made additional money available, and would do so at key moments that suited his purposes. He revolutionized the comptroller's office, brought it into the modern age of computers and technology. His staff members were highly sought after by other agencies. People who had graduated from the Bob Bullock school of public service were hardworking, knowledgeable, and tough. Bullock had a network of people loyal to him throughout state government.

Bullock was a lifelong Democrat, and as Lieutenant Governor, he was the leader of the Texas Senate, which still had, at the time of my election in 1994, a Democratic majority. Bullock was not of my party or my generation; he was a crafty master of the political process, not inclined to think much of a rookie like me.

Yet I knew that if I became the Governor of Texas, somehow, I would have to get along with him. Visiting his home during the final weeks of the 1994 campaign was the first step. I thought I was going to win, and I hoped Bullock would be impressed by my overture, would think the visit was a bold move. We spent a couple of hours talking about our mutual love for Texas; we talked about policy, not politics.

Mostly, I listened, and he talked. Conversations with Bullock were often a monologue. But by the time I left, I felt confident that we could work together. After I won the election, I continued my outreach. I called Governor Bullock and the Speaker of the Texas House of Representatives, also a Democrat, Pete Laney. I told them I respected them and wanted to work with them for the good of Texas. I knew that only by working together could we all be successful. Joe Allbaugh and I met with Speaker Laney at the Four Seasons Hotel a day or two after the election. The Speaker, a West Texan who I think was proud to see a fellow West Texan as Governor, telegraphed an important willingness to work with me for the good of our state: "Governor, we're not going to let you fail," he said.

Pete Laney is a cotton farmer. He's a man of the land. It's hard to overstate what that means. He understands storms and insects and bad luck and bad weather. Pete has had to work hard for everything he has accomplished in life. He is steady, a patient tiller in the soil of the legislative process. He knows that good legislation, like a good crop, requires work and time; he knows the need for sun and care and watering between planting and harvesting. Pete brought a touch of prairie populism to the Texas House. We differed on key issues, including school choice, home equity lending, and some tort reforms, but we respected our differences and became friends.

Pete is the strong leader of a dying breed, the rural conservative Democrats who have dominated Texas politics since Reconstruction. The Texas House still has a narrow Democrat majority, but that is changing. Conservative Democrats are being replaced by Republicans; the safe Democratic districts are now more likely urban, inner-city, majority minority, and moderate or liberal. Republicans have seen a dramatic increase in our numbers, from nineteen out of 150 in 1978 to seventy-two today. Pete recognized the changes by sharing power and delegating a lot of authority and responsibility to key committee chairmen, most of them Democrats, but some Republicans. Some don't think he shares enough; those he shares with usually think he handles it just right. Laney commands great loyalty; his team likes and respects him.

Pete and Bob came to see me in the transition office when I was setting up the administration, the first of many regular get-togethers. We agreed to meet each week during the legislative session for breakfast, and I invited them to the Governor's mansion for the first Wednesday morning. Bullock complained that the food was too healthy, not greasy enough, so from then on we alternated between the speaker's apartment on the west side of the capitol and Bullock's office on the east side. We usually had biscuits, gravy, and eggs, and my favorite, pancakes. We had some indigestion and it wasn't always because of the food. We were strong-willed people who sometimes had strong differences. But we met and we talked. We kept each other's confidence and our commitments, and gradually we built trust and friendship.

Bullock and Laney have challenging jobs. Leaders of the legislative branch of government work to bring diverse individuals and causes to a common conclusion. Someone once compared it to herding cats, trying to guide and direct independent creatures who tend to wander off in a lot of different directions. The goal is to get to the end of the session with good legislation and no unnecessary partisan catfights. Sure, there may be some hissing and spitting, but no blood. The Texas legislature meets for only 140 days every two years. I joke that some Texans would rather that the legislature meet for only two days every 140 years. We like to say in Texas, "If government doesn't meet, it can't hurt you." Short legislative sessions force discipline and focus. They also require legislators who want to get things done to check partisanship at the door.

There is a natural tension, some competition, between the house and the senate in any legislative body. The house believes it is the home of true debate, that only the house, with 150 members and more committee chairmen than the senate has members, gives legislation the thorough, nitty-gritty scrubbing it needs. Debate is more rambunctious in the house, where members line up at the microphone to have their say. Senators each have their own microphones. The senate believes it is more statesmanlike, that its members see the bigger picture. Senators represent five times as many people, have bigger budgets, bigger staffs, and, some house members would say, bigger egos. Pete Laney likes to remind senators who first served in the house that they are "housebroke."

Laney is a master of brinksmanship. What some people don't know about Pete is that in addition to farming, he also owns a used-car dealership. He knows how to negotiate. The house withholds action, takes its own time, as the senate passes a lot of bills. Then, power shifts to the house. The house can work the legislation, wait until the last possible moment, and with the pressure on, the senate may be forced to accept house changes or face losing the legislation altogether.

And so many of our meetings consisted of Bullock urging Laney to get moving. Bullock was a talker. He played his cards; Laney held his cards close to his vest. Bullock would try to dictate a solution; Laney would finesse one. At the table were two very different Democrats and a new Republican Governor, all with key roles in the process.

Our early meetings were push and pull. Bullock would thrust, and I'd jab back. We were testing each other, probing. Bullock always kept you on edge. He could surprise you with an insight, antagonize you suddenly with an unexpected shot, talk forever, then abruptly end the meeting. Laney was calmer, harder to read. He didn't wear his emotions as much on his sleeve. The meetings were sometimes tense, always interesting, and often full of laughs. Pete had a story to fit every situation; Bullock had stories, too, outrageous ones that you could never repeat in polite company.

I worked hard to learn the legislative process and get to know individual legislators. I knew if I had strong relations with members, I would have stronger relations with their leaders. I would unexpectedly drop by their offices, surprising receptionists and young legislative aides. I invited them to breakfast or lunch or dinner. I was accessible, always willing to see members who told my legislative staff they wanted to talk with me. I met with the house Republican caucus and spent a lot of time with committee chairs from both bodies and both parties. Hugo Berlanga, a Democrat and house committee chair, later told me he spent a lot more time with me than he ever had with any Democratic Governor.

I'm an observer, a listener, and a learner. We had all run for office for a reason. I wanted to hear what was important to each member, what he or she hoped to accomplish during the session. I was convinced that through patience and respect and listening to each other, we could find common ground.

My staff jokes that you can tell what the legislature thinks of the Governor, because the legislature begins its session before the Governor is even inaugurated. But because I had campaigned on specific reforms, I felt I had a good start on the legislative process. The public had, after all, endorsed my agenda by electing me. I used my state-of-the-state address to underscore the point. My campaign had focused on four key areas: reforms in education, welfare, juvenile justice, and tort law. The press was tired of my single-minded focus on the same four. They were ready for number five. Here it is, I joked during my State-of-the-State address: Number five, I said, is to pass the first four. Bullock loved it.

There were some moments of high drama, moments when legislation hung in the balance. Early in the session, Bullock decided he was going to take the bull by the horns and get the issue of tort reform resolved or out of the way for good. During my campaign, I had outlined a package of tort reform bills designed to curb frivolous and junk lawsuits, stop excessive punitive damage awards, and end the practice of "forum shopping" that allowed plaintiffs to file their cases almost anywhere they thought would give them a friendly judge or jury. I took on the trial lawyers directly, and won. Trial lawyers gave millions of dollars to my opponent; yet the public had agreed with my call to "end the frivolous and junk lawsuits that clog the courts and threaten our small business owners and entrepreneurs." The trial lawyers had lost the election, but they hadn't lost the legislative battle, at least not yet. I knew they wouldn't quit without a fight. They are savvy veterans of the legislative process, and I worried that the issue could be targeted for filibuster or killed on a procedural move. So I declared the tort reform package a legislative emergency, to highlight the issue's importance and make sure it didn't get bogged down in the legislative process.

"I want my man in there," I told Bullock, when he told me he was going to convene a working group to negotiate the details of tort legislation. "The Governor wants his man in the negotiations, so he's going to be here," Bullock had said, introducing my policy director, Vance McMahan, to the group of key senate and house members and plaintiffs and defense attorneys. Bullock had assembled the group, as only Bullock could do, and ordered them to work it out, as only Bullock could do. (Years later, while eulogizing Bullock, I joked that I was glad I was not Saint Peter. "Bullock's got him locked in a room and he's not going to let him out until he's happy with the details of his plan for eternity,"

I said, to knowing laughter from the crowd of Bullock's closest friends.)

The first issue on the tort reform table was punitive damages, and the negotiators were stuck. Punitive damages have nothing to do with a victim's actual damages. They are intended to punish a defendant for extraordinarily negligent or malicious behavior. But too often, that was not how they were being used; they were being used to terrorize small-business owners and force higher and higher out-of-court settlements. Punitive damages of tens of millions of dollars became all too common, even when the dispute involved actual damages that were much smaller. A major employer had closed its Fort Worth plant and moved six hundred jobs out of Texas in 1992 because, its chairman said, of Texas's liability laws and "the excessively large awards routinely given by Texas juries." The negotiators were stuck on a number I thought was too high. Over their dead bodies, they said, would the cap on punitive damages be anything lower than two times actual damages plus $1 million.

Vance McMahan came to me, warning that the negotiations were tense, and Bullock might pull the plug on the whole package if we didn't agree. It was my first legislative test; one of the four cornerstones of my campaign was at a critical juncture. "A million dollars is too high. I can't agree," I told Vance, who agreed that as a matter of good public policy, the amount needed to be lower. "We may lose everything over this," Vance warned. "Explain we are willing to work with them, but I just cannot accept one million," I replied.

Later that night, Republican Senator David Sibley was having dinner with me at the Governor's mansion, discussing a different issue. During the middle of the meal, he was summoned to the phone. It was Bullock. "You tell your friend the Governor he's too stubborn and bullheaded for his own good. He's not doing the state right," Bullock told Sibley, who delivered the message. Sibley asked me what the problem was, then suggested a cap of $750,000. I said I could live with that, and Sibley called Bullock, who agreed. "You're the greatest Governor ever," said Bullock, when Sibley put him on the phone with me to seal the deal. Later, some of my tort reform supporters tried to persuade me to work to lower the amount even further. But I had given my word. Bullock learned quickly that I could solve a problem, and I would not be pressured, even though some who had contributed to my campaign were putting on the heat. Bullock and I had agreed, and I would not back down. Bullock later told people that it was during the tort reform negotiations that I first earned his respect.

That moment also showed me how powerful a Governor can be. When the Lieutenant Governor and Governor, or Speaker and Governor, or even better, all three can agree on something, it's a tough combination to beat.

Our roles, however, are different. The Speaker and Lieutenant Governor are horse traders, lining up votes. The legislative process is one of give-and-take, of agreement and disagreement. Their job is to figure out how to shape and mold legislation, to put together the pieces into a whole that can gather enough votes to pass.

My job is different. A Governor is a chief executive officer. I believe my job is to set its agenda, to articulate the vision, and to lead. That hasn't always happened in Texas. Often, Governors propose and legislators ignore. Each legislative session, the Governor sends a budget message to the legislature. It is usually greeted with a yawn, dutifully reviewed, then shelved.

The office of Governor of Texas has frequently been described as "weak," but I reject that label. The role is constitutionally limited, but there are plenty of weapons in my arsenal. A Governor signs or vetoes every piece of legislation. A Governor makes thousands of appointments of citizens who govern state agencies, boards, and commissions. Only a Governor can call a special session and set its agenda. Most part-time legislators have full-time jobs and don't like special sessions. As the end of a legislative session approaches, fear of a special session becomes an increasingly powerful negotiating tool. And the Governor has the power of the bully pulpit, the ability to communicate with the public to articulate a message, an idea, an agenda. A Governor sets a tone, both for the state in general and for the legislative process. A strong person can make a powerful difference.

Part of the tone I wanted to set was one of constructive government. I was helped by a Lieutenant Governor and Speaker who were committed to doing what was right for Texas, and a history of bipartisanship in the Texas Legislature. I worked hard to foster that spirit of cooperation. I invited the Speaker and Lieutenant Governor and all the legislative sponsors, Republicans and Democrats, to join me when I signed the tort reform laws. I wanted to share credit, to commend them for their hard work. Without them, it would not have happened. I knew that, and wanted the public to know that as well. I invited the entire legislature to a picnic at the Governor's mansion to celebrate my first hundred days as Governor. I knew the press would define the date as an important marker, and I wanted to share it with those who were working with me to change Texas.

With tort reform finished, education took center stage for much of the session. I had campaigned on restoring local control of schools, reducing the regulatory authority of the state education agency, setting high standards, demanding accountability, and injecting competition and choice into the education system. Separately, an interim committee of the legislature, led by a friend and ally, Republican Senator Bill Ratliff, was drafting language for a major rewrite of the state's education code. Mike Moses, who would later become education commissioner but was then still the superintendent of Lubbock schools, served on the committee, as did State Representative Paul Sadler, a Democrat from East Texas who would become the sponsor of the education package in the house.

It's hard to imagine two more different legislators than Bill

Ratliff and Paul Sadler. Both are from East Texas, both are hard-working and intelligent, but the similarities pretty much end there. Bill Ratliff is the gray eminence of the Texas Senate, a calm, ramrod-straight, low-key Southern gentleman affectionately known to his colleagues as Obi-Wan Kenobi, after the wise adviser in *Star Wars*. Paul Sadler is a scrappy and fiercely independent trial lawyer, stubborn and known for an insistence on doing things his way.

They spent thousands of hours in committee meetings and hearings. I met regularly with both Sadler and Ratliff. I would invite Paul over to the Governor's mansion. We would talk for hours. We had a different political philosophy, but we shared a strong commitment to public schools and we wanted excellence for every child. The end result was the Ratliff-Sadler bill, the first complete overhaul of the Texas education code in almost fifty years. It was a massive, masterful job. "The new code is both strong and flexible," I said, commending legislators for their work. "It is strong because it sets clear education goals and holds school districts accountable for achieving them, and it is flexible because it lets local folks chart their own course to excellence. I like to say it offers a menu of opportunity to parents and teachers and educational entrepreneurs. Those who don't like the status quo can set up a charter school, attend a different public school, or, in the ultimate reform, have an election and form a home-rule education district, declaring independence from state authority."

The session was a successful and substantive one that achieved fundamental reform for Texas. The morning after it ended, I awakened to a lousy headline in *The Dallas Morning News*. It made me furious. GOVERNOR VIEWS LEGISLATIVE SESSION AS PERSONAL VICTORY, it said. To the contrary, I had worked hard throughout the session not to take credit, but to share it. I called my communications director before 7:00 A.M. and wrote a letter to the editor the very same day:

"Your headline and front-page story attempting to give me credit for the success of the 1995 legislative session missed the mark. As I have said repeatedly, no one person deserves credit for the success of this legislative session. This session was successful because Democrats and Republicans, representatives of big cities and small rural communities and representatives of the many diverse regions of Texas worked together, in a spirit of bipartisan cooperation. We found common ground and forged consensus based on our conservative philosophy. Much of the credit belongs to two outstanding leaders, Governor Bullock and Speaker Laney, as well as to all 31 members of the Texas Senate and 150 members of the Texas House of Representatives. The people of Texas told us they wanted better schools, tougher juvenile and criminal justice laws, a reformed welfare system, and fairer tort laws. The people of Texas can be proud that working together, we delivered."

After the session, I set up a series of bill-signing ceremonies in members' home districts. I traveled to San Angelo, home of the chairman of the House Appropriations Committee, to sign the state budget. I signed the juvenile justice laws in the Dallas–Fort Worth metroplex, the home of Republican committee chairs Toby Goodman and Chris Harris. It was a way to share credit, to bring praise and attention to the work of legislators in front of their friends and supporters and local media in their hometowns.

I asked Paul Sadler if I could come to Henderson to sign the education bill. Henderson is his hometown and is also located in Senator Ratliff's East Texas senate district. The ceremony was in the auditorium of the junior high school. School was already out for summer, but the cheerleaders donned uniforms and came, parents brought their children, hundreds of people in the small town turned out. They put red, white, and blue bunting across the stage. The principal introduced the education commissioner, who introduced the Governor, on down the line. When it came time for the person next to Paul Sadler to speak, Paul's four-year-old son, Sam, standing onstage holding his daddy's hand, urgently pulled his father down to his level and asked, "What do I say when it's my turn?"

I thanked Paul and Bill and all the legislators. I applauded the success of the session. And in that line, on that day, I told Paul and Bill to get ready for next time. We had addressed one-half of the equation. We had changed the way we governed our schools. During the next session, we needed to fix the way we funded them.

That fall, I went to see Pete Laney in his district. It's a big deal in small-town Texas when the Governor comes to town, and I wanted to visit Pete in front of his friends and supporters. We went to a pancake supper at the school, then the Friday-night high-school football game. I later joked it may not be the only time a Governor and Speaker went to a ball game together, but I know it's the only time a Governor and Speaker ever watched Hale Center play Morton, two small and remote West Texas communities.

That same fall, we developed the reading initiative and began planning for the next session. I had an idea, a big, bold idea.

I worried that rising local school property taxes were threatening the Texas and American dream of owning a home. I saw senior citizens who had paid off their mortgages struggling to pay property taxes higher than their original house payments had been. I saw young people who were not able to afford their homes because of rising property taxes. The problem stemmed in part from the state's failure to pay its fair share of the costs of education. The state share of public school costs was at a record low of 44 percent when I was elected; growing school enrollment forced local districts to raise local property taxes to cover increased costs.

The state's method of taxing businesses was also unfair. Some businesses paid high taxes, while others paid none, just because of differences in how they were structured. The only way to correct these problems was to overhaul the entire tax system, to reduce reliance on property taxes while making the state's business tax simpler, flatter, and fairer.

Everyone told me my idea was too ambitious and too bold. "People who play with taxes get burned," warned Cliff Johnson, a wise and cagey former state representative who worked on my staff during my first legislative session. "Things are going good. You're crazy to take on tax reform."

Almost everyone's view was that I had built up a lot of goodwill and I should not risk it. I had a different view. I believe you have to spend political capital or it withers and dies. And I wanted to spend my capital on something profound. I didn't come to Austin just to put my name in a placecard holder at the table of Texas governors. I came to do what I thought was right for a state that I loved. And I thought the way we paid for our schools was dead wrong.

I wanted to cut local school property taxes, increase the state's share of education funding, and make our tax system flatter and fairer, all in one big package. We spent much of 1996 developing the plan. My staff assembled a working group that included representatives from the offices of the Lieutenant Governor, the Speaker, and the Comptroller. Later, I appointed a citizens' committee that conducted fourteen hearings across the state to seek public input and mobilize support.

By November, budget director Albert Hawkins brought me good news. The combination of a growing economy and good fiscal stewardship from our state agencies meant the state would end the year with a billion dollars in surplus funds. I viewed it as a down payment toward fundamental reform, an opportunity to make the tax reform package an overall tax cut package as well. Others viewed it as easy money, there for the spending.

I decided to seize the money and freeze any plans to spend it by having a news conference to announce that the budget I would present to the legislature would include a $1 billion tax cut. I called it a "billion-dollar beginning." "Texas state government has achieved substantial savings during the last two years and we expect that trend to continue," I said. "By holding the line on spending and insisting on leaner and more efficient government, we can raise the state's share of funding for our schools while lowering taxes for Texans. I view this as a down payment toward what I hope will be even more substantial property tax relief during the legislative session."

Publicly, legislators were cautious. Privately, a few were furious. And my announcement provoked a mini–feeding frenzy among the press. No one was accustomed to a Governor taking the lead on a budget matter. How could I possibly know the money would be available? Surely I was going to hurt schools, cut programs, do something terrible and drastic. (As you read on, tuck away in the back of your mind that at the end of the session, when we cut taxes by the billion dollars I outlined in November, it would be characterized as an easy task. It's always interesting to watch how perspective changes during the course of a debate.)

The *Austin American-Statesman* reported:

Gov. George W. Bush staked out his territory in the tax reform debate Wednesday, saying he wants to use extra money in the state budget to reduce school property taxes for Texans. Bush's proposal, which would have to be approved by the Legislature, is raising questions. . . . Where will the money come from? . . . If the state gives local school districts an additional $1 billion, how will it ensure that they reduce their taxes by a commensurate amount? . . . If the state spends $1 billion on tax relief, will important educational programs go unfunded? House Speaker Pete Laney, D-Hale Center, questioned whether the governor's budget projections are overly optimistic. "We won't know if the governor's proposal is feasible until we have seen the details of his plan and examined all the needs for state services to see what monies are available," Laney said. Lt. Gov. Bob Bullock, a Democrat who presides over the Senate, said demands for money will be great as the Legislature makes its appropriations decisions for 1998-99. "I've been working on property taxes, and I've given a rough draft of the plan to the governor and his staff," Bullock said. "I have not received a plan from them. I will continue to work with the speaker and the governor on a plan, but I don't want to get the cart before the horse."

Bullock talked with my staff and advisors and gave them grim predictions of huge political consequences if I pursued the idea. He took a couple of my senior staff members aside and warned them this could cost me reelection.

And those who wanted to spend the money lined up quickly to denounce my idea. "We are very concerned that if there is $1 billion, it should be used to address reading, teacher salaries, extend-a-year and alternative education programs," said Richard Kouri, president of the Texas State Teachers Association. "Does this mean that billion dollars is off the table?"

"It's money that would have gone somewhere else," said Dick Lavine, fiscal analyst for the liberal Center for Public Policy Priorities. "What agencies and what sections of the budget aren't going to get funded that might have been otherwise?"

"I would like to see him take that $1 billion and do something in the way of health insurance for schoolteachers," said Doug Rogers, executive director of the Association of Texas Professional Educators.

The Fort Worth Star-Telegram reported: "Some key legislative leaders said they were caught off guard by the governor's announcement and were skeptical of his optimistic revenue projections. 'I can cut a budget,' said Rep. Rob Junell, D-San Angelo, who heads the House Appropriations Committee, which initiates legislation related to the state budget. 'But there's going to be a lot of people who are not going to be very happy.' Among the possible targets for budget cuts, he said, are higher education, prisons and human services." But my reaction was different. I knew it was possible to fund essential priorities and cut taxes, and I intended to do just that.

The curtain was rising on the 1997 legislative session. And my announcement had ensured that tax cuts would take center stage. I unveiled my specific plan during my state-of-the-state speech, calling on legislators to cut local school property taxes by almost $3 billion a year. My plan also proposed eliminating the corporate franchise tax on Texas businesses, in essence a business income tax, and replacing it with a fair and flat tax on business activity, and raising the sales tax by one-half cent. The net effect was a net $1 billion overall tax cut and a fairer tax system that made the state the primary funding source for our public schools. Property taxes would have been cut by $3 billion a year with strict caps to keep them from increasing. The new business tax I proposed was capital-friendly, with a flat, low rate of $1\frac{1}{4}$ percent, a generous $500,000 small-business deduction, and a 100 percent deduction for capital investment to encourage job creation. Because of the generous small-business deduction, fewer businesses would have paid the business flat tax than had paid the existing corporate income tax, and the plan would have been fairer. It more evenly distributed the tax burden among larger enterprises, including many major Texas businesses who had paid nothing under the current system.

I believed it was a fair and comprehensive approach that achieved a lot of important public policy goals, and I set about selling it with a vengeance. I brought legislators into my office, one by one, to ask for their help and their support. I traveled the state, giving speeches and news conferences to explain the plan. At one stop, in Beaumont, a firefighter approached me at the airport. I knew his name was Tommy because it was written on his shirt. He thanked me for working to cut property taxes and told me high taxes were making it hard for him to afford his home. *Newsweek* reporter Howard Fineman was traveling with me, and I called him over. "I want you to meet a Texan who is worried about his property taxes," I told him, introducing him to my new friend Tommy.

Speaker Laney surprised me one day, calling to let me know he was going to appoint a special committee of key house leaders to take up the property tax plan. The committee would be chaired by Representative Paul Sadler. It became known as the "committee from hell," although it had some unprintable nicknames as well. Lobbyists and staff members soon dreaded attending the meetings or, even worse, being called to testify, because they were grilled. Committee members worked tediously, laboriously, and studiously, examining the Texas tax code. I tried hard to convince the members that a flat tax was needed, but they soon shelved my plan and wrote a different one of their own.

The first week in March, many of us gathered at a ceremony rededicating the state cemetery, which had been refurbished and restored. The cemetery was one of Bullock's favorite places and restoring it was one of his pet projects. In my remarks, I alluded to a legislator, Ben "Jumbo" Atwell, who was still living, but had already purchased a headstone at the cemetery. "Over in the southwest corner—there's a particularly interesting tombstone," I said. "The epitaph reads: 'Lawyer, legislator, and author of tax bill.' Most of the elected officials here today would probably agree with me we would prefer ours to read: 'tax cut bill,' " I joked. Bullock got up to speak, thanked everyone, then turned to me with a twinkle in his eye. "By the way, Governor," he said, "Jumbo Atwell is not near as dead as your tax plan is."

It lived a few more months, not my plan, but the house version. When it came to the floor, I had two options. One, to kill the plan, which would have doomed the billion-dollar tax cut I had spoken for, or two, to preserve the billion dollars and keep the process alive to move it to the senate. I chose the latter. I felt the issue of cutting taxes was so important that I needed to spend every dollar of my political capital to keep the process alive. I knew if I threw in the towel, legislators would find a way to spend the money rather than cut taxes. The senate didn't like the house plan at all and passed its own version.

Finally, it all came down to a meeting in my office. Bullock was there, and Laney, and senate leaders Teel Bivins and Ken Armbrister, and house leaders Paul Sadler and Mark Stiles, and some of my staff. Other members came in and out; we worked until 11:00 P.M. on Friday. When we left the capitol late that night, we thought we had reached an agreement that would cut property taxes by $4 billion at a cost of only $2 billion. The remaining $2 billion would be funded through budget savings, including the $1 billion I had outlined in November.

"The rest of you may want to drink poison Kool-Aid, but I'm not," said the state senator in my office the next morning. The compromise we had carefully crafted the night before—dramatic property tax cuts, a different way to fund schools through $2 billion in budget savings, and expanding the sales tax base—was falling apart. Bullock called state senators in, and he and I met with them one by one in the back room of the Governor's office to see if they would support the plan. One by one, they would not. It was most dramatic and most disappointing. By early afternoon it was clear that we could not get the votes we needed to pass sweeping reform. But there was a silver lining: legislators would agree to cut property taxes by the $1 billion my budget director had originally identified. And the cut would be especially significant for people on the outskirts of poverty, people with low incomes and senior citizens living on a fixed income.

I went before the press to face the music. I started by thanking Lieutenant Governor Bullock, Speaker Laney, and all the legislators who had worked so hard. "This issue was enormously complex," I said. "Every member brought to our discussions legitimate principles from which he or she could not waver. . . .

Despite the hard work of a lot of people and the direct involvement of leaders of the legislative and executive branch, I am
disappointed to say we simply cannot get the votes to pass this
plan. . . . We still have the opportunity to cut property taxes this
session—in a smaller way, but in a way that is real and ongoing.
We have $1 billion in savings from a leaner and more efficient
state government. I ask the legislature to join me in giving that
billion dollars back to the people of Texas. . . . I thank all the
members of the legislature and especially the conferees, who
wrestled with difficult issues in a respectful and courteous way.
We all worked hard to do what we thought was right—and we
can join together to give Texans a billion-dollar tax cut—an
accomplishment we can all be proud of."

We passed the billion-dollar tax cut, which allowed us to triple
the homestead exemption from local school property taxes to
$15,000, from $5,000. It cut Tommy's taxes by almost 30 percent. Because the increased homestead exemption required a
change in our Texas Constitution, the voters had to approve it
in an election. I campaigned vigorously for it, and voters approved it overwhelmingly. I went to the Beaumont Airport fire
station to sign the enabling legislation with Tommy at my side.
"I never forgot Tommy during this debate," I told reporters.
"This was for Texans like Tommy who have the dream of owning a home. Some cynics say $1 billion is not much of a property
tax cut, but it is for Tommy." I'm convinced that one of the
reasons I did well during my 1998 reelection campaign in places
like the Rio Grande Valley was that low-income homeowners
knew I had fought for their interests and provided meaningful
tax relief.

I'm glad I tried the major overhaul. I wouldn't do it differently.
I did learn some interesting lessons. First, it's hard to win votes
for massive reform unless there is a crisis. If the courts had declared the school funding system unconstitutional, we would
have been under the gun. With no consequences for inaction,

action was difficult. The status quo is powerful, especially jux-taposed with fear of the unknown. Second, Texans appreciated bold leadership. I had earned political capital by spending it. All the dour predictions of damage for trying a bold reform were wrong.

I'm not sure Bullock, ever the shrewd reader of the Texas Senate, had ever thought we could succeed. I also think he was tired, didn't have the heart for the fight. His health was deteri-orating. And maybe he knew better than I did that state govern-ment didn't respond well to major change unless there was a major crisis.

Six months later, in November 1997, I had just landed in Flor-ida for the Republican Governors' conference when the office paged to tell me Bullock had publicly endorsed my campaign for reelection. He had actually done so the day before, when he joined me at a private fund-raiser for Senator David Sibley in Waco, but now the capitol press had gotten wind of it and Bul-lock had confirmed that yes, the highest-ranking Democrat in Texas state government would be supporting the Republican Governor for reelection.

It sent a powerful message. State Land Commissioner Garry Mauro, a fifteen-year incumbent Democrat state officeholder, had announced his campaign against me just weeks before, and Bullock was the godfather of one of Mauro's children. But in a sense, Bullock had adopted me, almost as a son. I think he trusted my heart, he trusted my instincts, he knew when I made deci-sions, I would do what I thought was right for Texas.

Jan and Bob Bullock had Christmas dinner with us that year, and his daughter's wedding was held at the Governor's mansion. It was important to have a Lieutenant Governor who put Texas first. He helped set the tone. He and Pete Laney deserve a lot of credit for our success.

Almost two years later, in the summer of 1999, I was wrapping up my first presidential campaign trip to Iowa and New Hampshire when we got the call that Bullock was dying. Doctors had predicted that before, but this time, it was true. The first thing Laura and I did when we returned to Austin was to visit Jan and Bob. He was at home, surrounded by a few friends, feisty to the end. He wanted to know all about the campaign swing. What had I said? How many people turned out? What was the press asking? He wanted to know why I didn't smile in the photograph on the *Newsweek* cover.

He cleared the room. Jan and Laura went into the living room to have coffee, I remained behind. He asked me to give the eulogy at his funeral. I was hugely honored. I was so proud to call him my friend. I was fortunate to have gotten to know him.

In the end, we wept together. He was so proud, so eager, so convinced that I had a great chance to become the next President. He had told friends that he looked forward to watching me take the oath of office. Bullock, a man who had lived for years on his sheer strength of will, realized that if it happened, he would not be there to see it. If it happens, he will have been a huge part of making it so.

10

THE BIG 4-0

MUCH, probably too much, has been made of my fortieth year. Despite the barbs some political opponents
like to toss, I don't believe life begins at forty. Mine
certainly didn't. Long before I turned forty, I went to school, got
an education, served in the National Guard, earned a graduate
degree, got married, had children, met a payroll, raised and risked
money in the oil business, campaigned for office. I was active in
my community. I coached Little League. I taught Sunday school.
I raised money for my church, and I led a United Way campaign.

But there are turning points in life, and one of mine was quitting drinking, which I did shortly after my fortieth birthday. My
wife and friends later joked that, notoriously frugal, I quit after
seeing the bar bill. Several of us turned forty that year, and we
gathered in Colorado Springs on the weekend of Don Evans's
birthday for a collective celebration. Don and Susie were there,
and Joe and Jan O'Neill, Laura, and our friend Penny Sawyer.
My brother Neil drove down from Denver to join us, and we
had a big time at a dinner at the Broadmoor Hotel. People later
asked whether something special happened, some incident, some

argument or accident that turned the tide, but no, I just drank too much and woke up with a hangover. I got out of bed and went for my usual run. For the past fourteen years, I had run at least three miles almost every day. This run was different. I felt worse than usual, and about halfway through, I decided I would drink no more. I came back to the hotel room and told Laura I was through.

"I'm quitting drinking," I told her, then never said much else about it. I'm not sure she believed me, at first. But I can be pretty stubborn with myself. I've always been a disciplined person. Even when I was drinking, I drank only after work, at night, never during the day. I always worked hard; I met my responsibilities as a husband, father, and employer. My friends laugh about the image of me as a party animal, an image they think is vastly overblown.

It all started when a reporter asked why I had quit drinking. "Because I thought I was drinking too much," I frankly replied. I set off another round of rumors when I was asked to itemize my youthful misdeeds. I famously, and perhaps foolishly, said, "When I was young and irresponsible, I sometimes behaved young and irresponsibly." I thought it was a humorous way to acknowledge that I am not perfect, that as a young man I did some things I am not particularly proud of today.

I am still amazed by the rumormongering set off by that off-hand remark, all apparently spawned by my refusal to itemize a laundry list of things I wish I hadn't done. Perhaps a better way to put it is to say I engaged in some of the excesses of youth of my time, things I wouldn't have wanted my mother to know then but that she would probably laugh about now that I've survived them. Things I don't want my own daughters to do, yet worry they probably will, before age and maturity help counter the sense of invincibility that comes with being young and the life of the party.

Many reporters who ask me about this do not approve of my

reluctance to itemize misbehavior. They worship at the altar of public confession, demanding that candidates tell all. They want to conduct a public strip search, throwing out a question here and a rumor there, hoping it will bare another layer.

I think they forget that children are watching, including my own. I believe parents who choose to recount their misadventures run a great risk that their children will imitate them. I also think some parents of my generation make the mistake of telling their children too much, of trying to be friends rather than parents and examples. I have chosen a different path. I don't want my own daughters or any other young people to imitate anything foolish I once did or use me as an excuse for misbehavior. I believe leaders have a responsibility to send a clear message to our children: Don't abuse alcohol. Don't use drugs. Don't have a baby out of wedlock. Make smart and healthy choices.

And so, much to the disappointment of some of the purveyors of gossip and innuendo, I will not play the game of political "gotcha." I will not respond to the rumor du jour. I have told people what they need to know about me. I have made mistakes, and I have learned from them. I have been a devoted dad and a loyal husband. And when I took an oath to become the Governor of Texas, I swore to uphold not only the laws of my state but also the dignity and integrity of the office. I have done so. And should I be fortunate enough to be elected President of the United States, I will uphold the dignity and high honor of that high office, too, so help me God.

I hope my stand will help purge the system of its relentless quest for scandal and sensation. I worry that when gossip spread on the Internet is repeated on the front page of respected newspapers, we are undermining our American democracy. The political process is only as good as the people who are willing to enter it. Too many good people tell me they would never seek office because they would never subject themselves to the scrutiny of the public strip search.

I have talked about my marriage and my decision to quit drinking because those speak to the way I have conducted my life as a mature adult. I am a person who enjoys life, and for years, I enjoyed having a few drinks. But gradually, drinking began to compete with my energy. I'd be a step slower getting up. My daily runs seemed harder after a few too many drinks the night before.

Drinking also magnified aspects of my personality that probably don't need to be larger than they already are—made me more funny, more charming (I thought), more irrepressible. Also, according to my wife, somewhat boring and repetitive. What may have been funny in moderation was not so funny in exaggeration. I don't want to leave a mistaken impression of late nights or wild parties. The truth is, when we had a get-together, I was usually the first to arrive and the first one out the door. Nine o'clock, and I'm gone. I have never been one to stay up late.

There were a few big parties. The Midland Country Club sponsored a three-day, member-guest golf tournament called the "wildscatter" that advertised seventy-two hours of open bar. It was renowned as one of the best parties of the year and people came from across the country to participate. I played some golf and attended the events, one of them a costume party. My friends allege that I showed up in a Nixon mask one year and that another time I dressed as Mahatma Gandhi in a toga that looked like a diaper by the end of the night. (Note to Jay Leno and other comedians who have had so much fun with the George-Bush-danced-naked-on-a-bar rumor. It's not true. The toga costume is about as close as you are going to get.)

I didn't advertise my decision to stop or make a big deal out of quitting; my friends just gradually noticed I was no longer drinking at our gatherings. Outwardly, nothing changed. Laura and I still went to parties and dinners with our friends. I didn't change habits or do anything different to help me quit. But inwardly, I felt different. I had more time to read. I had more energy. I became a better listener, and not such an incessant talker. Quitting drinking made me more focused and more disciplined. I now say it is one of the best things I have ever done.

Actually, the seeds of my decision had been planted the year before, by the Reverend Billy Graham. He visited my family for a summer weekend in Maine. I saw him preach at the small summer church, St. Ann's by the Sea. We all had lunch on the patio overlooking the ocean. One evening my dad asked Billy to answer questions from a big group of family gathered for the weekend. He sat by the fire and talked. And what he said sparked a change in my heart. I don't remember the exact words. It was more the power of his example. The Lord was so clearly reflected in his gentle and loving demeanor. The next day we walked and talked at Walker's Point, and I knew I was in the presence of a great man. He was like a magnet; I felt drawn to seek something different. He didn't lecture or admonish; he shared warmth and concern. Billy Graham didn't make you feel guilty; he made you feel loved.

Over the course of that weekend, Reverend Graham planted a mustard seed in my soul, a seed that grew over the next year. He led me to the path, and I began walking. And it was the beginning of a change in my life. I had always been a religious person, had regularly attended church, even taught Sunday school and served as an altar boy. But that weekend my faith took on new meaning. It was the beginning of a new walk where I would recommit my heart to Jesus Christ.

I was humbled to learn that God sent His Son to die for a sinner like me. I was comforted to know that through the Son, I could find God's amazing grace, a grace that crosses every border, every barrier and is open to everyone. Through the love of Christ's life, I could understand the life-changing powers of faith.

When I returned to Midland, I began reading the Bible regularly. Don Evans talked me into joining him and another friend,

Don Jones, at a men's community Bible study. The group had first assembled the year before, in the spring of 1984, at the beginning of the downturn in the energy industry. Midland was hurting. A lot of people were looking for comfort and strength and direction. A couple of men started the Bible study as a support group, and it grew. By the time I began attending, in the fall of 1985, almost 120 men would gather. We met in small discussion groups of ten or twelve, then joined the larger group for full meetings. Don Jones picked me up every week for the meetings. I remember looking forward to them. My interest in reading the Bible grew stronger and stronger, and the words became clearer and more meaningful.

We studied Acts, the story of the Apostles building the Christian Church, and the next year, the Gospel of Luke. The preparation for each meeting took several hours, reading the Scripture passages and thinking through responses to discussion questions. I took it seriously, with my usual touch of humor. Don remembers a time after watching a video on Luke's depiction of John the Baptist, when the speaker asked the class to define a prophet. He was serious, but I couldn't resist. "A profit is when revenues exceed expenses, and no one has seen one around here since Elijah," I answered. Once a speaker was joking about his upbringing and said, "It's not easy being a PK"—i.e., a preacher's kid. "You ought to try being a VPK"—a Vice President's kid—was my instant comeback.

Laura and I were active members of the First Methodist Church of Midland, and we participated in many family programs, including James Dobson's Focus on the Family series on raising children. As I studied and learned, Scripture took on greater meaning, and I gained confidence and understanding in my faith.

I read the Bible regularly. Don Evans gave me the "one-year" Bible, a Bible divided into 365 daily readings, each one including a section from the New Testament, the Old Testament, Psalms, and Proverbs. I read through that Bible every other year. During the years in between, I pick different chapters to study at different times. I have also learned the power of prayer. I pray for guidance. I do not pray for earthly things, but for heavenly things, for wisdom and patience and understanding.

My faith gives me focus and perspective. It teaches humility. But I also recognize that faith can be misinterpreted in the political process. Faith is an important part of my life. I believe it is important to live my faith, not flaunt it.

America is a great country because of our religious freedoms. It is important for any leader to respect the faith of others. That point was driven home when Laura and I visited Israel in 1998. We had traveled to Rome to spend Thanksgiving with our daughter, who was attending a school program there, and spent three days in Israel on the way home. It was an incredible experience. I remember waking up at the Jerusalem Hilton and opening the curtains and seeing the Old City before us, the Jerusalem stone glowing gold. We visited the Western Wall and the Church of the Holy Sepulcher. And we went to the Sea of Galilee and stood atop the hill where Jesus delivered the Sermon on the Mount.

It was an overwhelming feeling to stand in the spot where the most famous speech in the history of the world was delivered, the spot where Jesus outlined the character and conduct of a believer and gave his disciples and the world the beatitudes, the golden rule, and the Lord's Prayer.

Our delegation included four gentile governors—one Methodist, two Catholics, and a Mormon—and several Jewish-American friends. Someone suggested we read Scripture. I chose to read "Amazing Grace," my favorite hymn.

Later that night we all gathered at a restaurant in Tel Aviv for dinner before we boarded our middle-of-the-night flight back to America. We talked about the wonderful experiences and thanked the guides and government officials who had introduced us to their country.

And toward the end of the meal, one of our friends rose to share a story, to tell us how he, a gentile, and his friend, a Jew, had—unbeknownst to the rest of us—walked down to the Sea of Galilee, joined hands underwater, and prayed together, on bended knee.

Then out of his mouth came a hymn he had known as a child, a hymn he hadn't thought about in years. He got every word right:

> *Now is the time approaching*
> *By prophets long foretold*
> *When all shall dwell together*
> *One Shepherd and one fold.*
> *Now Jew and gentile, meeting*
> *From many a distant shore*
> *Around an altar kneeling*
> *One common Lord adore.*

Faith changes lives. I know, because faith has changed mine.

11

KARLA FAYE TUCKER AND
HENRY LEE LUCAS

Governors of states that have the death penalty share an awesome responsibility: life and death. Of the many thousands of decisions a chief executive makes, capital punishment decisions are by far the most profound.

I am a decisive person. I get the facts, weigh them thoughtfully and carefully, and decide. I took an oath to uphold the laws of Texas, including the death penalty, and enforcing it is part of my job. I recognized that, and thought about all the ramifications, before I decided to run for Governor.

I support capital punishment for those who commit heinous crimes. That does not mean enforcing the death penalty is ever easy. My legal counsel usually come to my office first thing in the morning of a scheduled execution to review the facts of the case, always grim and brutal. Then we wait, usually all day, for the courts to either act or not. And finally, if all the legal appeals are exhausted and I am convinced there is no reason to delay the execution, I give the final authority to go forward, to allow a warden at a prison unit in Huntsville to administer a lethal injection and enforce the judgment of a jury of Texans.

I review every death penalty case thoroughly. And early in my administration, I decided the standards by which I would decide whether to allow an execution to proceed. In every case, I would ask: Is there any doubt about this individual's guilt or innocence? And, have the courts had ample opportunity to review all the legal issues in this case?

The death penalty has been carried out numerous times since I've been the Governor of Texas. Each case is major, because each case is life or death. Yet two stand out. In trying to do what was right, I presided over the execution of a woman who seemed to have changed her heart and her life, yet stopped the execution of a despicable, remorseless killer.

Karla Faye Tucker put a face on the death penalty, for me and for much of the nation and world. Hers was a pleasant face, a smiling face, a sympathetic face. At five three and 120 pounds, with wavy brown hair and large, expressive eyes, Karla Faye Tucker did not fit the public image of a typical death-row inmate. She seemed contrite and sincere. She had found Jesus and salvation. She had also, she freely admitted, helped murder two people with a pickax. It was a brutal rampage, full of awful, lurid details. And, on a tape played in court during her trial, she had openly boasted to friends about the murders, claiming she had experienced sexual thrills with each swing of the ax.

The crime started with a plan to steal a motorcycle. When Karla Faye Tucker and her boyfriend, Daniel Garrett, arrived at Jerry Lynn Dean's apartment late on the night of June 13, 1983, they were high on drugs, at the tail end of a three-day orgy. Dean, the motorcycle's owner, was not supposed to be home. But once inside the apartment, Tucker and Garrett discovered Dean was there, along with a woman he had picked up earlier that night at a party. Garrett began beating Dean with a hammer.

When the battered man started to gurgle, Tucker grabbed a three-foot-long pickax and plunged it into his body again and again.

The woman, Deborah Thornton, had been in the wrong place at the wrong time. She had argued with her husband and had decided to get out of the house for a while. She dropped by a party and went home with Dean. It was a deadly decision. She lay under bedsheets, trying to hide from the awful sounds of Tucker and Garrett killing Dean. She was still under the covers when the two found her, and Tucker turned the pickax in her direction. Tucker later testified that she was trying to make sure the woman would not be a witness. Tucker was convicted of capital murder and received the death penalty. Her boyfriend, also sentenced to death, died in prison of liver disease in 1993.

Thirteen years later, Karla Faye Tucker's interview with Larry King from the Mountain View Unit of the Texas prison system captured the attention of much of the nation. I saw part of it, too, and it affected me more than I wanted to admit.

KING: What happened on that terrible day?
TUCKER: The details of what happened that night, I don't share. I mean, that's the worst night of my life, and I don't—with how I feel now, I don't relive that night.
KING: Do you think it was another person?
TUCKER: Yes, it was definitely.
KING: For the facts, for the benefit of the audience, two people were murdered that night.
TUCKER: Two people were brutally murdered.
KING: By you and your boyfriend?
TUCKER: Yes.
KING: What were you doing there?
TUCKER: We were there to do—there's a term called "case the joint out."

George W. Bush,
born July 6, 1946

The Bush family at Odessa airport, circa 1950: (left to right) *Barbara*
Bush, George W. Bush, George Bush, Dorothy Walker Bush, Prescott S. Bush

*Aspiring ballplayer in
Midland, 1954*

*Young George W. Bush
with his sister, Robin*

The Bush family, 1956: (clockwise from the top)
George Bush, Neil Bush, George W. Bush, Jeb Bush,
Marvin Bush, and Barbara Bush

Father and son, Midland,
circa mid-1950s

George W. Bush at Yale University, 1964–68

Texas Air National Guard, 1968–73

*Texas Air National
Guard, 1968–73*

Wedding Day, November 5, 1977: (from left to right) Dorothy Walker Bush, George Bush, Barbara Bush, George W. Bush, Laura Bush, Jeb Bush, Columba Bush, Neil Bush, Doro Bush, and Marvin Bush

Running for Congress, 19th District, 1978

George and Laura Bush campaigning in 1978

Midland oil fields, 1978

Midland oil fields, 1978

"Marching and singing Yale songs" to newborn twin daughters, 1981

At a Reagan-Bush rally in Midland, May 31, 1984: (from left to right) *Laura Bush holding daughter Barbara, George W. Bush holding daughter Jenna, and Barbara Bush*

*At Arlington
Stadium with
the girls,
April 1990*

*With then Governor Bill Clements casting the Texas delegation's vote for
George Bush at the 1988 Republican National Convention*

Bush family reunion, August 1992

George W. Bush and George Bush fishing, August 13, 1991

With baseball legend Nolan Ryan

Signing tort reform bills as Governor: (from left to right) *Lt. Governor Bob Bullock, Sen. David Sibley, Rep. Todd Hunter, Speaker Pete Laney, Rep. Rob Junell*

Taking the oath of office, 1999

Governor Bush with his Communications Director, Karen Hughes, on inaugural day, 1999

At the Del Mar Fair, June 29, 1999, San Diego County, California

Governor Bush promoting reading

Senior staff Christmas dinner, December 1998

KING: Look it over.

TUCKER: Right, yes.

KING: You were going to rob?

TUCKER: Not that night, no. We were looking the place over to at some point in time that night go back there, and go in and steal a motorcycle. That night was a spur-of-the-moment decision to go over there. And unfortunately, two people were killed with—

KING: And brutally killed?

TUCKER: Brutally, yes.

KING: How, to yourself, do you explain that? I know you don't want to—so forgetting the details, how do you explain it to yourself that I was involved in a violent slaying?

TUCKER: I can't—I can't make sense out of it. I don't know how to make sense out of it except that the choices that I made to do drugs, to buckle to peer pressure and everything else—it was inevitable that something like that was going to happen in my life.

Tucker told King she had been high on drugs that night, and as she told the jury during her trial more than a decade earlier, she had enjoyed the violence.

TUCKER: I said I did. I was—at that time in my life, I was very excited about doing different crazy, violent things, yes. It was a part of me that was used to fit in with the crowd that I was hanging around to be accepted.

KING: Did you walk around with any guilt?

TUCKER: No.

KING: None?

TUCKER: I not only didn't walk around without any guilt, I was proud of thinking that I had finally measured up to the big boys.

KING: Your boyfriend was proud of you?

TUCKER: Yes. Isn't that sick? That's crazy.

KING: No guilt?

TUCKER: None, none back then. I didn't—I didn't care about anybody. I didn't care about myself. I didn't place any value on myself or anybody else.

Karla Faye testified that her mother had given her drugs and had enticed her to become a call girl at an early age. She did not, however, attempt to dodge responsibility.

What she had done, she said, was terrible; she was just a different person now. The jury that had assessed the death penalty thirteen years earlier had had no doubts; in court, they had seen a boasting, remorseless killer. Karla Faye Tucker was saying that she had changed, and the state of Texas should take that into account and change her death sentence.

The case was destined for media attention. On top of the shocking nature of the crime, Karla Faye Tucker was a woman, and a woman had not been executed in Texas since Chipita Rodriguez was put to death in 1863 for murdering a horse trader. In fact, a woman had not been executed in the entire United States for more than ten years, since 1984, when a North Carolina grandmother was put to death for poisoning her fiancé.

The execution had been scheduled twice before, once in 1992 and again in 1993, but both times it was postponed. My office first began hearing about the case in the fall of 1997. The Harris County District Attorney's Office contacted us to let us know the high-profile prisoner Karla Faye Tucker would be scheduled for execution after the first of the year. The pressure began. In late November, an attorney for my friend Pat Robertson, founder of the Christian Coalition, called my general counsel, Al Gonzales, to inquire about clemency. While in prison, Tucker had met and married the prison chaplain, and Christian conservatives took up her cause. On December 18, the week before Christmas, the

Harris County District Attorney's Office notified us that the execution had been set for February 3, 1998.

On New Year's Day, *The New York Times* ran a front-page story by Texas-based reporter Sam Howe Verhovek. In bold type, the headline conveyed the discomfort: AS WOMAN'S EXECUTION NEARS, TEXAS SQUIRMS. Texas had put thirty-seven men to death the previous year, the article said, the most executions in a single year in any state in the modern era of capital punishment. "But even for a state with the nation's busiest execution chamber, the looming lethal injection of prisoner No. 777 at the Mountain View Unit here is a milestone," the article continued. "As the execution date nears, an unlikely array of sympathizers ranging from Christian conservatives to a juror in her trial are lobbying to save her life in a case that offers a stark political quandary for Mr. Bush and an equally stark picture of society's reluctance—even in a law-and-order state—to execute women."

I'm sure it was fair for the article to note the politics, but that isn't how I make decisions. I would apply the same standards to this case as I do to any other, as my communications director told the newspaper.

"The gender of the murderer did not make any difference to the victims," said the Governor's spokeswoman, Karen Hughes, who added that Mr. Bush asks two primary questions in his review of commutation petitions: is there any question about the individual's guilt, and has the individual had fair access to the courts and a full hearing on all legal issues?

Al Gonzales, whom I had recently appointed as Secretary of State, was upset by the news story. Al had been my general counsel during the first three years of my administration. He was now doing two jobs, still acting as general counsel while we searched for a replacement. He felt the story put Texas in a bad light, made us look bloodthirsty. He also worried that the article had made it appear that I might bow to political pressure in this case. "Don't worry, Al," I told him. "We will do the right thing when the time comes."

Throughout the country, a drumbeat began: spare the life of Karla Faye Tucker. I first recognized the passions unique to this case when a young television reporter confronted me in Waco. Clearly distraught, she proceeded to grill me about how I could possibly preside over the execution of a wonderful Christian soul. I tried to explain that I would be fair and would make a decision based on the facts and the law, but the reporter was emotional and unconvinced. Journalists from around the world also began to descend on Austin. They waited with cameras outside the Governor's office, and went to visit Karla Faye Tucker at the Gatesville unit, where she granted interviews, which generated more letters and more protests.

People's reactions were strong and heartfelt. Opponents of the death penalty seized on this case as a way to generate publicity for their cause. Bianca Jagger flew to Texas on behalf of Amnesty International; an emissary of Pope John Paul II wrote me a letter. Large groups of demonstrators began to picket at the capitol and at the Governor's mansion. A lot of my friends in the evangelical community were also deeply concerned. They felt Karla Faye Tucker was a living witness to the redeeming power of faith, and they were praying for her. I could feel their anguish. The environment became more and more charged.

Opponents of the death penalty are a principled minority in Texas. I disagree with them, but I respect their convictions. A few are always present on the nights when executions take place. They gather at the back gate of the Governor's mansion, where I live with my family. They light candles and hold signs. Sometimes they chant. I see them when I return from the office at the end of the day.

The death penalty is a difficult issue for its supporters as well as its opponents. I have a reverence for life; my faith teaches that life is a gift from our Creator. In a perfect world, life is given by God and only taken by God. I hope someday our society will respect life, the full spectrum of life, from the unborn to the elderly. I hope someday unborn children will be protected by law and welcomed in life.

I support the death penalty because I believe, if administered swiftly and justly, capital punishment is a deterrent against future violence and will save other innocent lives. Some advocates of life will challenge why I oppose abortion yet support the death penalty; to me, it's the difference between innocence and guilt.

These are difficult subjects, even more difficult in the implementation than the discussion, and I recognize that good people can disagree. Two days before Karla Faye Tucker's scheduled execution, one of my own daughters, obviously troubled by this case, looked up at the dinner table and told me she had decided she opposes capital punishment. I told her I was proud that she was thinking about the issue, that she had a right and a responsibility to make her own judgment, and she should always feel free to express her opinion. I welcomed the moment. Current events are great teachers, and I was pleased for the opportunity it gave her to express her opinion and independence. As a dad who was also Governor, it made my heart a little heavier, knowing I might have to carry out a sentence with which my own daughter disagreed. I explained to her the rationale for my support of the death penalty, that I believed the threat of being put to death might deter someone from taking another life. I explained the law: Texas executes those who commit heinous crimes, a punishment aimed at prevention. And I explained its application: once you have a death penalty statute, it must be applied fairly. I have a duty as Governor to uphold the laws of my state. I told my daughter that sometimes in life you have to make decisions that are not easy, but they should always be based on principle. In this case, the principle was to uphold the law of the land. I took an oath to do so.

I believe decisions about the death penalty are primarily the responsibility of the judicial branch of government. The process begins with a crime, an arrest, and a trial in a court of law. Only a jury can impose a death sentence in Texas, and if death is their verdict, the case is reviewed for years, by appellate courts, and usually, ultimately, by the United States Supreme Court. The executive branch role is much more limited. I view it as a fail-safe, one last review to make sure there is no doubt the individual is guilty and that he or she has had the due process guaranteed by our Constitution and laws.

I don't believe my role is to replace the verdict of a jury with my own, unless there are new facts or evidence of which a jury was unaware, or evidence that the trial was somehow unfair. Yet Karla Faye Tucker was making a different argument when she wrote to me and the Texas Board of Pardons and Paroles in late January. She was not claiming she was innocent or that her trial had been unfair. She acknowledged the horror of her crime and the appropriateness of her punishment. "I also know that justice and law demand my life for the two innocent lives I brutally murdered that night. If my execution is the only thing, the final act that can fulfill the demand for restitution and justice, then I accept that. . . . I will pay the price for what I did in any way our law demands it."

And again, Karla Faye did not attempt to dodge responsibility. "I used to try and blame my mother because she was my role model and she fashioned and shaped me into what I was at an early age. . . . At 14 she took me to a place where there was all men and wanted to 'school me' in the art of being a call girl. I wanted to please my mother so much. I wanted her to be proud of me. So instead of saying no, I just tried to do what she asked. . . . The thing is, deep down inside I knew that what I was doing was wrong. It may have been the norm for the crowd I was in, but it was not the norm for decent, upstanding families."

However, she said, she no longer blames her mother or society. "I don't blame drugs either. . . . Had I chosen not to do drugs, there would be two people still alive today. But I did choose to do drugs, and I did lose it, and two people are dead because of me."

But then Karla Faye explained that she was today a different person than the violent woman who had been sentenced to death by a jury of her peers. "It was in October, three months after I had been locked up, when a minister came to the jail and I went to the services, that night accepting Jesus into my heart. When I did this, the full and overwhelming weight and reality of what I had done hit me. . . . I began crying that night for the first time in many years, and to this day, tears are a part of my life."

Faith had taught her right from wrong, Karla Faye argued. She was a changed woman, and that required a changed punishment. "I feel that if I were in here still in the frame of mind I got arrested in, still acting out and fighting and hurting others and not caring or trying to do good, I feel sure you would consider that against me. . . . I don't really understand why you can't or won't consider my change for the good in my favor."

She wanted us to spare her life, she said, to allow her to help redirect other lives. "I see people in here in the prison where I am who are here for horrible crimes, and for lesser crimes, who to this day are still acting out in violence and hurting others with no concern for another life or for their own life. I can reach out to these girls and try and help them change before they walk out of this place and hurt someone else.

"I am seeking you to commute my sentence and allow me to

pay society back by helping others. I can't bring back the lives I took. But I can, if I am allowed, help save lives. That is the only real restitution."

It was a compelling argument. But did it erase my responsibility to enforce the laws of Texas, to make a decision in this case based on the same standards I applied to every other case? If I accepted that Karla Faye Tucker was a changed person because of her faith, how should Texas respond when a Muslim or Jew— or a Christian man—made the same argument?

And there was another side to this story, the story of the victims. I always try to remember the victims, who were not here to make their case.

On February 2, the Texas Board of Pardons and Paroles voted to deny Karla Faye Tucker's request for clemency; sixteen of the eighteen voted to deny clemency, two abstained.

Despite the call being sounded around the country and world, I could not convert Karla Faye Tucker's sentence from death to life in prison. Unlike many other Governors in death penalty states, the Governor of Texas does not have the unilateral authority to commute a death sentence. The reason is rooted in scandal. In one of the many colorful chapters of Texas politics, "Pa" Ferguson had been impeached for financial misconduct three years after being elected in 1915. Undeterred, in 1922, he helped his wife, Miriam, "Ma," win election as Governor. She subsequently signed several thousand grants of executive clemency. Relatives of the forgiven inmates returned mercy with cash, which she reportedly accepted.

To avoid a repeat of the scandal, the Texas Constitution was amended, creating a citizens' board of pardons and paroles as a buffer between inmates and the Governor. If the board of pardons and paroles recommends that an execution go forward, the Governor has only two options: accept the recommendation and allow the execution, or grant a onetime thirty-day delay. If the board recommends commuting a sentence from death to a different punishment, the Governor can either overrule the board and allow the execution, or accept the board's recommendation of a lesser punishment.

The board's membership has expanded over the years, as the prison system has grown. In 1989, the legislature approved the current structure. A Governor appoints eighteen members to staggered six-year terms; at the time of the Tucker execution, twelve members were my appointees and six had been appointed by my predecessor. I had named the chairman, Victor Rodriguez, formerly the chief of police in the border city of Brownsville, a good and conscientious man with a total of seventeen years of law enforcement experience.

Despite the intent of the constitutional change, theoretically, I guess I could have tried to tell the board how to vote. The members were, after all, mostly my appointees. But that isn't how I operate. I tell all my appointees that I want them to exercise their best, independent judgment. I know that I cannot possibly know all the information necessary to make good decisions about all the matters that come before different agencies, boards, and commissions. I select people who are qualified, who share my conservative philosophy and approach to government, and then I expect them to make the calls as they see them.

My appointees to the board of pardons and paroles reflect my no-nonsense approach to crime and punishment. They believe people who commit crimes against innocent Texans should pay the consequences; they believe sentences imposed by juries should be carried out. The Texas prison system had become a revolving door earlier in the 1990s, when the prison population had far exceeded the capacity of the system. One of the best things the Texas Legislature and my predecessor, Governor Ann Richards, accomplished was a major prison expansion program that provided more jail space to lock up those who dared to violate our state's laws. And with additional space now available, my parole board slammed shut the revolving door. I am proud that Texas today has virtually eliminated parole for violent criminals; I believe that making violent criminals serve longer sentences has made Texas a safer place.

Because of the vote of the Board of Pardons and Paroles in this case, as the day of the Tucker execution approached, I had only two choices: I could allow the execution to proceed, or I could delay it for thirty days. On the afternoon before the scheduled execution, the United States Supreme Court declined to act in the case of Karla Faye Tucker. My attorney told me her lawyers would try to seek help from the courts again the next day.

When Al Gonzales arrived at the office at 7:00 A.M. the next morning, I was already there. After a restless night, I had headed for the office. I was traveling to Bonham in North Texas that day, to announce a grant to help restore the home of legendary Texas Democrat Sam Rayburn. Speaker Rayburn, "Mr. Sam," as he was affectionately known, was first elected to represent North Texas in the United States House in 1913 and had served as Speaker for all but four years between 1940 and 1961. The $216,000 grant I was announcing would renovate his Bonham home, which had been damaged a couple of months earlier in an electrical fire.

My press office had told the media I would have nothing to say about the execution until I returned to Austin later that day, but that didn't stop the television crews in Dallas from driving the two hours to Bonham. A national network crew was there as well, and it wasn't because they were interested in the tribute to Speaker Sam. All the press wanted to talk about was the execution, but I had nothing new to say. I would wait for final word from the courts before announcing a final decision.

Two women in big hats showed up, first as I toured at the home, and later as I spoke to citizens gathered for the dedication. They carried signs: MURDERER. Other citizens whispered to me quietly. The comments ran the gamut. "We know you'll do the right thing." "She's a good Christian woman, surely you can spare her." "Don't pay any attention to the media and all those outsiders. She did the crime, she has to suffer the consequences." Best of all: "This must be so difficult. I'm keeping you in my prayers."

By the time I returned to the capitol at 4:00 P.M., our press staff was frazzled. Hundreds of reporters had thrown thousands of questions all day long. Rumors had been flying, each one sparking a whole new round of questions and answers. There were false reports that the attorney general's office was prepared to move forward with the execution but the Governor's office was not, reports that Governor Bush had decided to spare Karla Faye Tucker, reports that Governor Bush had decided to allow the execution to proceed. Early in the day, we had thought, and told the press, that the final United States Supreme Court review of the case would be conducted by one justice, Justice Scalia, acting on behalf of the Court. The press was now reporting that the entire Court had assembled to review the case, underscoring the publicity and interest.

At 5:00 P.M., Al Gonzales called Karla Faye Tucker's lawyer, David Botsford, to ask about the Supreme Court's decision. Once again, the Supreme Court had denied his request to halt her execution, but Mr. Botsford said he was on his way to file more appeals with the court of criminal appeals in Texas. Thirty or forty minutes that seemed like three or four hours later, we learned that the Texas court had denied the requests. At that moment, the phone rang. It was the lawyer, Mr. Botsford, calling to let Al know that he had run out of venues and would not be filing any more pleadings in court. After reviewing all the facts one final time, I made up my mind.

It seemed like a long walk across the reception room to the press conference room just outside. The television lights were hot, and the room was packed. Reading my statement was one of the hardest things I have ever done. It would have been far easier to announce my decision in writing. I had considered it but decided that would not be right. The world was watching, and I was accountable for my decisions.

"When I was sworn in as the Governor of Texas, I took an oath of office to uphold the laws of our state, including the death penalty. My responsibility is to ensure our laws are enforced fairly and evenly without preference or special treatment," I told the assembled reporters.

"Many people have contacted my office about this execution. I respect the strong convictions which have prompted some to call for mercy and others to emphasize accountability and consequences.

"Like many touched by this case, I have sought guidance through prayer. I have concluded judgments about the heart and soul of an individual on death row are best left to a higher authority. Karla Faye Tucker has acknowledged she is guilty of a horrible crime. She was convicted and sentenced by a jury of her peers. The role of the state is to enforce our laws and to make sure all individuals are treated fairly under those laws.

"The state must make sure each individual sentenced to death has opportunity for access to the court and a thorough legal review. The courts, including the United States Supreme Court, have reviewed the legal issues in this case, and therefore I will not grant a thirty-day stay.

"May God bless Karla Faye Tucker, and may God bless her victims and their families."

My communications director had told the press I would not answer questions. They were surprised, because it was the first time I had ever done that. They had protested when she told them, but once they saw my face, they didn't try very hard. I think they recognized that there was nothing else to say.

I returned to my office, where Al and a few other members of the staff had gathered. I felt the weight of the decision. I was heavy of heart, sad for those who had believed and prayed for Karla Faye, but I knew I had done the right thing in upholding the laws of Texas. Clay Johnson tried to make me feel better. "You should worry if you didn't think this is a hard thing to do. It's a good thing, not a bad thing, that this affects you this way."

We sat in my capitol office, waiting, as prison officials led her to the death chamber. We patched the phone line into the general counsel's office, where my deputy counsel, Donna Davidson, quietly repeated the words of the warden as she heard them. "6:25, prisoner led from cell." Joe Allbaugh, my chief of staff, Al Gonzales, Clay Johnson, and I sat there, not moving. "6:26, prisoner strapped to gurney." Karen Hughes wandered in and out, periodically leaving to brief the press on the status, then returning, worried, to look at me. I felt like a huge piece of concrete was crushing me as we waited. "6:28, needle inserted." No one said another word. "6:35, lethal dose administered." Finally, what seemed like hours later: "Prisoner is pronounced dead."

I sighed and picked up the phone to call Laura. I said I called to tell her I was on my way home, but the truth is, I wanted to hear her voice. On the way out the door, I paused and looked back in my office at Al Gonzales. "Thank you," I said somberly to the lawyer who had guided us through this difficult capital case. "You did a good job."

Karla Faye Tucker was pronounced dead at 6:45 P.M. Those remain the longest twenty minutes of my tenure as Governor.

Henry Lee Lucas was a totally different matter. He was contemptible, a one-eyed drifter, a proven liar, and a killer who wore a surly scowl and at one time confessed to police that he had committed more than six hundred murders, including that of his own mother. At the height of his confession spree, in the mid-1980s, the media portrayed him as the worst serial killer in United States history.

It's hard to imagine two more different cases. Karla Faye

Tucker had asked for clemency because she was a changed person; Henry Lee Lucas was asking because he had changed his story. He now claimed that he had been lying when he confessed to the brutal rape and murder the police referred to as the "Orange Socks" case.

On Halloween Day in 1979, a young woman was murdered in Texas, her body dumped just north of Austin off Interstate 35 in Williamson County. She was naked except for two orange socks. To this day, she has never been identified.

Four years after the murder, Henry Lee Lucas was arrested in Montague County on a gun charge and began confessing to a number of murders, including that of "Orange Socks." Just before his trial in this case, Lucas tried to recant his confession, but at the trial, the prosecution played tapes of Lucas bragging that he had killed people in every way imaginable. "I even filleted some of 'em like fish," he said. His story had changed, evolved somewhat, throughout a series of four separate confessions involving the young woman known only as "Orange Socks." His explanation for the differences was, "I had killed so many people that I couldn't keep the details straight." The jury heard, on tape, as Lucas described picking up the woman as she was hitchhiking in Oklahoma, killing her during the drive south toward Austin, then having sex with her dead body before dumping it on the side of the road.

The confession was the only evidence linking Henry Lee Lucas to the crime, but it was appalling and powerful. His last-minute attempt to recant didn't have nearly the credibility of his taped confession. Lucas's defense lawyer produced payroll records that indicated that on the day the young woman was killed in Texas, Mr. Lucas was actually working at a roofing job almost a thousand miles away in Jacksonville, Florida. He had cashed a paycheck in Jacksonville the next day. Prosecutors claimed the Florida evidence was falsified. The jury, no doubt horrified by Lucas's graphic taped confession, sentenced him to death.

For years after the trial, Lucas continued to proclaim his innocence. "I never knew her," he told a reporter from *The Dallas Morning News* from his prison cell in June 1998. "They showed me pictures of her laying in that culvert or whatever it was. But I never seen her alive in my life."

My legal counsel gathered in my office. For every death penalty case, they brief me thoroughly, review the arguments made by the prosecution and the defense, raise any doubts or problems or questions. And until today, when asked their recommendations, they have given them with certainty. This time was different. They were worried, uneasy.

"What do you think, Johnny?" I asked Johnny Sutton, my criminal justice policy advisor, a smart and tough former felony prosecutor who had himself successfully prosecuted several death penalty cases. Johnny usually has the black-and-white view of a law enforcement veteran; he knows, emphatically, the difference between the good guys and the bad guys. And Henry Lee Lucas was a very bad guy, the worst of the worst. "I've got a bad feeling in my gut about this case," Johnny surprised me by saying. "Even some of my strong-as-horseradish law enforcement friends have doubts about whether he committed this crime."

The prosecutors in Williamson County had no doubts, my lawyers told me. They felt they had their man. Henry Lee Lucas had confessed to this murder four different times. The prosecutors argued Lucas knew facts about the crime that proved he must have been the murderer. He identified the correct location of the body. Was it the true confession of the murderer, or clever guesswork by an experienced con?

Police throughout Texas had been asking that question for years. As the number of murders Lucas claimed to have committed grew, some law enforcement officials became increasingly skeptical. Jim Henderson and Hugh Aynesworth, investigative reporters for the now defunct *Dallas Times Herald,* had spent years looking into Lucas's crimes and claims. It had become obvious to them that Lucas was a devious man and that he had tried to glean information about crime scenes from investigators to help his fabricated confessions sound more real. Henderson, now writing for the *Houston Chronicle,* described the growing concerns of police officials about the trustworthiness of the Lucas confessions:

> "He [Lucas] started out with an effort to interview me," James Dunlap, a Michigan detective testified at a hearing in El Paso, where a murder charge against Lucas was dismissed by the court. Phil Ryan, a former Texas Ranger who investigated the only two Texas murders in which there was physical evidence implicating Lucas—those of his 15-year-old traveling companion, Becky Powell, and Kate Rich, the elderly Montague County woman who took them into her home—acknowledged that Lucas "had us over a barrel." "He could be very vague with his answers," said Ryan, now sheriff of Wise County. "So we would have to give him a few details to try to pin down the dates and locations." Over time, Lucas became skillful at gleaning information from those interviews and from crime scene photographs shown to him. Still, Ryan said, he became convinced early on, when Lucas's confessions count was a mere 77, that most of them were fabricated. He tried to warn the cops who were streaming into Texas to interview Lucas. Most of those warnings were ignored. "I know he did my two," Ryan said last week, "but I wouldn't bet a paycheck on any of the others."

As Henderson continued to report in his article:

Eventually, Lucas's confession count reached levels that set off alarms among many investigators. "I didn't know enough [about the crimes] to make a judgment," said Dallas detective Linda Erwin, who interviewed Lucas for three days in the summer of 1984, when he tried to confess to 13 murders in her city. "But when I heard it got to be hundreds and hundreds, it was unbelievable to me." Her initial skepticism was fortified once she began interviewing him. "He didn't know enough to convince me that he was involved," she said last week, as Lucas was just days away from execution. To test him, Erwin fabricated a case using random photographs from old murders long since solved and details pulled from her imagination. He claimed credit for the phony crime, and his confession, containing facts she had dribbled out to him, probably could have convinced a jury to convict him, she said. "It wasn't something I wanted to do [try to trick Lucas]," Erwin said. "But the department felt that, to make certain, it was necessary to take the steps we took." Lucas was not charged with any crimes in Dallas.

My lawyers told me about other concerns about Lucas's claims. In 1985, Texas Attorney General Jim Mattox, a Democrat whose politics are at the opposite end of the political spectrum from mine, had conducted a yearlong investigation into the Lucas confessions. He concluded that Henry Lee Lucas had committed three murders. But he believed that in the other cases, law enforcement officials had been so anxious to resolve unsolved crimes that they had unwittingly helped Lucas with suggestions that he incorporated into his "confessions."

As the execution date approached, the current attorney general, Democrat Dan Morales, sent two investigators from his office to Florida. The Texas Attorney General's Office has significant responsibility in a death penalty case; its appellate section represents the state in the federal courts as Texas seeks to enforce its death penalty statute. The investigators verified the previous Florida records and added a new twist. When Lucas recanted his confession in the Orange Socks case, he said that he had been in Florida on October 30 and had witnessed a car fire that day near his home in Jacksonville. The investigator verified the burning car incident with a Duval County fire/incident report; there had been no published reports in the newspaper or elsewhere about the fire. But the outcome of this investigation had shades of gray: the investigators concluded that while it was possible for Henry Lee Lucas to have been in Texas to commit the Orange Socks murder, it was not probable.

Of significance to me, the jury had already reviewed the earlier Florida evidence, including the payroll records; everything except the car fire. As I've said, I try not to substitute my judgment for a jury's verdict, unless there is new evidence or information that the jury did not know. And in this case, what the jury during his trial in 1986 did not know was that Henry Lee Lucas had a habit of confessing to crimes that he did not commit.

Hugh Aynesworth, the reporter, wrote me a long letter. He understood that deciding to spare a despicable killer would not be easy. "I am fully aware—as a journalist for fifty years—of the political ramifications of whatever decision is made in the next few days. But I do have faith that you, of all people involved, have the courage to do what your heart believes is just and proper. . . . The biggest problem here is that Lucas is not a man for whom most people would ordinarily go to bat. He is a colossal liar, a dirt-ball—and a killer."

He was also, said Aynesworth, innocent of this crime. "There is absolutely no way he could have been in Texas the night that the victim called 'Orange Socks' was killed and dropped in Georgetown. If anybody would take the time to read his confessions, he would note that Lucas missed the location of the crime by more than one hundred miles, the date of the murder by several months, and the manner of death, though he was given more chances to come up with the right answers by a sheriff who went to great ends to make his case. There is strong evidence he was in Jacksonville, Florida, that entire week. I personally traveled there and found a grocer who cashed his check a few hours after the murder and interviewed two men who had supervised Lucas's work at a roofing company that week," Aynesworth's letter said.

He ended by asking me not to let a man talk himself to death. "For more than a year, even before the Rangers task force took charge, I was in frequent contact with Lucas and he would relate to me the next town or state where he was headed to confess to more murders. I would warn him that he should not confess to crimes he didn't do. 'You will not be able to get out of it later,' I told him several times. 'You can't just stop and say, "Hey fellows, I was just kidding." You're embarrassing them and they won't ever forget it.' A few weeks ago when I visited him at Huntsville, he said, 'I guess you were right. They're gonna kill me for lyin'.' I don't believe Texas will do that. Sincerely yours, Hugh Aynesworth."

Mass murderer or mass hoax? Henry Lee Lucas had led law enforcement on such a confusing chase of multiple confessions, claiming he had committed so many murders in so many different places, that ultimately the only possible conclusion was that he could not possibly have committed them all.

But I clearly wasn't going to solve the many mysteries of Henry Lee Lucas in the few weeks before his execution. It was not clear that he was innocent, and a jury, after hearing the evidence, had sentenced him to death. On the other hand, it was not clear that he was guilty, and the jury had not known that Lucas had also confessed to many crimes he had not committed. (In one case, he was in jail during a murder he claimed to have committed; in several, he was in different states thousands of miles away from the scenes of the crimes.)

My staff was agonizing over the prospect of sparing a serial killer. In the back of their minds, I'm sure, was concern about political criticism. It was less than five months before the November election. How could the law-and-order Governor spare the life of a convicted murderer? On the other hand, the worst nightmare of a death penalty supporter and of everyone who believes in our criminal justice system is to execute an innocent man. "As a prosecutor, your worst fear is that someone will be put to death for something he didn't do," Johnny Sutton told me.

Opponents of the death penalty did not seize upon Henry Lee Lucas as a poster child for their cause. This time, Bianca Jagger did not visit Texas. The publicity in this case was very different, less emotional and more matter-of-fact, mainly confined to Texas, where many journalists had covered the Henry Lee Lucas saga and were very familiar with the conflicts in his confessions. I was asked about the execution during a June 15 news conference. I said that the Board of Pardons and Paroles and my office would have to give this case a very thorough, full review. Ten days later, on June 25, the Board of Pardons and Paroles voted to recommend that Henry Lee Lucas's sentence of death be commuted to a lesser penalty of life imprisonment. I could accept the recommendation or decline it and allow the execution to go forward; I would make the final decision: life or death.

This case would never have a smoking gun. It was never crystal clear. This was not a decision I had invited, yet it was my job to make it. In the end, I put the case to my fundamental test, the two questions I ask in every death penalty case: is there any doubt about the guilt of the individual, and has the individual had a fair hearing and full access to the courts? For the first time since I have been the Governor, the answer to the first question was yes. There was real doubt. I didn't know whether Henry Lee Lucas was innocent; I also did not know that he was guilty.

I asked my new general counsel, Margaret Wilson, whether we could make sure Lucas would never get out of jail. The answer came back, "Yes. We can make sure he never gets out of prison so he will never have an opportunity to kill again."

I was in Brownsville for the Border Governors' Conference when I announced my decision, explaining that for the first time since I had been Governor, there was doubt about guilt or innocence in a death penalty case. "I am reluctant to second-guess a verdict of a jury and the courts," I told the gathered reporters. "However, the clemency process is intended as a fail-safe for unusual or exceptional circumstances. In this case, at the time it made the decision, the jury did not know and could not have known that Henry Lee Lucas had a pattern of lying and confessing to crimes that evidence later proved he did not commit. His confession, now recanted, was the only evidence that linked him to this crime. Today's knowledge about his pattern of lies raises doubt." Not enough doubt to declare him innocent of the crime, I explained, but "enough doubt about this particular crime that the state of Texas should not impose its ultimate penalty by executing him. I concur with the recommendation of the Board of Pardons and Paroles and hereby commute his sentence to life in prison, which shall begin after all five of his other life sentences are served."

I reassured my fellow Texans that this meant Henry Lee Lucas would never get out of jail. "Henry Lee Lucas is unquestionably guilty of other despicable crimes for which he has been sentenced to spend the rest of his life in prison."

And finally, I explained my obligation in this case. "As a supporter of the death penalty for those who commit horrible crimes, I feel a special obligation to make sure the state of Texas never executes a person for a crime they may not have committed. I take this action so that all Texans can continue to trust the integrity and fairness of our criminal justice system."

The newspaper headlines told the story:

BUSH SPARES MURDERER, said *The Dallas Morning News.* "Serial killer Henry Lee Lucas was saved from death Friday by Gov. George W. Bush, who said he wasn't sure that Mr. Lucas committed the murder for which he faced execution next week. By commuting Mr. Lucas' sentence to life, the governor guaranteed that the once-fearsome, one-eyed murderer will never leave prison alive. 'He will serve until he is dead,' Mr. Bush said. 'There is no chance he will ever walk free. And he should not walk free. He's a very bad man.' "

BUSH SPARES LUCAS' LIFE; GOVERNOR TAKES POLITICAL RISK IN COMMUTING SENTENCE, said the *Austin American-Statesman.* "Gov. George W. Bush, in a rare and politically risky decision, on Friday spared the life of Henry Lee Lucas, once considered the nation's most prolific serial killer after he confessed to murdering hundreds of people. Pronouncing Lucas 'unquestionably guilty of other despicable crimes for which he has been sentenced to spend the rest of his life in prison,' Bush commuted Lucas' death sentence to a life term in the Halloween 1979 slaying near Georgetown of a still-unidentified woman known only as Orange Socks. His decision was apparently the first time since the 1930s that a Texas governor has commuted a death sentence based on a convict's claims of innocence without a court intervening first."

CITING FACTS, BUSH SPARES TEXAS INMATE ON DEATH ROW, said *The New York Times.* "Gov. George W. Bush of Texas agreed today to save the life of one of the nation's most notorious multiple murderers rather than see him executed for a murder he may not have committed."

The decision made for strange political bedfellows. The former attorney general, Democrat Jim Mattox, running for election to the office he had previously held, applauded the decision. "Governor Bush's decision will make our death penalty punishment stronger than ever," he said. "But it was still politically risky, and I'd be glad to stand up and defend him against any attack."

His Republican opponent, John Cornyn, an ally and friend of mine, disagreed and said I should have allowed the execution to proceed.

And my opponent, Democrat Garry Mauro, attacked me and tried to make political hay out of my decision, a strategy that ultimately backfired.

"There is no doubt in my mind that Henry Lee Lucas is guilty of enough of the murders he confessed to that he earned the death penalty," Mauro told the *Austin American-Statesman* on Monday. The paper said it then asked Mauro whether he meant the death penalty should be imposed on what a person might have done in other cases and Mauro replied: "That's what I said."

My campaign press secretary responded. "Although Henry Lee Lucas is unquestionably guilty of other despicable crimes, Garry Mauro's disregard for the law and the facts of the case in applying something like the death penalty is alarming," Mindy Tucker said. "Tuesday, Mauro said the paper may have quoted what he said but not what he meant," dryly noted an article in the *Houston Chronicle*.

Some of the victims' families were understandably upset by my decision, and in the short run, I'm sure it cost me some support. But my staff had done their homework; they had briefed representatives of victims' groups on the rationale for the decision, and they generously spoke up for me. Justice for All, a leading advocacy group for crime victims' rights, praised the decision: "The state of Texas should not execute anyone whose guilt they doubt—and that was the case here," President Dianne Clements said.

In the end, I think most people felt the system had worked; that the clemency process had performed as the fail-safe it is meant to be; that in a state that regularly carries out the death penalty, we had an obligation to be extra careful in times of doubt.

I could not have imagined making life-and-death decisions in the difficult cases of Karla Faye Tucker or Henry Lee Lucas when I first ran for governor. Yet making decisions is what governors and chief executives do. I try to do so thoroughly, thoughtfully, and fairly. I have assembled a top-quality staff that gets me accurate information and comprehensive briefings. I base my decisions on principles that do not change. And whether they agreed or not, in the end, I think my fellow Texans knew that in each case, I had tried to do the right thing for the right reasons.

12

TIDES

I WAS following in some very big footsteps when I lost my first political campaign for Congress in 1978. My dad lost his first political race for the United States Senate in 1964. And my grandfather Prescott Bush lost the first time he ran for the United States Senate. I don't know whether that means members of the Bush family are stubborn or merely persistent. I'm joking. There are tides in politics as in history. Sometimes you run a bad campaign and lose; sometimes you run a good campaign and lose anyway. Sometimes you catch the wave, and sometimes you don't.

My grandfather Prescott Bush believed a person's most enduring and important contribution was hearing and responding to the call of public service. Money and material things were not the measure of a life in the long run, he felt, and if you had them, they came with a price tag: the obligation to serve. He served for eighteen years as moderator of the Representative Town Meeting, the 148-member governing body of Greenwich.

Grandfather was a stern and formal man. Imposing would be a polite way of describing what we kids sometimes called "scary."

As a young boy, I once made the mistake of pulling my grand-parents' dog Plucky's tail. My grandfather's reaction was so swift and forceful that I never did it again. Today my family laughs about it, but for a chastened little boy, it was far from funny. When I think of my grandfather, I think of rules and respect. He expected guests in his home, including his grandchildren, to be on time, well behaved, and properly attired, which meant a coat and tie for dinner, something I never wore at home in Midland except for church. My grandfather also had a great laugh and, for such an imposing man, a huge heart.

He had such high standards, for himself and others, that I cannot imagine what it must have been like for him to lose. His first Senate race, in 1950, was very close. He won the Republican nomination but lost the general election to William Benton by a margin of only 1,102 votes, 431,413 to 430,311. Two years later, when the state's other United States Senator died, and party leaders came to my grandfather to urge him to run once again, he was not inclined. "I've had it," was his initial reaction. "I'm not going around the state again with my hat in my hand." But he finally was persuaded. He won with 51.3 percent of the vote, defeating Democrat Abraham Ribicoff in a close contest, and served in the United States Senate until 1962.

I was six years old when he began serving in the Senate and sixteen when he resigned, his failing health forcing him into retirement. I remember going to visit my grandparents after they moved to Washington. They lived in a townhouse in George-town, and from there, my grandmother took me to visit the monuments and see the sights of Washington. I vividly recall going to a predinner gathering where I met a Texan named Lyndon Johnson. He seemed so big, a larger-than-life-size man; of course, so was my grandfather. "Lyndon, I've got one of your constituents here," my grandfather said. "Georgie, I would like for you to meet Lyndon Baines Johnson, your United States Senator." His hand was huge, and I shook it, looking up at the legendary Texas politician who would later become Vice President and President. Lyndon was larger than life in person, and his view of government was similarly expansive. He used government to change much of Texas, bring electricity, create reservoirs and lakes such as Lake LBJ, and build the Johnson Space Center. His brand of activism extended far beyond public works. History has condemned Johnson because of the Vietnam War, but it should praise him for his concern for civil rights and the disadvantaged. His insistence on equal opportunity for all Americans was bold and just. His programs to lift people out of poverty, however, while well intentioned, proved costly and created too much dependency on government. More than thirty years after Johnson's "War on Poverty," the new Congress and a new generation of governors, including me, began to change "welfare as we know it" and replace dependency on government with work and charitable choice. Senator Johnson was just beginning to build his legacy at the time my grandfather introduced him to me.

But we lived far away in Texas, so my grandfather's political activities did not affect me very often. My first real exposure to the political process came when my dad ran for the United States Senate two years after my grandfather stepped down, in 1964. I was at Andover, the spring of my senior year, when Dad led the primary against three Republican opponents, then defeated Jack Cox in the runoff. It was a tough contest. Dad was decried as a "Rockefeller dupe" and a tool of the Eastern establishment. The same charges would be leveled against me fourteen years later when I ran for Congress in West Texas. Mother was described as a "Cape Cod heiress." She wrote her father, Marvin Pierce, saying she didn't recall ever visiting Cape Cod, but please wire immediately if she was an heiress.

I spent the summer between my senior year at Andover and my freshman year at Yale working on Dad's campaign. It was a great lesson in grassroots politics. I looked up phone numbers, delivered signs, and did anything else that needed to be done that nobody else was doing. One of my jobs was to organize a series of briefing books on each Texas county. The books listed the names of local campaign leaders and information about the county's agricultural products, main industries, and employers. I remember driving the campaign van to Dallas to deliver Bush signs to the big state Republican convention; Barry Goldwater Jr. was there to speak for his dad.

I helped with a series of rallies around the state that featured the Bush Belles, a group of women volunteers who distributed George Bush literature, and the Black Mountain Valley Boys from Abilene. We would roar into town and set up the flatbed truck. The Boys would play country music while the Belles and I worked to draw a crowd, then Dad would speak. One of our stops was in Quanah, in West Texas, where Dad gave a speech in the town square. The trip would have a sequel more than thirty years later when I was Governor of Texas. Laura, the girls, and I were on a nature tour, promoting Texas parks and family vacation destinations. We were on our way to Caprock Canyons State Park for a horseback tour, and we stopped on the way to visit the Main Street project in Quanah. Main Street is a program sponsored by the Texas Historical Commission to revitalize the downtowns of small-town Texas, and Laura has actively pro-moted it. We toured downtown and were heading to the square, where I had been asked to give a speech, when a man stopped me and introduced himself. "You know something, son, I saw your daddy speak right here in this same spot years ago when he was running for the Senate against Ralph Yarborough." I had been there then, too, the son of the candidate, and now I was in the same place more than thirty years later as Governor, my own daughters at my side. It was a sentimental moment, weaving a thread of politics and history through the Bush family past and present. My teenage girls were not impressed. They were bored, and hot, and ready to get on to the horseback ride.

I flew back to Texas from Yale for Election Day in November of 1964. My grandfather came down, too, but the evening was over before it started. At 7:01, as we were pulling into the parking lot of the hotel for our victory party, the radio announcer canceled it: "In the race for U.S. Senate in Texas, Senator Ralph Yarborough has defeated George Bush," he reported. I remember walking into the ballroom, decorated with all the balloons for the celebration we would not be having. Typical of my dad, he shook every hand, thanking volunteers for their support and hard work. I think he felt he had let them down. But the tide was too big. Barry Goldwater was routed by Texan Lyndon Johnson in the presidential race at the top of the ticket, and even though my dad ran eleven points better than Goldwater had, it wasn't enough.

When Dad ran again for the Senate in 1970, after two terms in Congress, the tides turned in a different direction. Senator Yarborough's liberal politics were increasingly out of step with the conservative philosophy of most Texans, and Dad was well positioned as the conservative alternative. I was in the car with him on primary night in Houston, getting ready to drive to Channel 11 for an interview, when we heard the news, again by radio: "In a major upset today, former Congressman Lloyd Bentsen has defeated incumbent United States Senator Ralph Yarborough for the Democratic nomination for U.S. Senate. . . ." All the planning had been based on Dad running against liberal Senator Yarborough; suddenly the opponent was a different and more centrist Democrat, Lloyd Bentsen. In that moment, the entire campaign changed.

I was living in Houston that year, learning to fly the F-102 and flying in the Texas Air National Guard. I helped some in the general election campaign. I did some surrogate speaking, visited college campuses, and traveled with a bus tour trying to build momentum and support for Dad. But again, it was not to be. Early in the evening on November 3, 1970, I walked into the ballroom of Houston's Shamrock Hotel and began doing my election-night duty, manning the telephone connected to my dad's command post high above in suite 1758. Our county chairman would call in to give me the vote totals; my dad's spokesman, Peter Roussel, was on the other end of the hotel line to relay the good news we expected to flow between me and the candidate's suite. There was little of it. The hours passed with mostly bad news, and only a few random rays of hope. "Rou, hang in there . . . tell Dad to hang in there," I said into the mouthpiece. "We're still waiting for returns from Dallas County . . . keep thinking victory. We haven't lost yet. . . ." I was the last to concede defeat.

People often ask me what it was like to have a dad in politics. Other than helping in those two campaigns, for much of my life, he wasn't. I was away at school when he served in Congress in the late 1960s, and when he became Vice President and later President, I was married and had my own children. And by the time he ran for President for the first time, in 1980, I had already jumped into politics with my own campaign for Congress.

I had inherited an understanding of the importance of public service, and I was deeply concerned about the drift toward a more powerful federal government. I was particularly outraged by two pieces of legislation, the Natural Gas Policy Act and the Fuel Use Act, which had mandated wellhead price controls on most categories of domestic natural gas and had determined which industries could use natural gas. Washington had substituted its judgment for the marketplace. It seemed to me that elite central planners were determining the course of our nation. I wanted to do something about it. Allowing the government to dictate the price of natural gas was a move toward European-style socialism, as far as I was concerned. If the federal government was going to take over the natural gas business, what would it set its sights on next?

From the examples of my grandfather and father, I knew that when you are not happy with the direction of the government, you can do something about it. I brought that sense of mission and purpose to a meeting with my friends. The longtime local Congressman had just announced he would not run for reelection, creating an opening. "So who's going to run?" I asked, and we went around the table. Everyone said "not me" until it got to me. Joe O'Neill later told me he remembers thinking, "Hey, wait a minute, I've been here longer than Bush. Maybe I should run instead." "But I changed my mind," Joe told me, "the next week when I saw you work the crowd."

I had a tough primary against two opponents. One was the former mayor of Odessa, who had run a credible race two years earlier against the incumbent Congressman, and was therefore considered the heir apparent for the Republican nomination. My other opponent was very credible as well, a hardworking candidate and retired Air Force officer. When I made it into the runoff, Ronald Reagan endorsed my Republican opponent. Some of Reagan's strategists later hinted he did so because he feared my victory could give my father another foothold in Texas if he challenged Ronald Reagan for the Presidency in 1980. It's an interesting reminder for those who claim I've always benefited from my father's political career. When I won the Republican primary, President Reagan was very gracious and personally called to congratulate me and offer to help.

Long before the primary season, I had a chance meeting with Allan Shivers, the respected former Governor of Texas. He told me the political tides were against me. "Son, you can't win," I remember him saying. "This district is just made for Kent Hance. It's rural, conservative, and Democrat, and he's a rural, conservative Democrat." It turned out Governor Shivers was exactly right, though I put up a good fight. I worked hard and enjoyed the campaign. I met people who are still some of my closest friends; my wife and I enjoyed traveling the back roads of West Texas together.

It's interesting to look back at that campaign twenty years later. It's like listening to an echo of myself. I spoke out for increasing exports of agricultural products, and called for balancing the budget by reducing federal spending while cutting taxes to stimulate job creation. The educational system, I said, should provide more alternatives to parents and students. Our nation will take care of those who cannot help themselves, I said, but we must not reward people for idleness and we must purge the welfare rolls of those who try to cheat the system.

In late October, I was campaigning in Lamesa when a guy came running up to me as I was finishing a radio interview. "How dare you use alcohol to try to influence voters?" he asked. I didn't know what he was talking about. He pulled a "Dear fellow Christian" letter out of his pocket which alleged I had tried to use beer to influence the votes of college students. What actually happened was that I had attended a Bush for Congress campaign reception near Texas Tech University in Lubbock at which beer was served. The letter was sent to Baptist and Church of Christ congregations throughout the district, and it created quite a stir. Laura and I called together our team in Lubbock, and a number of my supporters urged me to condemn my opponent as a hypocrite. Kent Hance was the part owner of a piece of land that had leased space to a bar called Fat Dogs, where some Texas Tech University students drank. Some of the senior Republicans in Lubbock said they were willing to stand up and condemn the hypocrisy of his supporter's attack on me. But I asked them not to. I thought people would appreciate a campaign that stayed focused on the issues. I learned an important lesson. When someone attacks your integrity, you have to respond. I should have countered with an explanation that laid out all the facts. I believe in positive campaigns; I don't engage in personal attacks or gossip or innuendo. But if someone attacks me, I will never again fail to fight back.

I doubt responding would have changed the outcome of the election, however. As Governor Shivers had predicted, I was swimming upstream in the rural district. I will never forget the Fourth of July parade in Muleshoe. Laura and I sat in the back of a pickup truck, smiling and waving the entire route. No one smiled or waved back. I was in trouble in rural Bailey County.

I was also in trouble with members of the American Agriculture Movement. Low prices and high costs had lit the fire of prairie populism; economic distress was sparking political outrage. I attended one of their conventions, and was literally surrounded and peppered with questions when I walked into the big hall. Was it true I was part of the international banking conspiracy that was threatening the American farmer? Because I had been educated up east, the farmers wanted to know if it was true that the Rockefellers had sent me to West Texas? Some farmers made the point that I was not really from here because I had not been born in Texas. "No, I was not born in Texas," I replied, "because I wanted to be close to my mother on that day." Clearly, someone had sown the seeds of conspiracy propaganda, the kind of connect-the-random-dots charges that are virtually impossible to refute. I tried my best to explain why I was running, that I thought the federal government was becoming too big and too powerful, that I was worried about their problems in agriculture, but I don't think I made much headway. As I left, I saw my opponent in the crowd, hugging babies, shaking hands and slapping the backs of the old boys he'd known for years.

On election night, I carried my home county big, and two surrounding counties, but I was unable to crack the entrenched popular state senator on his home turf, which turned out to be virtually all of the rest of the district. Governor Allan Shivers had been right. But so were Prescott and George Bush. Life doesn't end with a loss.

I had poured my heart and soul into the campaign. I'm a hard worker and a tough competitor, and I do not like to lose. But Laura and I were heartened that our home community had turned out big, and that we had done well among the people who knew us best, our friends and neighbors in Midland. I had a lot of people to thank, and I spent weeks writing personal notes and making phone calls. Laura and I took some time off; I dusted myself off and turned my attention back to building my business.

But it wasn't long before politics beckoned again. My dad was running for President. Would I mind spending a few days in Iowa to speak on his behalf? Congressman Tom Tauke from Iowa and I went to people's living rooms, met their neighbors, urged them to turn out to caucuses to vote for my dad. We flew to Des Moines on caucus night. Dad had come out of nowhere to win, and it was exciting. He came flying out of Iowa, on top of the world, with "Big Mo," as he called the momentum he had gained. The next morning we ran into political strategists John Sears and Charlie Black, and I remember being impressed by how polite and gracious Charlie was, even though his candidate, Ronald Reagan, had been defeated.

But momentum was not enough to sustain the campaign through the snows of New Hampshire. Ronald Reagan won their primary.

I was working in Midland and missed most of the rest of Dad's slow spring slide out of the presidential contest. Even though Dad fought fiercely, it became clear that Ronald Reagan would be the nominee of the party. As convention delegates gathered in Detroit that summer, the big question was who would be selected as the candidate for Vice President. I was not in Detroit, but I paid close attention to the unfolding drama and negotiations between Ronald Reagan and former President Gerald Ford. At the time, I felt there was little chance my dad would be selected to run for Vice President; I was surprised and thrilled when President Reagan chose him. Despite the misgivings of some of Ronald Reagan's loyal supporters, I knew that Dad would be an excellent Vice President and a loyal member of the Reagan team. History proved me correct.

Laura and I went to Washington for the inauguration. It was a great honor to meet President-elect Reagan. He has a strong handshake, and I remember thinking he was taller than I expected. He is privately just as he seems to be publicly, a man with deep convictions and a great sense of humor, a kind and decent man of principle who also always has a twinkle in his eye. It was reassuring to know that he was about to be our nation's leader and that Dad would be there to help and support him.

President Reagan was resolute in his goals and confident in his philosophy. He set a clear agenda of limited government, of economic growth through tax cuts, and of peace through strength. His Presidency was a defining one. Before President Reagan, the trend in the modern presidency had been toward bigger and more centralized government. President Reagan realized the greatness of America was found not in government in Washington, but in the hearts and souls of individual Americans.

I admired President Reagan's optimism. He had a sunny spirit and a contagious faith in the goodness of our country. He lifted our national spirit, inspired people, and brought out their best. He articulated the values that made America great. And he was able to unite our country. Some on the left still carped, but most Americans were eager to follow this great leader.

My dad had great respect for President Reagan and served him well. He was always loyal, not only as the Vice President, but also as a friend. The President knew he could confide in George Bush and he would never read about the conversation in the newspaper. It's often hard to find that kind of loyalty in Washington, D.C.

Dad had a vast reservoir of knowledge and experience, and he was a team player, willing to battle for the administration. He was a loyal soldier who toiled in the political vineyards, helped make the administration's case, worked hard to build the Republican party, and attended funeral after funeral with never a complaint.

Throughout Dad's years as Vice President our family would gather for holidays and special occasions at the vice presidential mansion in Washington or at the family home in Maine. By this time, my brothers and sister and I were adults, and the years had faded our differences in ages. I am seven years older than my closest brother, Jeb, eight and a half years older than Neil, ten years older than Marvin, and thirteen years older than my sister, Dorothy. Jeb was eight when I went away to boarding school at age fifteen; Dorothy was only two. They had been little kids when I first left home; now, we were all adults, building our own families and having children. We are a close family. I love my brothers and sister and count them among the most important people in my life.

I didn't attend many political events during those years; I went to see Dad speak when he came to Texas as Vice President a couple of times, but I was busy in the oil and gas business, and Laura and I were raising our own twin daughters. I was not really involved in policy or politics, but that all changed at a family gathering at Camp David in late 1986.

Dad called us all together to introduce us to the people who would run his campaign for President. My brothers and I were a little suspicious. I know a lot of national political consultants who think candidates are a burden they bear on the way to winning an election; I wanted to make sure the political managers of Dad's campaign were there to help elect a great man as President, not to make themselves look good.

I remember getting right to the bottom line by asking Lee Atwater, the young brilliant strategist, "How do we know we can trust you?" Lee had business partners and friends in other political camps, which made me very nervous. He had a reputation for being aggressive and flamboyant. My brother Jeb followed up, "What he means is, if someone throws a grenade at our dad, we expect you to jump on it." After the meeting, Lee came over to me and issued a challenge of his own. "If you're so worried about my loyalty, why don't you come to Washington and help me with the campaign?" he asked. "That way if there's a problem, you'll be there to solve it."

It was an interesting invitation at an interesting time in my life. The oil industry was in the midst of a depression; later that year, I would merge my company into another and leave my daily management duties behind. Over the course of several months, Laura and I talked about it and ultimately decided to move to Washington on a great mission: to fight for a man I loved and admired and to help elect my dad as the next President of the United States.

The next eighteen months were exciting ones, not only because I learned a lot about politics, but also because it was a joy to have the two George Bush families in the same city at the same time. We had hamburger lunches at Mother and Dad's every Sunday. We threw horseshoes. We talked politics. Our girls got to see their grandparents at least every week and sometimes more often.

One night, Laura and I were out of town campaigning, and Barbara and Jenna spent the night at the vice presidential mansion. Dad had spent the day preparing for a debate with Michael Dukakis. Unfortunately, Barbara lost her sleeping companion, Spikey, her favorite stuffed dog. She complained loudly that she could not sleep without Spikey, so "Gampy," better known as Vice President Bush, spent much of the night before his debate searching the house and grounds of the vice presidential residence, flashlight in hand, on a mission to find Spikey. Finally, he did, and Barbara slept soundly. I don't know if my dad ever went to sleep that night.

At work, I learned the pressures and pulls, the ups and downs, the strategy and organization of a presidential campaign. This was the first time I had worked full-time for a national campaign; I had worked as a travel aide in a Senate campaign in Florida and spent several months as the political director for a Senate campaign in Alabama in 1972. My job was to convince people to sign up as county chairmen for Winton M. "Red" Blount. We were well organized, but we lost anyway. Our opponent was supported by former Alabama Governor George Wallace, who taped a radio commercial turning Blount's own home against us. Blount was a successful businessman and owned a large house on the outskirts of Montgomery, Alabama. The commercial basically said that old Red owns this *fancy* house which has *a lot* of bathrooms; in other words, he was a rich man, not one of us. I remember watching the cars drive by, and seeing people gawking at that big house, looking for all those bathrooms. I witnessed firsthand the effects of populist campaigning and knew our candidate was in trouble. Election night proved me right. A good man went down to defeat.

For Dad's presidential campaign, I had no formal role or title; I didn't need one. Atwater and I jogged and strategized together; I was a loyalty enforcer and a listening ear. When someone wanted to talk to the candidate but couldn't, I was a good substitute; people felt if they said something to me, it would probably get to my dad. It did only if I believed it was important for him to know. A candidate needs to focus on the big picture, his message and agenda, and let others worry about most of the details. Through the course of the campaign, I became great friends with Lee Atwater. I grew to admire his strategic abilities and his loyalty to my dad. Our whole family was deeply saddened years later when he suddenly passed away, far too early.

I became the screen for reporters who wanted to interview Dad. "Why you? Give me one reason why I should let you talk with George Bush?" It was the first question I asked, every time. I earned and deserved a reputation for being feisty and tough, sometimes too tough. My blood pressure still goes up when I remember the cover of *Newsweek,* in October 1987. It pictured my dad, in his boat, with the caption: "Fighting the Wimp Factor." They were talking about George Bush, war hero, youngest pilot to earn his wings in the Navy, a pilot who had been shot down and rescued by a submarine near an island occupied by the Japanese. How could they say that about the former director of the Central Intelligence Agency, ambassador to the United Nations and China, loyal Vice President to Ronald Reagan, and wonderful dad and grandfather? I felt responsible, because I had approved the interview. I was livid, and I let a lot of people know exactly how I felt.

In his excellent book about the 1988 presidential campaign, *What It Takes,* Richard Ben Cramer described me as the "Roman Candle" of the Bush family, quick to spark, and that's true when it comes to defending my dad.

I was reminded of that recently, during one of the first trips of my own presidential campaign, when I walked into the second-floor Lincoln Library of the Illinois Governor's mansion and introduced myself to the reporter waiting there to interview me. "Actually, we've met before," he said, during 1988, just after my dad had announced his selection of Senator Dan Quayle as his vice presidential running mate.

The announcement was quite a surprise. Dad made the decision on the airplane, on his way to the convention in New Orleans, then announced it immediately when he arrived. No one was really prepared to brief the press on the reasons for the decision, and it was quickly condemned. As the reporter recalled it, he and a colleague were in a broadcast booth, questioning Dad's choice, when I walked over from a neighboring booth. My father's staunchest defender, I was on the warpath against someone who had not known he had entered a battle. "I'm George W. Bush. I'm the Vice President's son and I want you to know I resent what you all said about my dad," the reporter still remembers me saying, now more than ten years later. At the time, he was taken aback, he told me. He remembers wondering, "Who does this guy think he is?" "Now that I'm older," he told me, "now that I have teenage children, I think that's pretty admirable for a son to do for his dad."

The years may have mellowed the reporter's reaction to the fierce loyalty of a proud son; they've added some embarrassment to mine. "I was exuberant beyond the call sometimes," I told him somewhat sheepishly.

"Your dad himself would have never been that feisty, he was too polite," the reporter told me. And he's right. My dad is not one to provoke a confrontation. He is milder-mannered, more thoughtful than that. He could be tough when he needed to be, but he rarely ever raised his voice, and certainly never had the challenge in it that is frequently heard in mine.

"We are different; he grew up in Greenwich, I grew up in West Texas," I told the reporter, as I frequently say to sum up the inevitable question about our differences. "I went to Sam Houston Elementary School, and he went to Greenwich Country Day."

"Yes, he got to Texas a little late," the reporter wryly replied, "he was already well bred." The Texans in the room broke into laughter, knowing immediately what he meant. There is a brashness, an honest directness in Texans that is sometimes viewed as too direct. I can be blunt, probably sometimes too blunt for my own good.

"I was a warrior for George Bush," I explained. "I would run through a brick wall for my dad. And I was feisty about it. When I thought he was being treated unfairly, I didn't like it one bit and I let people know it."

As I finished the interview with the television reporter and left the room, I noticed a huge, blue-and-white porcelain fishbowl that had been a gift to President Lincoln in the White House. The reporter had reminded me how difficult it is to watch someone you love be criticized, exactly the reason I had worried so much about putting my own family into the fishbowl of a campaign for President.

I hated the criticism of my dad, and I know my brothers and sister felt the same way. "The world knows George Bush as a master of personal diplomacy. We know him as the world's greatest dad," I said at the dedication of his presidential library, summing up our private affection for this public man.

My dad has never tried to influence me except through his example, and it is a powerful one. I have his name, all but the Herbert, and people tell me I look a lot like him. "George W., you have your daddy's eyes and your momma's mouth," a supporter in Houston once said, and that's a pretty accurate assessment. My mother and I are the quippers of the family, sharp-tongued and irreverent. I love her dearly, and she and I delight in provoking each other, a clash of quick wits and ready comebacks. Occasionally, our comebacks are too quick, too ready. I sometimes get in trouble for jesting with reporters, and who can forget Mother's infamous quip, "rhymes with witch"?

Mother has always been the front line of discipline in our family, something my own children and the other grandchildren are learning quickly. If she sees something she doesn't like, she makes sure you know about it. She quickly blows off steam and clearly lays down the law. Mother is also easy to talk with. She's a great conversationalist, not only because she listens but also because she is insightful and direct. Mother loves her family, her dogs, her garden, and my dad.

And America loves her. One of the most memorable moments of my first term as Governor involved my mother. We were in the small central Texas city of Fredericksburg, at a parade to celebrate the fiftieth anniversary of the end of World War II in the Pacific Theater. Mother and Dad were there, and I had been asked to speak. I had looked forward to it, because it was a wonderful opportunity to say thank you on behalf of the sons and daughters of my generation to all the moms and dads of my parents' generation for the incredible sacrifices they made for our freedom. I went to the microphone, acknowledged Dad with a "Mr. President," and everyone gave him a nice round of applause. Then I said, "Mother," and the crowd went wild. I said, "Mother, they obviously still love you here in Texas," and there were more cheers, "and I love you, too. But after fifty years, you're still telling me what to do." And a guy in a big cowboy hat stood up in front of thirty thousand people, cupped his hands, and yelled out, "And you better be listening to her, too, boy." I do listen to her and I am a better person for it.

Dad is an intelligent man of boundless energy. He is a product of a great generation that lived the values of duty, honor, and country. Those values, which caused him to hear the call to serve his country at age eighteen, are an indelible part of Dad's being. He is a principled man who has a clear view of right and wrong. He loves to laugh and has a very tender heart. My dad personifies the Golden Rule.

Dad loves his family. Just this last summer, during an outdoor church service in Maine, the preacher asked whether anyone in the congregation thought they had a perfect family in this imperfect world. The minister asked for a show of hands. Only one hand went up without hesitation: Dad's. He thought we had a perfect family, warts and all.

For Dad, that was an expression of his enormous love for all of us, not any show of pride. "Don't brag," was one of the mantras his mother drilled into him. I respect his humility and try to emulate it in my private life. In the public arena, though, if you don't define and promote yourself, someone else will define you. During the 1988 campaign, my dad was able to define himself. In 1992, Bill Clinton and Ross Perot and Pat Buchanan defined him, and he lost in a long and miserable year. You die a death of a thousand cuts in politics, and his opponents inflicted them. One cut was self-inflicted, by my dad's famous statement: "Read my lips. No new taxes." Several years after he made that pledge, he and his advisors decided to forge a compromise with Congress. He traded some tax increases for spending restraints. Dad knew it would cost him politically, but decided to do it nonetheless. Many economists argue that the compromise laid the groundwork for economic recovery. No one can argue that it hurt Dad. Breaking his pledge cost him credibility and weakened his base.

Elections are about issues and ideas. They are also about earning the voters' trust. During his 1988 campaign, Dad defined himself as a leader Americans could trust to make major decisions about peace and war. By 1992, the cold war had thawed, and people's attention returned home. Bill Clinton managed to convince people, I think unfairly, but nonetheless convincingly, that he had a plan to improve the economy but my father did not. Dad never spent the capital he earned from the success of Desert Storm; the economy was recovering as he lost the election, but people didn't know it. I'm convinced objective history will judge his Presidency far more kindly than the 1992 election did.

I learned a great deal from my dad's Presidency and campaigns, lessons large and small. Laura and I watched Mother make a tremendous difference by focusing on one huge goal, family literacy, as First Lady. We watched Mom and Dad build a spirit of teamwork and camaraderie among friends and staff and security officers by hosting special parties and receptions and roasts, and always treating people with kindness and respect.

I learned the value of personal diplomacy as I watched my dad build friendships and relationships with foreign leaders that helped improve America's stature in the world. I learned firsthand the importance of surrounding yourself with smart, capable, and loyal people, friends who are not afraid to tell you what they really think and will not abandon ship when the water gets choppy. I learned you must give your senior advisors direct access to the boss, or they become frustrated and disillusioned.

I learned you must spend political capital when you earn it, or it withers and dies. I learned that it is difficult to protect incumbency. That lesson would make me work even harder in my 1998 reelection campaign than I did in my first campaign for Governor in 1994. I learned voters are interested in what you have done, but they are more interested in what you will do next.

Based on my work in my dad's campaigns, reporters and my opponents spent much of my 1994 campaign waiting for me to blow up, to lose my temper. It never happened. They expected I would react the same way when they criticized me as I had when they criticized my father. But there is a big difference between being a loyal son and being the candidate. One is a follower, the other a leader. And from a great leader, my dad, I learned the most important lesson of all: you can enter the arena, serve with distinction, absorb the slings and arrows, and emerge with dignity and integrity and the love of your family intact.

13

THE VETO

O NE of my closest friends called to warn that I would be a fool to veto the bill. It was late, nine or nine-thirty at night, and the call was unusual. "Sorry to bother you," Charlie said, but "this is important." He had heard I might veto a bill important to doctors and patients across Texas, and that would be a big mistake, he warned. I should sign it. If I didn't, I risked a huge backlash that could erode the goodwill I had earned during my first five months as Governor of Texas.

People will be surprised that this does not happen very often. A Governor hears a lot from a lot of people, but they are usually fairly predictable constituencies. State employees write asking for a state employee pay raise, lobbyists line up on all sides of a complex business regulatory matter, police chiefs and prosecutors or defense attorneys call about changes in criminal laws. Yet the times when friends or family or political supporters or contributors have asked me to sign or veto a specific piece of legislation are rare, far rarer than public cynicism about politics might lead one to imagine, so rare that they stand out amid the tug-of-war of opinion that takes place on every major piece of legislation.

And Charlie was asking for the right reasons. He wasn't seeking a special favor or an opportunity to personally profit. He knew something about this legislation, and he was dead set for it. Charlie is a doctor, the respected Dr. Charles Younger to patients in Midland who visit him for orthopedic advice and surgery. I sought his advice myself when I was told I needed a knee operation. The doctor in Austin had a great reputation, but Charlie is a friend and I value his judgment. And his emphatic medical opinion was that I needed to sign this bill.

Like many doctors, Charlie is fighting mad at insurance companies. He thinks they've meddled far too much and too often in the way he treats his patients. They've changed the way he practices medicine, subjecting him to countless forms, preclearances, and claim denials. He feels in many ways they've made him a glorified benefits advisor, forcing him to guide patients through a labyrinth of insurance consequences for each treatment option. Most of all, he believes, they are more worried about their profits than about the care of his patients.

The piece of legislation Charlie was asking me to sign was the medical profession's way of fighting back, a stick in the eye of the dispensers of forms and formalities, the intruders in the relationship between doctor and patient.

And doctors weren't the only ones feeling frustrated. Public resentment was beginning to bubble up. Many people were still happy with their own insurance plans, but increasingly, they were beginning to hear the horror stories: "drive-by deliveries" where young mothers were sent home the day after childbirth; patients with serious illnesses forced to change doctors in the midst of their treatment; patients who waited weeks, even months, for an appointment with a specialist; women angry because they had to go through a gatekeeper doctor before seeing their gynecologist.

Health care was changing rapidly, dramatically, and more and more people wanted someone to do something to stop it. That's why Charlie believed I had to sign this bill, to force the insurance companies to turn back the clock on managed care.

The legislation had a great name: the Patient Protection Act. How noble. How sound. How difficult to veto. How could anyone possibly be against protecting patients? Everyone, at one time or another, has been a patient. Everyone, instinctively, believes patients should be protected. What bad Governor could possibly veto a bill protecting patients, especially from unfair and unscrupulous HMOs? Of course, there was a lot more to it than that, but I knew that was what the critics would say.

My policy director has a saying that some legislation is a television commercial waiting to happen. He was warning that the title or issue is so inflammatory that if you dare veto it, it almost certainly becomes a television commercial that your opponent can and will use against you. It's a sad fact of political life today that bad legislation sometimes becomes law for this reason. In an era of sound-bite politics, no one wants to be the bad guy who vetoes a bill with a good-sounding name.

Even worse, this bill not only sounded good, it did some good as well. Many of Charlie's points were right. Some insurance companies had gone too far, and government does have a responsibility to protect public health and safety. I thought it was wrong for insurance companies to impose gag rules to attempt to limit or restrict doctors' best medical advice. I believed all patients should be able to receive emergency care, at any facility, in cases of true emergency. I believed patients should be able to choose their own doctors, so long as they were willing to pay the additional costs of that choice and didn't force the costs onto other members of the health care plan. But this bill had a host of mandates and regulations not directly related to patient care; it dictated everything from how managed care companies hired and fired health care providers to who paid for copying charges for patient records. I worried that this legislation might actually hurt patients by driving up health care costs and forcing some small companies to drop health insurance coverage for their employees altogether. It also had some disturbing provisions, hidden deep in the bill, that would have unfairly created two sets of HMOs—one group subject to the state regulations and the others completely exempt.

As I said, health care was undergoing revolutionary change. Just as doctors were reluctant to let insurance companies decide how they treat patients, I was worried about having the Texas Legislature, which meets for only five months every two years, attempt to regulate a market that was changing daily. Health maintenance organizations were a response to the high costs and inefficiency of the current market; but I also knew that because of consumer dissatisfaction, HMOs were unlikely to survive in their current form. Doctors, I believed, would get more involved in the business side of medicine (they have) and the next wave of change was likely to provide greater consumer choice of health care plans, an increased emphasis on preventive care, and a focus on disease management. The challenge was to protect patients from unscrupulous practices while not stifling the ability of the market to adapt to meet consumer demand.

Insurance Commissioner Elton Bomer, a tough, straight-talking man I had named to the position in one of my first appointments, brought a chart to outline the problems with the bill. He listed more cons than pros. The legislation's mandates would drive up health care costs by almost $500 million, by some estimates; he was especially worried those increased costs would cripple the ability of small businesses to offer affordable health care to their employees. And he didn't like the fact that powerful lobbyists had worked to completely exempt two of the largest HMOs in Texas from the rules in the legislation, claiming their management structure made them different. Bomer felt if you were going to regulate managed care companies, you had to regulate everyone equally.

"The bottom line is you have to sign it," said Bomer, the man who had just outlined all the reasons I should not. "Why?" I asked, surprised by the unexpected conclusion to the briefing. "The Texas Medical Association is powerful, legislators want cover on this issue before going home to their districts, and news-paper editorials across the state say sign it. And so do I—even though it may not be the best public policy," said Bomer. "Po-litically, you just have no other choice."

Bomer is no stranger to politics. A native East Texan, he has served three terms in the Texas Legislature, earning a reputation as tough, honest, and fair. He's not one to shrink from a fight. Elton was the only incumbent Democrat in the Texas Legislature to endorse my campaign against the incumbent Democratic Gov-ernor, Ann Richards, so he certainly has political fortitude.

Bomer also knows the facts of life in the legislature, and the facts are that no one likes a Governor to veto a bill, especially not one that has a nice name, and especially not one that is pop-ular with the press and the public and a powerful lobby group. Even worse, this bill was sponsored by a fellow Republican, Da-vid Sibley, one of the most respected members of the Texas Sen-ate, my good friend, and a strong supporter. Sibley is a maxifacial oral surgeon, a medical professional who felt as strongly as the other doctors who were now inundating my office with letters urging me to sign the bill. My staff and I had talked with him about our concerns about the bill earlier in the session, but like my friend Charlie Younger, he was unhappy with the insurance companies and was not willing to change the proposed bill.

One hundred and eighty of 181 Republicans and Democrats in the Texas Legislature voted for the legislation, eager to cast a vote for protecting patients and against the big bad HMOs. The business groups who were now lining up to oppose it had been asleep at the switch and had missed the opportunity to fix the legislation before it came to my desk. They were counting on me to take the heat. I didn't like having a bad bill land on my desk because they hadn't worked hard enough to mend it during the legislative process. I'm going to think about it some more, I said, ending the meeting. I'll let you know. That night, Charlie called.

My office was beginning to hear from small-business owners across Texas who were adamantly opposed to the legislation. "This bill, under the guise of protecting patients, is a hoax," wrote one small-businessman, the owner of an environmental consulting services business. "This bill is about protecting physicians and a laundry list of special-interest provider groups by giving these groups government-mandated contracting rights unavailable to any other worker in the American economy. . . . Keep the government out of it and let the market for health care and other services continue to respond to the needs of Texas businesses and Texas consumers."

I received a fax from the owner and employees of a welding and machine shop in Kamay, Texas: "For the first time in years we are able to have health insurance that is affordable and sufficient to meet our needs . . . we feel that the more regulated health care becomes in our great and wonderful state, the more expensive and complicated things become for the ordinary people you govern. Please take us into consideration no matter what pressure is put upon you to sign such a bill."

The president of a steel company in San Angelo wrote, "This year, we were offered a managed health care plan by a local hospital. The results have been overwhelming in acceptance by our people. . . . Our managed care plan was able to reduce the company as well as the employee cost by approximately 25 percent. We believe that there will be *no* less attention given under our new plan to our people's health risk. Basically, most of the 145 physicians in our community have signed on to taking care of our employees. Additionally, by paying an additional cost to other doctors, we allow our folks to use any doctor of their choice. In lieu of the Clinton Health Care Plan, we were able to take advantage of the free market system to bring down the cost of medicine within our company. Please do not allow this to be caught up in regulations."

"The way I understand it," a citizen from Arlington wrote, "this 'protection act' protects only the doctors who aren't part of my employer's management care network. As a taxpayer, I am asking for your support against the powerful special-interest doctors who have sponsored this legislation."

The members of my senior staff gathered for lunch at the long dining-room table at the Governor's mansion. We had hamburgers and continued indigestion about the patient protection act. Vance McMahan, the policy director who knew this bill would be used against me in a television commercial, was nonetheless convinced we had to veto it. It was excessive government intrusion into the private health care marketplace, he argued, exactly the sort of governmental overreach that an advocate of limited government must oppose. My legislative director, Dan Shelley, was certain I should sign it. Legislative directors generally encourage signing everything. They have to explain it to the legislators if you don't.

We talked about the intricacies and the repercussions. We talked for more than an hour. I asked Elton Bomer a lot of questions. Was there another way to approach this problem? Could he develop insurance regulations that would prevent unscrupulous practices and protect patients without the costly faults contained in this legislation? Elton believed he could.

In the end, it was a choice of good public policy versus politics. It would have been easy to sign the legislation; some small-business owners would have been unhappy, but everybody else would be pleased. I'd had a great legislative session. All four of my major priorities of education, welfare, juvenile justice, and tort reforms had become law. I knew a veto would call into question my leadership and ability to deal with the legislature, and would definitely be used against me in a future campaign. But I was willing to take the political heat rather than sign what I thought was a bad law.

I'm vetoing the bill, I said, rising from the table. It's the right thing to do. But I'm also going to direct Insurance Commissioner Bomer to develop tough rules to protect patients and health care providers in the right way. We need to write the veto message carefully, to explain it.

The outcry was swift and loud. "The honeymoon is over for George W. Bush," said *Texas Monthly* magazine, calling it my "first big political mistake." The Texas Medical Association was furious. Consumer groups condemned me. And quietly, Elton Bomer set about writing insurance rules to protect patients and providers.

Several weeks after the veto, I went to the Texas Medical Association's convention in Austin, into the den of the lion. They were still very unhappy that I had vetoed their carefully crafted attack on the insurance companies. Yet I would not shrink from them or from my decision. I explained why I had done what I did. And I asked them to work with Commissioner Bomer and me to develop tough and fair patient and provider protection rules that Bomer could implement through the Department of Insurance. Under Texas law, the insurance commissioner had broad power to enact rules governing insurance to make sure customers, in this case, patients, were treated fairly. Charlie Younger went to the medical association's convention with me, even though he wasn't happy with me either. It wasn't going to affect our friendship, he told me, but he was pretty skeptical about these rules.

The patient and provider protection rules that Elton Bomer developed were ultimately heralded as better patient protections than those contained in the original legislation. Even Charlie admits it. Bomer enacted them as insurance regulations, and I subsequently signed them into law in 1997, though few people paid much attention.

During the spring of 1998, ignoring the fact that I had subsequently signed patient protections, my Democratic opponent ran the negative and misleading television commercial Vance McMahan had predicted. "Governor George Bush has never had to pick a doctor from an HMO list. Yet he vetoed your right to choose your own doctor. . . . To choose your own doctor, you need to choose a new governor."

Yet by the summer of 1999, as the United States Senate was debating national patient protection laws, the patient protections I had signed in Texas, including the right to choose your own doctor, were lauded as a model for the rest of the nation.

Many associations and respected health publications have cited Texas as a national example as well. Larry Besaw, the Associate Editor for *Texas Medicine,* wrote: "While other states have enacted parts of the reform bills passed by the legislature this year, only Texas has adopted the full complement of legislation addressing patient and managed care liability."

Thanks to the rules Elton developed and laws that I signed, in Texas today HMOs are forbidden to enact "gag clauses" that discourage doctors from discussing all possible treatment options, insurance must pay for hospital emergency care in any circumstance that a reasonable person would define as an emergency, women can go directly to their gynecologist without having to go through a gatekeeper doctor first, and health plans that cover mastectomies must also cover postmastectomy breast reconstruction. Patients with lengthy, ongoing illnesses cannot be required to change doctors, and if cancer patients need treatment that is not provided within their health care network, their insurance must refer them to specialty hospitals and pay for that care.

And the Texas Medical Association that was so upset when I went to speak to their group eventually stated that, "the rules as adopted are, from the vantage point of a health care consumer or a physician, superb. We consider these rules far superior in content and intent to the vetoed legislation. . . . These patient protection rules should be held as a national model."

Politics, like life, is a strange endeavor. Things are sometimes not what they seem. I try to get the facts and weigh both sides. And I remain confident that most people, most of the time, can see beyond the sound bites to appreciate leaders who try to do the right things for the right reasons.

14

BASEBALL

I WAS standing near the pitcher's mound, looking up at the thousands of people who had been milling around Arlington Stadium for hours, standing in long lines to buy peanuts and hot dogs, watching as the hitters took batting practice, waiting with the hope-springs-eternal sense of anticipation and optimism of American baseball and its fans. This is our year, that optimism says every year, opening day of the season we win the pennant. No matter that the same scene is replayed in every Major League ballpark in America, on every opening day, it always seems entirely possible, imminently doable that this year, it's our dream, our team, our pennant.

In this way, baseball is much like the other major endeavors of my life. Baseball is a pursuit for optimists, just like drilling for oil or running for office. To come to the ballpark every day, you have to believe you can win. To drill another well after a dry hole, you have to believe this one will be successful. To run for office, especially after losing, you have to believe you can win.

Standing with me that spring day in 1989 in the infield were

Eddie Chiles, longtime owner of the Texas Rangers, Tom Landry, who had just been abruptly fired as head coach of the Dallas Cowboys football team, and Rusty Rose, my new friend and partner. Tom Landry was beloved by many people in Dallas, not only because of his winning football teams, but also because of the way he conducted himself, with integrity and decency. Eddie was angry that the new football owners had fired Tom, and he was honoring him by having him throw out the first pitch of the new baseball season. Rusty and I were about to be introduced as the managing general partners of the new group of owners that was purchasing the Texas Rangers from Eddie Chiles. A lifelong baseball fan, I was about to own a baseball team. I remember thinking, "This is as good as it gets. Life cannot be better than this."

I had pursued the purchase like a pit bull on the pant leg of opportunity. I was in Washington, working on my dad's 1988 presidential campaign, when my friend Bill DeWitt called from Cincinnati. When DeWitt and I worked together in the oil business, we would meet with investors during the day and at night we would go to baseball games. One night in 1985, we saw Pete Rose drill hit number 4,192, a single to left center off San Diego's Eric Show to break Ty Cobb's career record. Bill loved baseball and so did I. His dad, Bill DeWitt Sr., had once owned the St. Louis Browns and the Cincinnati Reds. DeWitt called because he had heard through baseball circles that the Texas Rangers might be for sale. "This could be a natural for you," he told me. "I know you want to get back to Texas, and you've always loved baseball."

When Dad won the election, I made plans to move back to Dallas. Some people were surprised. They figured I would stay in Washington and try to cash in on Dad's political success. They didn't understand I had come to Washington not for myself but to help my dad pursue his dream. I was ready to go home to Texas, to get back to my life.

Within weeks of returning to Dallas, I began reading the speculation in the newspapers. Television station owner Ed Gaylord might buy the team; a group of Florida investors was interested. And so was I. If they were selling, I was buying. Of course, I had more determination than money.

And that's exactly what Eddie Chiles told me when I went to see him. Eddie, who has since passed away, was a wonderful man. He and his wife, Fran, had long been involved in supporting Republicans and conservative causes and candidates. Fran was the Republican national committeewoman from Texas during much of the 1980s; Eddie became well known for the "I'm mad, too, Eddie" campaign he conducted to express his outrage at the big spenders in Congress. I don't remember specifically where I first met Eddie Chiles, although I'm sure it was growing up in Midland.

Eddie's health was deteriorating, and he wanted to sell the team. My job was to convince him to sell it to me. To Eddie, the Texas Rangers was much more than a business asset. The team was something he loved, almost like a child. I think he recognized I would love it, too. "I'd like to sell to you, son, but you don't have any money," I remember him saying.

And he was right. I had nowhere near the $80 million it would take to purchase the team. I am, however, a hard worker who catches a dream and refuses to let go. I had knocked at the door, and I would keep on knocking. I began making the rounds, calling on friends, calling on strangers, trying to string together enough money to buy the team. I kept in touch with Eddie, trying to make myself his buyer of choice.

I had assembled a good group of friends to be my investors. A few were from Texas, but most were friends from around the country—DeWitt and Mercer Reynolds from Ohio; Roland Betts, Tom Bernstein, and Craig Stapleton from the New York area; and others. When Baseball Commissioner Peter Ueberroth visited Dallas, he told the media that he was worried that my group did not have enough of a Texas presence. He strongly believed that more than half of a franchise's investors should come from the state in which the team was located to provide stability. I read in the newspaper that the commissioner met with Dallas businessman and investor Richard Rainwater, and he must have been a better salesman than I was. I had cold-called Rainwater weeks earlier, gone to see him out of the blue to ask if he might be interested in investing in the Texas Rangers. Richard told me he had no interest in baseball. But after Commissioner Ueberroth's visit, I thought that he might have changed his mind.

I called Richard immediately and went to see him. My hunch was right; the commissioner had interested him in the merits of owning a team. He was now excited about the possibility. Richard had called his longtime friend Rusty Rose to see if Rusty was interested in the baseball investment, and he was. We all met to look one another over and see if we could work together. We ended up merging our two groups and we became great friends. We worked out a partnership agreement: once all the investors received their original money back, plus a 2 percent return, they would split 85 percent of any profits. Rusty and I would share the day-to-day management responsibilities of the partnership and would split the remaining 15 percent of any profits—5 percent for him and 10 percent for me—in recognition of my role in putting the deal together and persuading Eddie Chiles to sell the team to us.

It was ironic later to watch how the political process would view this financial arrangement, one that is typical of many business partnerships. During my 1994 campaign for Governor, I was criticized for owning too little of the team. "He makes a big deal about running a baseball team. Fact is, he only owns a little more than one percent of the Texas Rangers," my opponent's television commercials said, failing to recognize both my management responsibilities and my managing partnership interest. Then, after my partners and I sold the Rangers in 1998, I was criticized during my reelection campaign that year for owning too big an interest and making too much from the sale.

Buying the baseball team was a financial risk for me. I put $600,000—almost a third of my entire net worth—into a team that had a twenty-five-year losing streak, sagging attendance, and an inferior ballpark. On the other hand, owning a Major League Baseball team was a dream come true.

Baseball has been a part of my life since before I can remember. Mother took me to see my first games as an infant when Dad and his teammates at Yale made it to the NCAA national championships his junior and senior years. I spent so much time at the Yale ball field that the groundskeeper, a man who loved my dad, also adopted me, taking me on field trips and adventures. He took me to the Peabody Museum once, and when I came home I asked my mother whether she remembered the dinosaur on display there. "Yes," she replied, and I asked, "Do you remember the tail? Well, here is a piece of it," I said, proudly pulling it out of my pocket. Mother was horrified and promptly returned it.

I went to my first Major League Baseball game during grade school when I visited my grandparents in Connecticut. My uncle Buck took me to the Polo Grounds to see the New York Giants play. The Giants became my team at age eight, the year they took the series 4–0. Eight years later, my dad and I went to spring training for the team that had replaced the Giants, the newly formed New York Mets. My grandmother's brother, my great-uncle George Herbert Walker, was one of the Mets' three owners. He invited us to spring training, where he introduced me to Casey Stengel, then the manager, and Rogers Hornsby from Winters, Texas, the batting instructor. His joy of ownership must have been infectious;

perhaps it was watching my great-uncle's delight that planted the first seed of desire to own a club.

Shortly after my family moved to Houston, baseball expanded to our new city. The Colt 45s came to town, and I became their number one fan. I sweltered through day games in the Houston summers, days when both the temperature and humidity were ninety-eight. I sweltered through night games where the lights attracted mosquitoes the size of swallows. I sweltered through several losing seasons. Some nights the heat was so bad and the score so lopsided that friends and I would go next door to the amusement park and ride the roller coaster. It was perfect training for the ups and downs of baseball. I will never forget my excitement when Judge Roy Hofheinz and the newly named Houston Astros built the eighth wonder of the world, the Astrodome. No more sweltering, but still no championships. I remained a loyal fan and am still friends with two of the initial Astros, Rusty Staub and Joe Morgan.

After years of rooting for National League teams, when we purchased the Rangers, I was suddenly in the American League, designated hitter and all. It did not take long to switch my allegiances. I was in baseball.

Rusty Rose and I planned out our business strategy. We would let the baseball people make the baseball decisions. We didn't tell our managers whom to play at third base, but we held them accountable for their decisions. We set the financial parameters and managed the business side of the operation, trying to keep the payroll reasonable and the ticket prices down. I instinctively knew that the most important part of our job was to make sure that our ballpark was family-friendly, so that moms and dads would enjoy bringing their children to see America's game.

Rusty and I are very different people, but we made our partnership work. He is methodical; I work more quickly. He is private; I am public. Rusty didn't like to give speeches or talk with the media, so I became the face and voice for the management of the Texas Rangers. I worked hard to sell tickets. I traveled the Rangers' market, which encompasses a huge part of Texas, speaking to civic groups and chambers of commerce. I did thousands of media interviews, touting baseball as a family sport and a great entertainment value.

I got to know all the hot-dog vendors and the ticket takers and the ushers by their first names. They were an important part of making sure our fans felt welcome and at home. I signed thousands of autographs, brought guests to the ballpark, and sat in the seats with the fans every night. I sat in the front row, not in the owners' box. I did so because I wanted to be close to the game, but also because I wanted our fans to see that the owners were willing to share in their experiences. Sometimes I paid a dear price. As the seasons wore on and the Rangers fell behind, the fans became more and more frustrated. "Hey, Bush, more pitching," they would yell.

I will never forget the time one fan was on my case, yelling about the lousy pitching for almost the entire game. After the sixth inning, I stood up and waved at the guy and invited him to come sit near me in an empty seat. I shook his hand and introduced myself. He was a teacher at a local school. I asked whether he liked having his name yelled out loud in public in a derogatory way. When he said no, I replied, "Neither do I." I talked with him about our pitching situation; he halfway apologized for yelling and I halfway apologized for the pitching, and we had a great baseball discussion. Several years later, after I became Governor, a man came over and tapped one of my security officers on the shoulder and said he needed to see me. It was George the teacher. We had become "ballpark friends." Even though time had elapsed and my job had changed, we shared the common bonds of baseball.

Even before we purchased the team from Eddie, it was obvious that we would need a new stadium. The Rangers were a Major League team playing in what was a minor league park; we could not sell enough premium tickets to remain financially competitive. So Rusty and I asked one of our partners, Tom Schieffer, to manage the process of building a new stadium. It turned out to be one of our best decisions. Tom, a former Democratic state representative, is a well-organized strategic thinker. He developed an ingenious plan and sold it to another big thinker, the mayor of Arlington, Richard Greene. Richard was adamant about keeping the team in Arlington, because he believed it would be good for his city and its citizens. He worked with Tom on a proposal for a public-private partnership, in which the Rangers would put up part of the money to construct a new stadium, and the citizens of Arlington would put up the rest, using a half cent of the sales tax allocated for economic development activities. I was comfortable with this type of public-private financing so long as the taxpayers of Arlington knew all the facts and were allowed to vote on the proposition. The people of Arlington supported the proposal overwhelmingly. Not only was the vote to build the ballpark large, but also the total turnout was the largest the city had ever known. The day after the election, we began work on the ballpark project.

We sat down and talked about what we wanted. We agreed that all seats should face the mound and the field had to be outdoors and grass. We wanted an old-style park, with modern accommodations, including plenty of concession areas and lots of women's rest rooms. We wanted unique architecture and unpredictable corners in the outfield to enhance triples, one of the game's most exciting plays. During one of the most interesting weeks of my life, we had architects from all over the country come in and meet with our partners to discuss their proposals for the ballpark. In the end, the decision was unanimous. Architect David Schwartz had captured our vision.

Opening day of the Ballpark in Arlington was another high-light of my life. It came in April of 1994, during my campaign for Governor. A record crowd came out to celebrate the opening, and they would not be disappointed. World-renowned pianist Van Cliburn of Fort Worth played the national anthem on a grand piano. Arlington Mayor Greene threw out the first pitch, and the first game was played in a magnificent monument to baseball and its fans. Our partners had had a vision, we developed a strategy, we picked good people like Tom to manage the project, and the proof was in the results.

Five years later, the Ballpark in Arlington is an unqualified success, a win for everybody involved. Arlington has seen tremendous economic growth, and tax revenues have increased for both the city and the state. The stadium added value for the fans. The Ballpark is an incredible place to watch a baseball game. The ambience evokes a simpler time of family and fun. The bonds are being paid off so rapidly that the city's half-cent sales tax will go away ten years earlier than projected. The Rangers have signed a long-term contract guaranteeing they will remain in Arlington at least through the year 2030.

After I was elected Governor, I was not able to attend many games. I continued to be a loyal fan, catching the Rangers broadcast whenever I could on radio or television from the Governor's mansion. I was surprised that I did not miss baseball more. My attention had been captured by my job as Governor of Texas, a job I love. I took great satisfaction in knowing that our franchise was well run and well established. We had significantly increased the value of the Texas Rangers. Our teams were winning. Our farm system had produced stars like Juan Gonzalez, Ivan "Pudge" Rodriguez, and Rusty Greer. We were regularly playing to huge crowds in our new ballpark. So I was not surprised when Rusty Rose and Tom Schieffer called to tell me that a Dallas business-man, Tom Hicks, was interested in purchasing the team. We all agreed we were ready to sell. We had had a great run, we had all enjoyed working with one another and the team, but it seemed time to move on and the offer was too good to refuse. As has been widely reported, when we sold the Texas Rangers, I made more than $15 million, more money than I ever dreamed possible. The sale was bittersweet, though, because I have so many wonderful memories of my time in baseball.

For five years, Laura and I went to fifty or sixty home games a year. I always say if you're going to a baseball game, you had better go with someone you like, because you have ample time to talk. I went with someone I loved. And talk we did: about baseball, about our girls, about life. It was a time of family and friends. Our girls grew up at the ballpark and we entertained friends from all across the country.

I'll never forget some of the magic moments, like the night Nolan Ryan struck out his five-thousandth victim. Cameras flashed all across the stadium, and my daughter Barbara said, "Hey, Dad, look at all the fireflies." It was an electric moment for my good friend Nolan Ryan, who joined the team the year we bought it. Watching him defy age and crown his Hall-of-Fame career was a privilege. Nolan is the epitome of a Texan, a hardworking family man who is a fierce competitor on the field and a gentle, humble soul off of it.

I remember when Robin Ventura charged the mound, and Nolan gave him what the sportswriters called a "Texas Whuppin'." He looked like a beast protecting his lair. Ventura must have been irrational to charge someone as big and tough as Nolan. After the bench-clearing brawl, Ryan went on to pitch seven innings, allowing only one earned run in a 5–2 Rangers victory. The Ventura incident cemented the legend of Nolan Ryan.

Nolan and I often exercised together. I would run on the warning track or on the streets around the ballpark, and then go to the clubhouse to lift weights. He was almost always there. I marveled at Nolan's work ethic and intensity. I watched him prepare for games, then come back to the clubhouse to work out again after a game. God gave him the talent to be a good player; his hard work and drive made him great.

I admit to almost mystical feelings about America's pastime. I give a speech to college graduates where I outline "fixed stars," essential truths that can help guide them through life. Most involve faith and family and how to live responsibly. I'm only partly joking when I outline fixed star number four: "Baseball should always be played outdoors, on grass, with wooden bats." I'm a traditionalist when it comes to our national sport. I voted against wild-card play, because I don't believe baseball should reward a second-place finish. I didn't like interleague play because I worried it would diminish the World Series. I thought the best future for baseball would be found in reverence and respect for its history and traditions.

Baseball inspires the Muses. Baseball does not have time limits or clocks; we are under no artificial deadlines except three outs to an inning. The true baseball fan loves the dull spots in a game, because they allow you to think and remember, to compare the present with the past. The competitor in me also loves the challenge of baseball, a challenge all of us can identify with, because baseball is a sport played by normal-sized people. Joe Garagiola, former catcher and broadcaster, said, "Baseball gives you every chance to be great. Then it puts every pressure on you to prove that you haven't got what it takes. It never takes away that chance, and it never takes away that pressure."

You could also apply that quote to a political campaign. I didn't intend it or think about it at the time, but in retrospect, baseball was a great training ground for politics and government. The bottom line in baseball is results: wins and losses. It's a people business. You have to attract customers in the first place, and you have to keep them with you and bring them back. We had to create trust with the fans that we wanted to win. And we had to provide a venue that was comfortable for families and children.

We succeeded in baseball because we had a vision and a message. From baseball, I developed a thick skin against criticism. I learned to overlook minor setbacks and focus on the long haul. I would find those skills invaluable in my campaigns and tenure as Governor of Texas.

15

A TIME TO BUILD

MAYBE we should burn it, I suggested, only half jokingly, looking at the stack of 25,000 pages of proposed
new curriculum my chief education advisor had just
dropped on the desk, an exclamation point to her concerns that
the recommendations were a bureaucratic nightmare. This curriculum was unacceptable, she told me, we had to do something
to stop it. The voluminous stack was the result of two years of
committee meetings, an arduous process launched by my predecessor and now landed quite literally on our desks, poised to
drown Texas schools under the weight of garbled expectations.

"It's even worse than I thought. Gobbledygook. A mess."
Margaret LaMontagne, my chief education advisor, was beside
herself at the thought of sending this curriculum into Texas
schools. A straightforward list of academic expectations, that's
what I wanted. A clear list of what students should know, and
when they should know it. That's what a curriculum should be.
I believe the role of the state is to set high education standards
and hold local school districts accountable for results. The standards should reflect what we expect fourth-graders to know be-

fore they move to the fifth grade, what body of knowledge a student should have to earn a high school diploma in Texas. It seemed straightforward, even simple. But the *only* thing these pages made clear was that it was anything but simple.

"The student analyzes the influence of the speaker's verbal and nonverbal behaviors on listener's perception and acceptance or rejection of the message, including speaker's use of language, voice and gestures," said one sentence, unfortunately representative of many in these 25,000 pages. "I don't know what that means," I said in a speech to educators. "Moreover, I don't know how you would test a child on that. We must say plainly what we want students to know and when we want them to know it. No touchy-feely essays on learning by osmosis. No holding hands till the karma is right. Just a straightforward list of state expectations."

I viewed the first major rewrite of our curriculum in more than a decade as a great opportunity. The curriculum, known as the Texas Essential Knowledge and Skills plan, was a new road map for learning in Texas. It would guide and direct our schools for years to come. The standards outlined in the new curriculum would become the basis for textbooks and tests, the foundation on which we measured student and school performance. The rewrite was a significant opportunity to raise standards and redirect the focus of every school in Texas, all at once. But the 25,000 pages on my desk did not achieve the mission.

I called together the Education Commissioner and his top deputies, along with members of the Governor's Business Council, a group of major business leaders who have been instrumental in helping reform education in Texas. I told them I needed their help to completely overhaul this curriculum. It was an interesting reminder of the role of the executive branch, a role that extends far beyond the legislative process. The final word on state policy often comes in the implementation. The process of rewriting the

Texas curriculum began before legislation required it; the process would end long after the legislature had gone home.

I would never claim to be an expert in the details of developing a curriculum. I did know the result I wanted: a clear, straightforward outline of high academic standards for Texas schools. And I gave our education leaders a new mission: Texas would assemble the most highly regarded scholars in the nation, experts who shared my belief in the power of high standards and basic education, and contract with them to review and revise and repair this curriculum.

I publicly denounced the curriculum as mush and said we would revise it. We contracted with experts in various subjects: Barbara Foorman, an expert in diagnosing and correcting reading problems; Marilyn Adams, the guru of research-based reading techniques; T. R. Fehrenbach, a much heralded Texas historian; Diane Ravitch, an expert in social studies; and Lynne Cheney, an education specialist and former chairman of the National Endowment for the Humanities.

I am grateful for their hard work. They overhauled the entire curriculum. They overcame opposition from advocates of the status quo, and they insisted on high academic standards. As a result, they developed a model for Texas schools that has won national recognition for excellence. By late 1996, Texas had adopted a new curriculum that has been praised as one of the strongest in the country.

A big part of a Governor's job is executing an agenda through executive branch agencies. My staff and I meet regularly with the directors of the criminal justice, health and human services, education, environmental, workforce, and other major agencies, to set a strategic vision and mobilize all our resources toward the same goals. I met a number of times with the director of our juvenile justice system to talk about my strong belief that discipline and love go hand-in-hand, that we must teach young people there are bad consequences for bad behavior if we hoped to change their bad choices. The director of the Texas Youth Commission, Steve Robinson, took the mission to heart.

We strengthened our juvenile justice laws during the 1995 legislative session, but Steve accomplished something just as important. He changed the culture and approach of our entire juvenile justice agency. Previously, juvenile offenders spent large parts of their day loitering or sleeping. They wore clothes promoting their gangs; guards often had to break up gang fights. Thanks to Steve's leadership, when juvenile offenders arrive at our intake facility today, they are issued bright orange uniforms and their heads are shaved. They get up early, exercise regularly, and help maintain the facility. They don't speak unless they are spoken to, and then they acknowledge their guards with a "yes, ma'am," and a "yes, sir." Every hour of their day is structured and productive. Steve called me one day to tell me he thought he was making progress in achieving his mission, because a young juvenile offender who had committed a serious crime had warned his younger brother to stay out of trouble because "you don't want to come here." He's right; we don't want our children to end up in juvenile jail in Texas, and when they do, we teach them discipline and try to redirect their lives. They spend time studying and learning, working, and talking about how to make better choices. We teach them they are accountable for their actions.

Texas has created a series of steps designed to rescue troubled children. We created strict alternative schools for students who caused problems in regular classes. We expanded boot camps, and tripled the number of beds in the juvenile detention system, giving us space to require longer sentences for violent juveniles. Law enforcement officials and juvenile judges have credited our tougher laws and different approach with substantial results: violent juvenile crime has decreased 38 percent and overall juvenile crime has decreased 7 percent—the first decline in a decade.

★   ★   ★

My faith-based initiative is another example of the power to implement change through the executive branch of government. Shortly after I was elected in 1995, state regulators tried to shut down a successful drug and alcohol treatment program, Teen Challenge of South Texas, because its faith-based approach didn't conform with the agency's bureaucratic rules. Teen Challenge didn't claim to offer medical treatment; it was saving lives through the transforming power of faith. Its program focused on Bible study and prayer and taught that drug and alcohol addiction were bad choices. And it had good results, much better results than many comparable secular programs. But the agency said Teen Challenge didn't meet its strict requirements for a "treatment" program. The agency compiled a forty-nine-page list of "violations," ranging from frayed carpets to torn shower curtains. One agency official, citing state law, insisted "outcomes and outputs are not an issue for us." In other words, the condition of the carpet was more important than the condition of people's lives.

What caught my attention was how ridiculous it seemed for the state drug and alcohol agency to shut down a drug and alcohol program that was successfully fighting addiction. "I'm results-oriented, and I worry about the state being so process-oriented that we stifle good programs. We need to judge programs on results, not on forms and process," I said during an interview. My office stepped in and helped work out an agreement to allow Teen Challenge to continue to operate while we looked for more permanent ways to address this problem.

Texas has many kind and loving people who follow a religious imperative to help neighbors in need. It seemed to me that a government that truly wants to help people should welcome the active involvement of people of faith, not throw up roadblocks or stifle their efforts with bureaucratic red tape and excessive regulation. I assembled a task force that met throughout 1996 to recommend ways that churches and synagogues and mosques and other faith-based or private institutions could work with government to help people in need without violating the important principle of separation of church and state, compromising the religious nature of their mission, or being shackled by government intrusion. The result was a landmark report that recommended a number of changes to our state laws. The legislature adopted many of them in 1997 and 1999. If drug treatment programs such as Teen Challenge rely exclusively on faith—and not any medical treatment—to try to cure addiction, they are now exempt from state regulation. Church day care or child care that meets or exceeds state standards may be accredited by nationally recognized private sector entities rather than licensed by the state. Texas enacted a "Good Samaritan" law, which protects medical professionals from frivolous lawsuits when they volunteer their services to help needy Texans. I signed legislation protecting Texans' right to free exercise of religion without government encroachment. These efforts are making Texas a national leader in allowing faith-based organizations to help government tackle our toughest social problems.

Just as important, I signed an executive order encouraging state agencies to take advantage of the 1996 "charitable choice" provision of the federal welfare reform law. This allows government agencies to contract or partner with faith-based organizations to deliver social services. I encouraged all our state agencies to look for ways to work with faith-based groups. And that is how I came to be pictured on the front page of the *Houston Chronicle,* singing "Amazing Grace" with a murderer.

Carol Vance, former Harris County District Attorney and former chairman of our Texas board of criminal justice, came by my office one day to tell me about a trip he had taken to Brazil, to visit a faith-based prison rehabilitation program that had achieved dramatic results. Traditional rehabilitation programs aimed at reducing recidivism have not been very effective. I believe in the power of faith to change lives, so I told Carol I was interested in giving this type of program a try. Chuck Colson, who founded a prison ministry after serving time in federal prison for his role in the Watergate scandal, approached Texas prison officials with a proposal to operate a values-based prerelease program in one of our prison units, and they agreed at my urging. The idea behind the InnerChange Freedom Initiative, as the program is called, is that changing hearts will change lives. Inmates participate in a rigorous program of Bible study, worship, exercise and physical fitness. Participation is strictly voluntary, and Colson's Prison Fellowship organization provides the staff and volunteers to run the program. The state of Texas provides what we would normally provide anyway: jail space, food, and guards. While I was visiting InnerChange during its first year of operation, a group of prisoners came around the corner singing hymns. I jumped in line and joined in.

The next day, I read all about it in the *Houston Chronicle*.

For an instant, two lives with nothing in common merged on a patch of prison blacktop Thursday as a group of men sang "Amazing Grace" under a cloudless Texas sky. Gov. George W. Bush put his arm around convicted murderer George Mason, 46, and joined him and 55 other Texas prison inmates in a most unusual blending of church and state. "Standing up there, singing that song, reminded me that all of us need to think about our hearts, think about our lives," Bush told a crowd of reporters, prison officials and members of the Houston-area religious community. "We're all human. We all make mistakes."

... Modeled after a successful program in Brazil, InnerChange is designed to focus on inmates who are nearing release and prepare them for life outside prison through a change of heart, or spiritual and moral transformation. Changing hearts, it is hoped, will decrease the recidivism rate—the numbers of ex-convicts who return to crime. The faith-based voluntary program has been called a Bible boot camp of sorts, with days and evenings filled with courses on subjects such as personal responsibility, parenting and financial management. The three-part program begins a year to a year and a half before an inmate is scheduled for release and continues outside prison with volunteer mentors from the community. "This particular program is being watched everywhere," Colson said, crediting Bush with having the courage to be the first in the nation to try it.

It's too early to tell the ultimate success of InnerChange, but the initial indications are encouraging. Once released, the inmates are "adopted" by volunteers from local area churches who help them assimilate back into society. A number of the graduates have been released and are working in the community. One InnerChange participant took the unprecedented step of voluntarily refusing parole and delaying his departure from prison to spend more time in the program. In his letter to the parole board, he said, "Each day when I wake up here at Jester II, inside the razor wire fences, I'll be crucifying my selfish wants and desires. I'll be saying to my brothers, here and on the outside, that I'm here because inner change is important to me. Maybe my decision to stay here will help others see that God is real—that He is the truth, and He changes people. This is God's program. He's really moving in the prisons, and He's got me right in the middle of it. I feel it an honor to stay here and complete the commitment I made when I signed up."

Increasingly, other state agencies are also welcoming the involvement of faith-based and private groups in areas such as job training and child care. The Department of Human Services and the San Antonio area work force board contract with the Lutheran Social Services of the South to mentor welfare clients who are transitioning from welfare to work. United Community Centers of Tarrant County, a mission of the Methodist church, contracts with the Fort Worth–area workforce board to go into the county's poorest neighborhoods and visit and help welfare recipients who have been sanctioned for failing to meet their training or education or work requirements. The Christian Women's Job Corps provides mentoring, nurturing, and job skills training to women who are trying to become self-sufficient. Tillie Burgin, a wonderful woman known as the Mother Teresa of Arlington, is helping provide transportation, food, shelter, and love to needy Texans in that city. Tillie's ministry started when she returned from Korea, where she had worked as a missionary, and realized there were major needs in her own neighborhood. I heralded Tillie in my State of the State address to the legislature in 1999; she is a leader in the armies of compassion who are changing Texas, one heart, one soul, and one conscience at a time.

During my first three years as Governor, with the hard work and help of a lot of people and through major changes in both law and approach, we were transforming Texas. We had laid the foundation, but as I told my fellow Texans in announcing my plans to seek reelection, now it was time to build.

"The choices we make today will determine whether tomorrow holds promise and opportunity for every single Texan," I said. "I want to be your Governor because I want Texas to seize the moment and usher in an era of excellence, responsibility, and opportunity for every single one of our citizens. I stand before you today with a sense of pride and purpose. Pride because much has been accomplished, and purpose because there is so much more to do."

On December 3, 1997, standing before a crowd of students and teachers at Sam Houston Elementary School in my old hometown of Midland, where I had attended grade school years before, I announced my plans to seek reelection. "I proudly offer my record to the voters of Texas, because I have done in office what I promised to do. We put control of our schools where it belongs, in the hands of local people. We have reformed welfare to insist on work. We've changed our civil justice laws to restore fairness. We have passed some of the toughest criminal justice laws in the country. And with a parole rate that is the lowest since the state began keeping records, Texas sends a clear message: If you break our laws, you are going to jail and you are going to stay in jail for a long, long time. Texas has funded our priorities. We put our public schools first, and I will continue to do so as long as I am your Governor. And we have lived within our means. Once we met our state's basic needs, we gave a billion dollars back to our taxpayers by passing the largest tax cut in Texas history."

But I knew the perils of incumbency. I remembered all too well my dad's 1992 campaign. I knew how quickly a constituency can forget success. Politics is not about the past or rewarding office holders for a job well done. Voters want to know a candidate's view for the future. I had earned political capital by doing in office what I said I would do during my first campaign. Now was the time to spend that capital on a bold agenda for change and reform in a second term. So as I announced for Governor, I told my fellow Texans that the only reason to look back was to determine who was best to lead us forward. I had more, much more, I wanted to accomplish. I outlined plans to intensify our state's focus on guns and gangs, and to require automatic jail time for any juvenile who committed a crime with a gun. I proposed mobilizing a vast array of resources to help young people make responsible choices in life. I called for tax cuts to stimulate small business and job growth. Perhaps most profound of all, I proposed an end to the practice of pushing children through the school system even though they are not prepared to do the work.

"Texas has a strong accountability system to let parents and taxpayers know exactly how our schools are performing. I believe in results. Our high school exit test is being challenged. I will fight efforts to undermine it, because a high school diploma must stand for something in Texas. But the strength of the accountability system is not merely to blow the whistle on failure. We must use it as an early warning system to find problems far earlier and address them before it is too late. I refuse to leave any child behind. I propose we begin the new century by putting an end to social promotion in Texas schools. We must recognize that self-esteem is not taught but earned by teaching our children to read, write, subtract, and add."

It was a frontal assault on the status quo, and it caused an immediate firestorm. Social promotion, the practice of promoting children to keep them with their age group, was rampant in Texas schools, although everyone pretended it was not. Each year, tens of thousands of school children failed the state's minimum skills test but were promoted anyway, even though state law and the policies of most school districts supposedly banned social promotions.

My plan called for building on the reforms we had already put in place. We had overhauled our education code to insist on local control of schools, safe classrooms for teachers, and an opportunity for innovation through charter schools and greater school choice. We had set clear goals: excellence in a core curriculum of reading, math, science, and social science. We had launched the reading initiative and developed a reading diagnostic tool to help kindergarten through second-grade teachers detect and correct reading problems early. We had approved a rigorous core curriculum that was knowledge-based, back to basics, and phonics driven, and the legislature had funded reading academies. It was time to make our accountability system count.

My plan said that children who did not pass the reading portion of the TAAS test, the Texas basic skills test, in the third grade must receive appropriate intervention and instruction, then pass the test, before moving to the fourth grade. My plan called for early diagnosis of reading problems and immediate corrective intervention, after which students would have additional opportunities to take the test. The type of intervention would be up to local school districts, which would choose after-school programs, individual tutoring, expanded reading academies, or summer school. Later, children would be required to pass reading and math tests in fifth grade—and reading, math, and writing tests in eighth grade. But by that time, only third-graders with good skills would be promoted, ensuring greater success in the fifth and eighth grades.

I proposed that the state would provide an additional $203 million for the early intervention programs and teacher retraining. I also called for an expansion of the advanced placement program that offers teachers intensive training in high-level math, science, and other subjects so they could challenge our best and brightest students.

"The message to our schools is: Do what it takes to teach our children to read. If a child is struggling with reading then stop, diagnose the problem, and fix it. If it takes reading all day long, fine by me," I told educators meeting in Austin. "To those who say, 'Too much is riding on one test,' I say, 'Stop the excuses.' We are asking children to score a 70—a minimum passing grade on a basic skills test—because if they have a problem learning, we want to help them correct it. As Gayle Fallon, a former teacher and current president of the Houston Federation of Teachers, said when she embraced this plan: 'A child does not survive if he can't read. . . . You don't get into the Army anymore without passing a test.' The voices of the status quo want to leave the system as it is and doom more children to failure. But that is unacceptable to me, and I know it is to you as well."

The educators listened intently but silently. Then the voices of the status quo began shrieking. "We'll have kids shaving in the third grade," one man protested at one of my speeches. The headline in the *Austin American-Statesman* on December 31, 1997, portrayed grim news for the new year: THOUSANDS WOULD

FAIL SCHOOL IN BUSH PLAN, read the headline. "More than half of Austin's eighth-graders would have flunked last year under a proposal by Governor George W. Bush to end promotions of students who can't pass the statewide basic skills test," the article reported. The article made a point, but it had it backward. As the article pointed out, thousands of students were already failing, but their failure was being ignored. I intended to do something about it.

My call to end social promotion became one of the defining issues of the 1998 campaign. My opponent said he was against social promotion, too, he just didn't think we ought to let a test decide who would be promoted. That was exactly the system that existed in Texas schools already, a system that allowed thousands of children to fail yet move on to the next grade.

We knew the plan was going to be controversial. Some of my advisors had warned it was too bold and that we should play it safer, not risk such a sweeping proposal in a reelection campaign where the polls showed me far ahead. I was convinced it was the right thing to do, and I wanted to use my campaign to build public support for the proposal. And in the end, it resonated with parents, who realized too many children were being trapped in failure. Parents like the baffled mother who wrote me, "If a child cannot read in the ninth grade, why was he given passing grades on his report cards for eight years? There should have been some awareness that he couldn't read several years before that and he should have been put in remedial classes."

The education world is often risk-averse and reluctant to change. As long as students make fairly good grades and pass at the end of the year, everyone is happy. Parents are happy, teachers are happy, administrators don't have problems, all is well. Except when the state test shows that little Melissa can't read. Some say we shouldn't test because the pressure forces students or teachers or school districts to cheat. To me, that's like saying we shouldn't have laws because some people will break them. Others decry "teaching to the test," as if some horrible fate befalls those who learn what they are expected to know. I believe that as long as the test is a straightforward measure of the body of knowledge we want children to learn we should welcome it. Of course, I want schools to teach more than the test. I want young language arts students introduced to great works of literature and ideas far beyond the basic curriculum. But I also want to know that they have learned to read. And so when I put my signature on a budget that sends more than $27 billion of Texans' tax dollars to our public schools, I knew I was representing thousands of Texans who want accountability for how their tax money is spent.

My proposal to cut taxes became the other major issue of my reelection campaign. Texas had a budget surplus, thanks to the good fiscal stewardship of the legislature and directors of state agencies. I argued we should meet the state's basic needs, fund the early intervention I had proposed for our schools, send money to local school districts to give teachers a pay raise, and reduce class sizes; then we should return money to the people who pay the bills, the taxpayers. I outlined $2.6 billion in tax cuts during my campaign, another sweeping proposal that many predicted would never happen. Ultimately, thanks to hard work and bipartisan cooperation, the next legislature would enact almost $2 billion in tax cuts, almost double the record tax cut we had approved in the previous legislative session.

I outlined my proposals in speeches throughout Texas in 1998. I refused to take a single vote for granted and worked harder in my reelection than I had in my initial campaign. I hosted community receptions in small towns throughout our state; a Governor had not visited many of them in years. Hundreds of people would gather at the courthouse or community center to visit and hear my proposals for the future of Texas. I always stayed to shake every hand. And at every stop, someone always asked THE question.

It all started in the summer of 1997, when Karen Hughes

walked into my office with a smile on her face and a scrap of paper in her hand. "You're leading in the poll," she said. It was almost a year and a half before the next statewide elections in Texas. "What poll?" I asked. "The poll that shows you are the front-runner for the Republican presidential nomination," she replied. At the time it seemed surreal, but the speculation soon began to mount.

By the fall of 1997, I couldn't get on an elevator or walk through the back of a hotel kitchen on the way to make a speech without someone saying, "Governor, please run for President." Reporters from all over the world asked whether I would run at every stop. I had been telling the media that I would address the question when I announced my campaign for reelection. But then I realized any delay meant the news coverage of my announcement would focus on the presidential question, not on what I wanted to accomplish during a second term as Governor.

The question had become a distraction, interfering with my attempts to deliver any other message at any other stop. So I called a news conference nearly a year before the 1998 election to deal with the issue. I did not know, I told the reporters, whether I would or would not seek the Presidency. Mike Holmes, the Associated Press bureau chief, was incredulous. "You called a press conference to tell us you haven't decided anything?" he asked Karen. But that wasn't the point. The point was I did not know whether I would run, I would not decide in the midst of a reelection campaign, and I would not mislead my fellow Texans. In the past, other candidates in similar situations had told their constituents they would not run for the Presidency, then changed their minds once they were safely reelected. That was not my style. I flatly stated that if my fellow Texans were concerned that I had not made up my mind one way or the other, they should vote for someone else. Of course, I hoped they would support me.

It might have affected some votes, but overall, I think most of my fellow Texans were proud to have their Governor considered a potential President. The election returns showed the people of Texas not only agreed with my agenda but also appreciated my positive, issue-specific campaign. I became the first Governor elected to back-to-back four-year terms in the history of Texas. I won reelection with a record almost 69 percent of the vote, including 65 percent of women, 49 percent of Hispanics, 27 percent of African-Americans and 73 percent of Independents. And I led a statewide sweep for the Republican Party, as all seventeen of my fellow Republican candidates won with me.

The major television networks carried my speech. "Tonight's victory is a victory of ideas built on a philosophy that is conservative and compassionate," I said, saying my reelection was a mandate for tax cuts and education reforms. "Tonight's resounding victory says my compassionate conservative philosophy is making Texas a better place. But today's election says something more. It says that a leader who is compassionate and conservative can erase the gender gap, open the doors of the Republican Party to new faces and new voices, and win without sacrificing our principles."

With the election behind me, the pressure to make a decision about seeking the Presidency began mounting. I wrestled with the decision. I was worried about my family, worried about exposing them to an environment that I know better than most. I know what it feels like to have someone you love torn up on the national stage, and I worried about putting my girls and my wife through that difficult process. On the other hand, I worried about my country, about an increasing drift that I felt threatened America's promise of opportunity for all at home and America's place as the keeper of freedom in the world.

Conventional wisdom warned that other candidates had been campaigning for years and if I did not launch a campaign immediately, I would be too late. I had to begin raising money and organizing in key states, many said, or I would have no chance to win. But I had a commitment to the voters who had reelected me in Texas. I had campaigned on a specific agenda of education reforms and tax cuts, and I wanted to make sure they were enacted. "We begin this session in the national spotlight," I told legislators during my State of the State message in Austin. "Let's use it to show the rest of the world what limited and constructive government can do." By the time the legislative session adjourned in May, legislators had approved major tax cuts, a plan to end social promotion in Texas schools, a parental notification law, and automatic jail time for juveniles who commit crimes with guns.

There was no magic moment of decision. After talking with my family during the Christmas holidays, then hearing the rousing sermon to make the most of every moment during my inaugural church service, I gradually felt more comfortable with the prospect of a presidential campaign. My family would love me, my faith would sustain me, no matter what. In March, I set up a committee to begin exploring the prospect of running for President. I would not leave Texas until June, until my work in the legislative session was finished, but I began to prepare to seek the most powerful office in the world, that of President of the United States of America.

16

A COMPASSIONATE
CONSERVATIVE

THE question was a haunting one. The young man who asked it had been silent up until then, his wide eyes watching carefully, taking it all in, as I talked with his fellow offenders at the juvenile jail in Marlin, Texas.

The meeting was awkward at first. I'm sure the guards had warned these juveniles to be on their best behavior during the Governor's visit. So they weren't exactly forthcoming when I sat down to talk with them about why they had ended up in jail.

I was there to see firsthand the changes in our Texas juvenile justice system. We had worked hard to instill discipline and accountability.

These kids were tough juvenile delinquents that you and I would be afraid to encounter on the streets late at night, yet when I sat next to them and looked in their eyes, I realized some of them were still little boys. They had committed grown-up crimes: burglaries, robberies, violent assaults. When I asked whether any of them had ever belonged to a gang, the hands slowly went up. I asked why. The kids seemed eager to respond to that question. The gang was like a family, one told me; another, that the gang looked out for you and took care of you when no one else did. But when they landed in jail, these young men had realized the gang didn't seem to care so much anymore. One boy told me his mother and sister were the only ones who had visited him at Marlin. No one from the gang had made the trip.

The question came at the very end of the conversation, as I was preparing to leave. The young man, probably fifteen, raised his hand and quietly asked: "What do you think of me?" The question sprang from the deep doubt of someone who was wondering whether his life had any worth or value. He was asking, do you, the Governor of my state, a successful white man sitting here in my jail cell, believe that this young African-American from a broken family and a poor neighborhood has any chance in life? He was asking whether there was any hope for him. It broke my heart to think that any young person in America should have such doubt.

I told the young man that he had made a terrible mistake and that he had to pay the consequences by serving his time in jail. I told him that if he learned from his mistake, if he went back to school and studied and worked hard and stayed out of trouble and stayed away from gangs and drugs that yes, he could succeed, he could realize the promise of America. I assured him that people cared about him and would try to help him. I am not sure he was convinced. Too many of our young people are not convinced.

We live in the greatest and freest and most prosperous nation in the world, yet too many of our citizens do not believe their lives have meaning or value. The American dream is a distant offer meant for somebody else, they think. They do not believe the fundamentally American conviction that you can be what you want to be, and achieve what you want to achieve, so long as you are willing to work hard and earn it. This gap of hope is found in the poverty of our inner cities, where neighborhoods have become urban war zones, a world of barred windows and gang violence and failed schools, a world of shattered glass and shattered dreams. But the gap of hope is also found in the large but sometimes empty houses of our affluent suburbs, where young people turn to drugs or alcohol or sex in a failed search for something they are missing. We see glimpses of this hopelessness in schoolyards where children inexplicably, tragically, horrifically murder other children. And we worry about our national soul.

This gap of hope threatens the very fabric of America. I worry that we are being divided into two nations, separate and unequal: one nation with the tools and confidence to seek the American dream; another nation that is being left behind. We risk becoming two societies: one that reads and one that can't, one that dreams and one that doesn't. Some think they can protect themselves through willful apathy. Some put up big fences and live in gated communities. Some close the shutters, turn on the television, and withdraw. But apathy comes with a risk, because when the American dream is diminished for any one of us, it is diminished for all of us. We are "one nation, under God, indivisible, with liberty and justice for all." I reject the thinking of those who would lump Americans into different groups based on characteristics such as skin color or ethnic heritage or economic circumstance. Group thought pits people against one another, and its political expressions, quotas, and preferences demean the individual and lower standards. Each of us is a unique individual, with a heart and a soul and a conscience, and each of us has ties to one another. We are united by a common bond of history and citizenship. President Lincoln reminded us that America is not just a collection of states or individuals. We are a single, moral community, with obligations to one another. We are America.

We must close the gap of hope, but the answer is not found in yet another government program. The answer begins with each one of us assuming our responsibilities as parents and neighbors and citizens. I want to usher in the responsibility era, an era when every American knows with certainty that each of us is responsible for our actions, that each of us is responsible for our family and our community, that each of us is responsible for loving a neighbor as we would like to be loved ourselves.

During the more than half century of my life, we have seen an unprecedented decay in our American culture, a decay that has eroded the foundations of our collective values and moral standards of conduct. Our sense of personal responsibility has declined dramatically, just as the role and responsibility of the federal government have increased. The changing culture blurred the sharp contrast between right and wrong and created a new standard of conduct: "If it feels good, do it" and "If you've got a problem, blame somebody else." Individuals are not responsible for their actions, the new culture said, we are all victims of forces beyond our control. We went from a culture of sacrifice and saving to a culture obsessed with grabbing all the gusto. We went from accepting responsibility to assigning blame. As government did more and more, individuals were required to do less and less.

The new culture said if people were poor, the government should feed them. If someone had no house, the government should provide one. If criminals are not responsible for their acts, then the answers are not in prisons, but in social programs. Every problem suddenly demanded a government solution.

Fathers moved out and Uncle Sam moved in. People became less interested in pulling themselves up by their bootstraps and more interested in pulling down a monthly government check. A culture of dependency was born. Programs that began as a temporary hand-up became a permanent handout, regarded by many as a right, an entitlement, something for nothing. The expanding role of government accelerated and sanctioned the changes in our culture. Not too long ago society knew without question that being unmarried and pregnant was cause for shame. Today, many say no problem, government will provide a rent-free apartment and send money to help; government condoned it with a check and society with a shrug.

We can now say, without question, that the belief that government could solve people's problems instead of people solving people's problems was wrong and misguided. That does not mean we should not help people. It means we should look for more effective means of help. We must reduce the reach and scope of the federal government, returning it to its proper, limited role, and push freedom and responsibility back to local governments, to neighborhoods, and to individuals.

Government can be a part of helping usher in the responsibility era. Government sends signals every day. It can pass laws that hold people accountable for their acts. In Texas, we passed a law that says the state will suspend any license it issues if you fail to pay court-ordered child support. And to show that we mean business, we included not only driver's licenses, but also professional licenses and hunting and fishing licenses as well. Government can pass tough laws that hold people accountable if they commit a crime with a gun or illegally carry a weapon. And government can do a better job of enforcing those laws by expanding programs such as Project Exile, where federal, state, and local prosecutors and law enforcement officials team up to rid our communities of illegal weapons. But government is only part of the solution.

We all have a role and a responsibility. Corporate America has a responsibility to treat its workers with respect and to give back to the communities in which it does business. Corporate America has a responsibility to work for cleaner air and cleaner water by cleaning up old plants that pollute and by developing new technologies to manufacture and produce in a more environmentally friendly way. Mothers and dads are responsible for remembering that the most important job any of us will ever have is being a good parent to our children. We have a collective responsibility to teach our children not only reading and writing, but also right from wrong. We must teach our children our common values, not the values of one faith or one religion over another, but the values shared by good people of all faiths from all walks of life: Give an honest day's work for an honest day's wages. Respect others, respect their property, and respect their opinions. Don't lie, cheat, or steal. Extend a hand to a neighbor in need.

We must celebrate and support and expand the institutions that nurture these values. The problem with government bureaucracies is not only that they are too costly. They are also too cold. Often when a life is broken, it can be rebuilt only by another caring, concerned human being—someone whose actions say, "I love you, I believe in you, and I'm in your corner." This is compassion with a human face and a human voice. On my first presidential campaign trip, I visited the Olivet Neighborhood Mission in Iowa. I met with some of the women whose families had been helped by the program. They had received food from the food pantry and their children had selected clothes from the clothes closet, and that material help was essential to helping them get back on their feet. But clothes and food were not what they talked about. They talked about the program's director, Ann Torticill. One woman told me about how Ann had helped her prepare for a job interview, another how a call from Ann had kept her going at a critical moment when she was feeling lost and helpless. The Anns of America are miracle workers, performing daily miracles of renewal in their communities. Government should direct resources to help these programs, programs that succeed because they touch human hearts in a human way. They are located in every community in America, and I want to lift the regulations that hamper them. Whenever possible, I would look to community programs, charities, and religious institutions that save and change lives to help Americans in need. I support charity tax credits and a change in tax policy to allow even those who do not itemize to deduct their charitable contributions, because I want to encourage an outpouring of charitable giving in America.

For our culture to change, it must change one heart, one soul, and one conscience at a time. Government can spend money, but it cannot put hope in our hearts or a sense of purpose in our lives. This is done by churches and synagogues and mosques and charities that warm the cold of life. They are a quiet river of goodness and kindness that cuts through stone. Some call their efforts crumbs of compassion; I say they are the greatness of America. I recognize their challenges are often greater than their resources. And I recognize that many religious institutions fear involvement with government, because they fear it will compromise their core values and spiritual mission. That's why I support alternative licensing procedures, so effective efforts aren't buried or compromised by government regulation. Participation in faith-based programs must be voluntary, and we must make sure secular alternatives are available. But government should welcome the active involvement of people who are following a religious imperative to love their neighbors through after-school programs, child care, drug treatment, maternity group homes, and a range of other services. Supporting these men and women—the soldiers in the armies of compassion—is the next bold step of welfare reform, because I know that changing hearts will change our entire society.

Finally, to close the gap of hope, America must make a solemn commitment: Every child will be educated and no child will be left behind. I want to take my passion for high standards and high hopes to the highest office in the land. The President is not a national superintendent of schools and should not try to be. But the President speaks for the common good, and much of our common good is found in our common schools.

We are a nation where a majority of fourth-graders in our cities can't read or understand a simple children's book; a nation whose ninth-graders too often have fourth-grade reading skills, and where the achievement gap between rich and poor, Anglo and minority, is wide. Reform of our public schools must begin with the mind-set that all children can learn. Some say it is unfair to hold disadvantaged children to rigorous standards. I say it is discrimination to require anything less. I refuse to condemn children to the soft bigotry of low expectations.

We know what works. Schools must have a few measurable goals, focused on basic skills and essential knowledge. We must measure to make sure the standards are met. Effective reform requires accountability. Someone should be praised when schools succeed, and someone must be responsible when they fail. Accountability is empty without local control. If we fail to align authority and responsibility at the local level, we create a convenient excuse for failure—just blame the central office. I trust local people to make the right decisions for their schools because I know local parents and teachers care far more about what happens in local schools than distant bureaucrats do. We should pass authority and flexibility from the federal government to the states. Finally, we must recognize the central role of competition in achieving better schools. All monopolies are slow to reform when consumers have no power to express their frustration. When we find failure, we should give parents different options, such as charter schools and greater school choice. When we created charter schools in Texas, the critics said they would be a haven for fleeing Anglo students. Yet 78 percent of the students enrolled in Texas charter schools are minorities. Charter schools encourage educational entrepreneurs to try innovative methods. They break up the monopoly of one-size-fits-all education. These diverse, creative schools are proof that parents from all walks of life are willing to challenge the status quo if it means a better education for their children.

The federal government should fund only what works in education, only those methods and ideas that prove their power to close the achievement gap. Much of what the federal government sponsors is sloppy and trendy, heralding self-esteem over basic skills. Self-esteem is not taught; it is earned when we teach children to read and write and add and subtract. Federal education programs should be required to prove results, or we should move money into different programs that are spending it successfully. In one area, the research is definitive: the best way to teach children to read incorporates phonics. We should put the research to work and help children develop building-block reading skills at a younger age. I want to reform Head Start to ensure it becomes an early reading and early learning program. Finally, we should not use taxpayer money to reward failure. If schools don't measure up, we will give them time to change. But if they fail to improve, there must be some final point of accountability. At the end of three years, if a school that receives federal Title I funds is not making progress, I would divide the money on a per student basis, match it with additional federal education funds, and make it available directly to parents. This grant of about $1,500 a year would allow parents to choose tutoring, or a different public school, or a charter school, or a private one. This would allow parents to choose hope over failure. I refuse to trap children in schools that do not teach and will not change.

The goal is to strengthen public schools by expecting performance. The goal is also to make sure our federal government no longer pays schools to cheat poor children. More competition and more choices for parents and students will raise the bar for everyone. Every child in America must have a first-rate education, because there are no second-rate children and no second-rate dreams.

This is what I mean by compassionate conservatism. The philosophy is ingrained in my heart. The words came from a discussion I had with a reporter several years ago. The reporter was trying to label me. I am a conservative, I told him. "But you have done things differently," he argued. "Insisting on educating every child and leaving no child behind is not a concept usually associated with conservatives," he said. "Well, then, call me a conservative with a heart," I replied. None of us can remember the exact date when that conversation took place, but from it grew the brand name my philosophy now wears. I didn't invent the phrase, but I adopted it, and I have made it my own. "I am a compassionate conservative," I said during my first presidential campaign trip to Iowa and New Hampshire in June. "I welcome the label. And on this ground, I will make my stand."

I am a conservative because I believe in the worth and dignity and power of each individual. My philosophy trusts individuals to make the right decisions for their families and communities, and that is far more compassionate than a philosophy that seeks solutions from distant bureaucracies. I am a conservative because I believe government should be limited and efficient, that it should do a few things and do them well. I am a conservative because I believe in a strong national defense to keep the peace. I am a conservative because I support free markets and free trade. I am a conservative because I believe government closest to the people governs best.

I am a fiscal conservative and a family conservative. And I am a compassionate conservative, because I know my philosophy is optimistic and full of hope for every American.

Compassionate conservatism outlines a new vision of the proper role for the American government. Government must be limited and focused, but it has an important job within its bounds. Government is too often wasteful and overreaching. But we must correct it and limit it, not disdain it. I differ with those who want to dismantle government down to the last paper clip—and with those who want to extend its reach. Government is neither the enemy nor the answer. The federal government has some compelling purposes: to defend our homeland, to help keep peace in the world, to help secure the retirement and health needs of our senior citizens, and to help our society confront human suffering.

State and local government must educate children, put criminals behind bars, and maintain roads and basic services. But in some cases, the job is best done not by government itself, but by directing government resources to neighborhoods and parents and schools and faith-based institutions that shape values and change lives.

Compassionate conservatism is neither soft nor fuzzy. It is clear and compelling. It focuses not on good intentions but on good results. Compassionate conservatism applies conservative, free-market principles to the real job of helping real people, all people, including the poor and the disadvantaged. My vision of compassionate conservatism also requires America to assert its leadership in the world. We are the world's only remaining superpower, and we must use our power in a strong but compassionate way to help keep the peace and encourage the spread of freedom.

The phrase "compassionate conservative" recognizes that a conservative philosophy has sometimes been mistakenly portrayed as mean-spirited. I like to joke that a compassionate conservative is a conservative with a smile, not a conservative with a frown. Some who would agree with a conservative philosophy have been turned off by a strident tone. I have set a different tone. I advocate limited government because too much government limits innovation, restricts competition, and crowds out the market. I know the role of government is not to create wealth, but to create an environment where entrepreneurs and small businesses and producers are willing to risk and dream and build. I worked to reform welfare because I believe it is far more compassionate to help individuals become independent than to trap them in a cycle of dependency and despair. I support local control of schools because I know local parents care far more about their own children than people in Washington do.

I also said in Texas that we should educate children, all the children who live in my state. Texas shares a huge border with Mexico. We share close ties of history and culture and geography; we have aunts and uncles and cousins on both sides of the Rio Grande. I believe we should trade and visit freely with our neighbors in Mexico. But we must do a better job of stopping those who seek to come into our country illegally. I support strict border enforcement programs such as Operation Hold the Line, which concentrate border patrol officers and resources at known border-crossing points. I believe it is far more compassionate to turn away people at the border than to attempt to find and arrest them once they are living in our country illegally. But I also believe we should educate children, regardless of the status of their parents. It is in our own best interests to do so. An educated child is far more likely to become a productive citizen. An educated child is less likely to commit a crime.

We have had a debate in Texas and throughout America about our national language. I believe people who live and work in America must learn to speak English. English is our common language and it reflects our common bond. The ability to speak and read and comprehend English is the gateway to success in our country. I call my philosophy "English plus." I want all of America's children to learn to read and write in English, plus I want my own daughters to learn Spanish. Plus, I make an effort to speak Spanish myself. Plus, I recognize that the Hispanic heritage and culture are important to my state and our country and make Texas and America a richer place. Those who advocate "English-only" poke a stick in the eye of people of Hispanic heritage. "English-only" says me, not you. It says I count, but you do not. That is not the message of America.

I am optimistic that the next century will be one of great prosperity. America will be prosperous if we cut taxes. Reducing marginal tax rates will increase economic growth and create higher-paying jobs. By returning money to the taxpayers, we can also limit government. Money returned to Americans will not be spent on new or expanded government programs. Americans now have greater consumer debt than at any time in our nation's history. Returning money to their pockets will allow them to strengthen their family finances. Our tax code must also be fairer. The current tax structure makes it difficult for people to move from near poverty to the middle class, and we should remove that barrier. I support reducing the marriage penalty because the tax code should not conflict with our core values. I support reducing the death tax to make it easier to pass a family farm or small business on to the next generation, an essential element of the American Dream.

America will be prosperous if we embrace free trade. I want to end tariffs and break down barriers everywhere, entirely, so the whole world trades in freedom. By opening markets for our producers abroad, we enhance our prosperity at home. The fearful build walls. The confident tear them down. I am confident in American workers and farmers and producers. I am confident that America's best is the best in the world. And America should not use food as a diplomatic weapon. We are too great a nation to starve people to achieve our foreign policy goals. As we export American goods and services, we also export American values.

America must be prosperous to keep our commitments to the health and security and dignity of our senior citizens. Medicare should be strengthened by providing more choice and more private sector alternatives for the elderly, including plans that offer coverage for prescription drugs. I support medical savings accounts and patient protections in federal health care plans similar to the ones I signed in Texas. I would not, however, support allowing the federal government to supersede the healthy reforms already enacted by states such as mine.

Social Security is a solemn commitment, and we must preserve its guarantee for our seniors. Modernizing it will require a bipartisan effort. Social Security money should go only to Social Security, not to other programs, and Social Security taxes should not be increased. I oppose government investment of Social Security funds in private stocks or bonds and believe we should trust individual Americans by giving them the option of placing part of their Social Security contributions into personal retirement accounts.

And America must be prosperous to keep the peace. This is a unique moment in history. A generation after the successful struggle against an evil empire, a new generation of American leaders will determine how American power and influence are used.

This is still a world of terror and missiles and madmen. And America's military is challenged by aging weapons, low morale, and failing intelligence. To keep the peace, we must rebuild America's military power.

Peace is not ordained, it is earned. Building a durable peace requires strong alliances, expanding trade and confident diplomacy. It requires tough realism in our dealings with China and Russia. It requires firmness with regimes like North Korea and Iraq, regimes that hate our values and resent our success. And the foundation of our peace is a strong, capable, and modern American military. Back-to-back deployments, poor pay, shortages of spare parts and equipment, and rapidly declining readiness have undermined the military's morale. Not since the years before Pearl Harbor has our investment in national defense been so low a percentage of our gross national product. Nearly twelve thousand members of the armed forces are on food stamps.

I support increased pay and better benefits and training for our citizen soldiers. A volunteer military has only two paths. It can lower its standards to fill its ranks. Or it can inspire the best and brightest to join and stay.

The long-standing commitments we have made to our allies are the strong foundation of our current peace. America must keep its pledges to defend friends from aggression. But our military should not become permanent peacekeepers, dividing warring parties. America should work with our allies to develop political solutions and a timetable to bring our troops home from places like Bosnia and Kosovo.

Rebuilding America's homeland defenses is an urgent priority. I support deploying antiballistic missile systems to guard against attack and blackmail. And America should modernize its military capability, not by reauthorizing all of the weapons of the past, but by investing in research and development to make our military more mobile, more agile, and more suited to the needs of the twenty-first century.

America cannot keep the peace alone. We must work closely with our friends and allies. As the Governor of Texas, I have reached out to our neighbors in Mexico. I have worked to build bridges of personal diplomacy. Mexico is our friend, and friends solve problems in a spirit of mutual trust and respect. America's foreign policy should respect and nurture our traditional alliances throughout the world and strengthen relations with countries in our own neighborhood. With Canada and Mexico and the countries of Central and South America, we have an opportunity to create a powerful free-market alliance.

The world seeks America's leadership, looks for leadership from a country whose values are freedom and justice and equality. Ours should not be the paternalistic leadership of an arrogant big brother, but the inviting and welcoming leadership of a great and noble nation. We have an individual responsibility to our families and our communities, and a collective responsibility as citizens of the greatest and freest nation in the world. America must not retreat within its borders. Our greatest export is freedom, and we have a moral obligation to champion it throughout the world.

I have many reasons to run for President and many things I want to accomplish for our country. I want to change the tone of our national discourse. Americans look at Washington and they don't like what they see. Who can blame them? They see partisanship and bickering. They see some who would rather score a point for the next election than get something done for the good of the nation. People often ask me, Can you do in Washington what you have done in Texas? Washington is different, they say, so partisan and bitter.

I recognize that it's a big challenge, but I believe an administration can change the tone of American politics, and I believe we must do so. Public cynicism about our government is a fundamental threat to our American democracy. Self-government is only as good as those who are willing to participate. Most people who seek election do so because they want to accomplish good for our country. This is the beginning of a common bond. Republicans and Democrats in Congress come from different places, different backgrounds, and different perspectives. Yet we all run for office because we want to make America a better country. That is a place to start.

I know that I am seeking an awesome responsibility. I know that serving as Governor of Texas is not anywhere near the same as being President. But if Texas were a nation, it would be the eleventh-largest economy in the world. I've had some success, and I've learned to lead. You cannot lead by dividing people. I am a uniter, not a divider. My campaign will be positive, hopeful, and inclusive. I want to show that politics, after a time of tarnished ideals, can be higher and better. I hope to give our country a fresh start after a season of cynicism.

I am running hard, and I am running to win. And I feel a remarkable sense of freedom. I know that no matter what happens during the months ahead, my wife will love me, my daughters will love me, the dog will love me, the cats will pretend they don't, but they really will. And my dad answered one of my doubts about seeking the office he once held in a letter to Jeb and me last year.

Your Mother tells me that both of you have mentioned to her your concerns about some of the political stories—the ones that seem to put me down and make me seem irrelevant—that contrast you favorably to a father who had no vision and who was but a place holder in the broader scheme of things. I have been reluctant to pass on advice. Both of you are charting your own course. But the advice is this. Do not worry when you see the stories that compare you favorably to a Dad for whom English was a second language and for whom the word destiny meant nothing. First, I am content with how historians will judge my administration— even on the economy. I hope and think they will say we helped change the world in a positive sense. It is inevitable that the new breed of journalists will have to find a hook in stories, will have to write not only on your plans and your dreams but will have to compare those with what, in their view, I failed to accomplish. That can be hurtful to a family that loves each other. But the advice is don't worry about it. At some point both of you may want to say, "Well, I don't agree with my Dad on that point" or "Frankly I think Dad was wrong on that." Do it. Chart your own course, not just on the issues but on defining yourselves. No one will ever question your love of family—your devotion to your parents—so do not worry when the comparisons might be hurtful to your Dad for nothing can ever be written that will drive a wedge between us—nothing at all, so read my lips, no more worrying.

This from your proud and devoted, Dad.

During the opening months of my presidential campaign, I have traveled our country and my heart has been warmed. My experiences have reinvigorated my faith in the greatness of Americans. They have reminded me that societies are renewed from the bottom up, not the top down. Everywhere I go, I see people of love and faith, taking time to help a neighbor in need. I met Mary Jo Coleman, a cheerful woman with a big smile and a bigger heart, whose Sharing and Caring Hands program provides shelter, transportation, food, dental service, and bountiful love to the homeless in St. Paul, Minnesota. I visited a church in downtown Columbus, Ohio, whose leaders have taken a former crack house and turned it into a house of faith and worship. I met farmers in Cape Girardeau, Missouri, who have been helped by the ADOPT-a-Farm family ministry during times of personal and financial crisis and who have in turn helped others. I met grandmothers who are helping kindergarten students learn to read at the Bruce-Guadalupe School, a private, nonprofit school run by Milwaukee's largest Latino social service organization, the United Community Center. And in Ohio, I met two more soldiers in the armies of compassion, Curt and Eileen Thomas, who humbly wash the feet of those less fortunate as directors of the Haven of Rest ministries.

These people and thousands more like them are the heart and soul and greatness of America. And I want to do my part. I am running for President because I believe America must seize this moment. America must lead. We must give our prosperity a greater purpose, a purpose of peace and freedom and hope. We are a great nation of good and loving people. And together, we have a charge to keep.

INDEX